1991

A HISTORY OF
WESTERN ASTROLOGY

FOR PHYLLIDA

A HISTORY OF
WESTERN ASTROLOGY

S. J. Tester

THE BOYDELL PRESS

First published in hardback 1987 by The Boydell Press, Woodbridge
Reprinted 1988
Reprinted in paperback and hardback 1990

The Boydell Press is an imprint of Boydell & Brewer Ltd
PO Box 9, Woodbridge, Suffolk IP12 3DF
and *for hardback copies only*
of Boydell & Brewer Inc.
PO Box 41026, Rochester, NY 14604, USA

ISBN 0 85115 446 8 hardback
ISBN 0 85115 255 4 paperback

British Library Cataloguing in Publication Data

Tester, S.J.
  A history of western astrology.
  1. Astrology – History
  I. Title
  133.5'09   BF1671
  ISBN 0-85115-446-8 hardback
  ISBN 0-85115-255-4 paperback

This publication is printed on acid-free paper

Printed in Great Britain by
St Edmundsbury Press, Bury St Edmunds, Suffolk

Contents

List of Illustrations

Preface

Books are sometimes fancifully treated as the offspring of their authors. If this one be so regarded, it is one to confound the obstetricians, since it is both premature and overdue. It is premature because until the masses of material buried in MSS – Greek, Latin, Pahlavi perhaps, Arabic, – have all been published, sorted, related, assimilated and distilled out, no history of Western Astrology is going to be possible, long or short. It is overdue, because it is badly needed; so many wrong things are written about astrology – especially in the Middle Ages – that some correction is necessary. It is partly that scholars like Thorndike, who did too much in one man's working life to get it all right, saw astrologers where there weren't any, and trusted gossips like Simon de Phares; partly that everyone seems to have seen astrology wherever the word *astrologia* occurred, or wherever an author began his work with a description of the zodiac and the characteristics and powers of the planets – though what followed was a wholly astronomical work; or saw astrology wherever, in MSS or windows or carving, a zodiac represented time, the calendar; for all these reasons it seemed that from the twelfth century on (or even the tenth!) Europe was full of astrologers. Which it was not. It is hoped that this book presents a plausible picture: it is honestly based on what evidence I have found, and it must stand or fall as my considered opinion. At the least it may provide a framework in which to slot new research and knowledge, until it cracks and breaks and becomes first inadequate and then wholly wrong, as it will.

I cannot provide a bibliography. One which merely lists in alphabetical or any other order all the books, articles, MSS, etc. referred to in the footnotes is worse than useless, if it is not merely an author's boast, since it presents the reader with a daunting wood and no guidance through the trees. A short select bibliography is very useful; but impossible for this book, because there are no other such works to refer to. The reader who pays attention to footnotes will, I hope, find all he wants.

There are some debts of gratitude to express: the obvious ones, but none the less very warmly felt for being obvious, to various librarians and libraries, especially of the University Library, Bristol; the Bodleian Library, Oxford; and the British Library. And there are personal ones.

I began this book years ago, when my mother was dying with cancer; it is ended, incomplete, with myself in the same condition. My wife has put up with this work for longer than either of us anticipated, and without her devoted nursing over the last months, and particularly over the last month, I should never have got even as far as I have. I apologise for the end of the last chapter. I have written under the pressure not of time, which is hard, but of eternity, which is inexorable. I am consequently more than grateful to Richard Barber and the others at the publishers who have been so understanding and so helpful and so kind in these last stages.

S. J. Tester
Bristol, June 1986

Publishers' Note

Jim Tester died shortly after completing this preface. We would like to thank his friend and colleague, Mr John Farrell, for compiling the Index and seeing the book through the press, with all the attendant difficulties, both personal and editorial, inherent in the circumstances.

I

Introduction

Thales of Miletus, the first philosopher in Western history, is said to have been strolling along, his head in the air, gazing at the stars, and so to have fallen down a well, from which he was rescued by a pretty servant-girl, who went on at him because he was so busy finding out what went on in the sky that he didn't see what was before his feet: a not inapposite remark to a philosopher. Perhaps it was because of his experience with the well that Thales said all things were made from water. Another of the early Greek philosophers said that the first stuff of the universe was air, and another, fire. Add earth to those three, and we have the four elements, earth, air, fire and water, which we shall meet again and again in this story. Thales lived in the sixth century B.C., before astrology was introduced into the Greek world. But he, and star-gazing, and philosophy, and indeed even the rescue by the servant-girl, are not irrelevant. Star-gazing is of course far older than philosophy, and older than history; and philosophers with their heads in the air are with us still, as is the common sense of servant-girls. But the conjunction of star-gazing and philosophy and Greece takes us very properly to the roots of our subject. For this is the story of Western European astrology, and that self-styled ancient art is today very much as the Greeks formed it. It was they who took the star-gazing and its magic and mumbo-jumbo and added philosophy, added geometry and rational thought about themselves and their universe, and produced the art of astrology. It was they who wrote the ancient textbooks of the art on which all later astrology has been based – even the two important Latin books on the subject are derived from Greek sources.

The literature of and on astrology is immense. Apart from specialist works on particular aspects or writers of antiquity and the Middle Ages, and Bouché-Leclerq's *L'Astrologie Grecque*, which remains the best introduction to that subject, it is almost wholly, except as source material, useless to the historian. Books on the subject fall generally into three categories. First, there are books by astrologers or sympathisers, which are sometimes useful in explaining how astrology works but are usually unhistorical – sometimes grossly so – and universally uncritical. Second, there are books by those attacking astrology. Those

1

of the past are occasionally useful sources of information, but they are for the most part at least as uncritical and unhistorical as those of the first group. Third, there are popular outlines and histories, which have lately been increasing in numbers though not in value. Practically none quotes primary sources, and most seem to have been copied one from another, generalisations, footnotes, mistakes and all. It is necessary, therefore, to go back to the primary sources, many of which have been printed, but few of which are easily accessible.

The first two categories of books, those by writers explaining or defending astrology, and those by its attackers, seem to have existed from very early times, when astrology became a skilled and public art, in the early centuries B.C. There has always been, in every Western society since the Greeks, more than one attitude towards astrology. But before rather simply categorising attitudes, it is necessary to be more precise about the subject itself. The name 'astrology' appears to cover anything from a vague acceptance of stellar 'influences' on the lives of men to precise and fatalistic predictions of the future. But keeping to the narrower sense in which it has been defined in the Preface, and not to anticipate its own proper divisions, there are and have been broadly two kinds of astrology, which we may call 'hard' and 'soft'. Hard astrology is that which assumes or accepts a firm determinism, so that sufficient knowledge and expertise should allow firm predictions to be made of events and actions which are 'written in the stars' and so must happen. Soft astrology allows for the moral freedom of man, and its attitude is summed up in the maxim, 'the stars incline, they do not compel'. The division between these two kinds of astrology is not always clear cut, nor do they always appear to be mutually exclusive, but can both be held by the same individual. This is particularly true of pagan antiquity, when the notion of free will was not itself very clear. A Stoic like Seneca can firmly assert man's moral freedom, and at the same time as firmly hold that fate rules all things, and that true freedom consists in following fate instead of opposing it, going with what is bound to happen instead of trying to go against it, and being dragged willy-nilly. Nevertheless the distinction between hard and soft astrology is a real one, of some historical importance, especially in later, Christian centuries.

There are consequently four possible, and three actual, attitudes towards astrology. One is to support hard astrology, to believe in a determinist fate and in the necessary links between the patterns in the heavens and events on earth in the lives of men. For those who hold this view, the value of astrology lies in foreknowledge of the inevitable, for as Ptolemy says (*Tetrabiblos* I, 3): 'Even with regard to things which are going to happen of necessity, their unexpectedness usually causes distraught confusion or joy beyond bounds, while foreknowledge accustoms and composes the soul by the rehearsal of things to come as though they were present, and prepares it to receive everything which happens in peace and steadfastness'. Then there are those who reject such determinism, and believe in man's freedom, and who consequently cannot accept hard astrology. These fall into two classes: there are some who reject fate, but do hold that the stars can give some guidance, either as to character or even as to future events, while leaving us free to modify our behaviour in the light of the knowledge we gain from astrology. These are the supporters of soft astrology, and most modern astrologers would seem to come into this category. Lastly, there are those who reject all astrology, hard and soft alike, whether on religious or other grounds, and whether they believe in man's freedom or hold to some scientific or other determinism. All three attitudes are ancient, and the Christianising of Europe made surprisingly little difference.

Ptolemy's *Tetrabiblos* has just been quoted. Its four books became for centuries the most influential textbook of astrology. Its author was that same second century geographer and astronomer who wrote the *Almagest*, the great textbook of astronomy for thirteen centuries. Ptolemy did for Greek astronomy what Euclid did for their geometry. Incidentally, what is now generally known as the 'Ptolemaic system', which is really a simplified and popularised, bastard form of an Aristotelian system of concentric spheres of aether or crystal, bears no real resemblance to the intricate and exact mathematical system of epicycles of the *Almagest*. The only real similarity between the system of Ptolemy and the Ptolemaic system lies in their geocentricity, and the continued use of the name is unfair to Ptolemy. He was an Alexandrian Greek of the mid-second century A.D., and Alexandria was the home of Greek astrology. In his *Tetrabiblos* (by which name, or by its Latin form, *Quadripartitum*, his *Apotelesmatica* is generally known) he summed up the astrology of his time, as he saw it in his scientific fashion. In that book he says that the astrologer must be a man 'who fully understands the movements of all the stars and the sun and moon, so that he knows the place and time of any configuration'. Under 'stars' Ptolemy was including the planets: the Greek, οἱ πλάνητες ἀστέρες, means simply 'the wandering stars'. They were so called because instead of moving in regular daily circles about the pole, as do the 'fixed' stars, they move across the heavens, against the background of the stars, and at times stand still or even move back on their tracks – when they are going back they are called 'retrograde'. Now it is not necessary to become an expert astronomer to understand astrology and its history, but it is important to have some idea of the mechanics of that celestial universe which provides the data for the astrologer.

For him, as indeed (for convenience' sake) for modern elementary textbooks of mathematical astronomy, the universe is a vast hollow sphere on the inside surface of which the stars appear to be fixed, and at the centre of which is the stationary earth. Between the fixed stars and the earth lie the courses of the sun, moon and planets. These last were, for much of the period of astrology's history, five in number, the five visible to the naked eye. Four – Saturn, Jupiter, Mars and Venus – are easy to see; the fifth, Mercury, is much more difficult to spot, since it stays so close to the sun. It is true that Uranus can also sometimes be seen without a telescope, if the night is clear and one knows exactly where to look; and there are astrologers who claim that it was known in antiquity, but there is no evidence of this, and all the ancients speak only of seven planets – seven, because for the ancients the sun and moon are also planets, for they also wander. The order of these seven planets, moving in from the outermost towards the earth at the centre, is Saturn, Jupiter, Mars, Sun, Venus, Mercury, Moon. This is to put them in descending order according to the time they take to pass right round the heavens, the basically correct assumption being that the longer they take to go round, the further from the earth they are.

These seven are the 'seven stars in the sky' of the old rhyme, 'Green grow the rushes O'. The 'April rainers' were almost certainly originally angels (possibly 'Gabriel's rangers'), the angelic 'Intelligences' which in Christian Neo-platonism turned the eight moving spheres – one each for the seven planets and one for the fixed stars: the sphere of the stars revolves round the earth once a day. The 'nine bright shiners' are these eight spheres and a ninth, the outermost, the Empyrean. The rest of this old counting rhyme has nothing to do with astronomy or astrology, though certainly it is full of interest and mystery.

Now take the seven planets in the order set out above, and then name the hours of each day after them, beginning with the first hour of Saturday, named after Saturn; the second hour belongs to Jupiter, the third to Mars, and so on round the twenty-four hours. Then the first hour of the next day goes to the Sun. If each day is then called after the name of its first hour, we have the names of the days of the week. It is best to look at the names in a Latin language like French or Italian, and compare them with the Latin, remembering that Sunday was renamed the Lord's Day (*Dominica dies*) in many Christian countries, though not in our own, despite (or because of?) the Puritans. The seven day week is thus partly a consequence of the fact that there were seven planets and twenty-four hours in the day, though it probably had as much to do with the phases of the moon – new, first quarter, full, last quarter – which recur roughly every seven days.

Let us return to the mechanics, and draw a circle to represent the sphere of the fixed stars, the dot in the centre being the earth (Fig. 1).

4

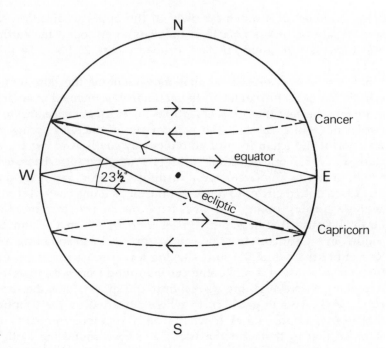

Fig. 1

Let us put the north and south poles at the top and bottom of the figure, and half way between them draw in the great circle of the equator. (A great circle on a sphere is one whose plane passes through the centre of the sphere.) This is the celestial equator, an imaginary line on the inner surface of the sphere; it is the projection on the sphere of the earth's equator. The whole sphere and everything in it except the earth, which remains stationary, revolves on the axis between the poles, in an east-west direction, taking 23 hours 56 minutes for each revolution. The Pole Star, which most people can find on a starry night from the 'pointers' of the Great Bear, is virtually at the celestial north pole, and the constellations can be seen to wheel round it in a circle during the night.

If we watch the western horizon at and just after sunset, and note which constellation sets with or just after the sun; and if we continue to watch and note the constellations for a year, we shall find we have made a list of constellations lying in a great circle on the celestial sphere, and that the sun has moved right round the heavens, *from west to east*, and is now back where it started. This great circle lies at an angle of about 23½° to the equator, and it is called the *ecliptic*, because it is where eclipses happen. The sun takes a year to travel round the ecliptic, in the opposite direction to that of its daily rotation round the earth, which it acquires by being part of the spinning sphere of the heavens. Since it is moving slowly in the opposite direction to that spin, it takes a little longer than the stars to go round the earth from east to west – 24 hours, in fact, instead of the 23 hours 56 minutes taken by the stars.

Since this west-to-east, annual movement of the sun round the ecliptic is not on or parallel to the equator, but inclined at an angle to it, during the year the sun seems (from the earth at the centre) to move north and south, crossing the equator twice: once, in spring, on its way north, and again in autumn on its way south. And twice a year it stops moving in one direction, north or south, and turns back, to move south, or north. The Greek for a 'turning' is *tropos*, and if we draw in Fig. 1 two dotted circles to represent the sun's daily, east-west rotation at these turning points, we shall have the *tropics*: of Cancer in the north, because that was the constellation in which the sun turned south, and Capricorn in the south, for the corresponding reason. Remember that while the sun is taking a year to go round the ecliptic from west to east, it is still being carried round from west to east every day, along with everything else on or in the sphere. Now the sun takes about 365¼ days to get back to where it started on the ecliptic; but that yearly motion slows down its daily rotation, compared to the stars, so that in that year the stars have been round the earth 366¼ times. So the stars' day is shorter than the sun's, which is why the constellations are not all in the same places at the same time every night of the year.

The fact that the true explanation of all this is that the earth is spinning on its own axis every day, and travelling round the sun in a year, does not affect the *relative* motions at all. The apparent motions of the stars and sun are as have been described. The description we now know to be right did in fact occur as a hypothesis to one Greek astronomer, Aristarchus, at the beginning of the third century B.C., but since it was (and is) less than obviously true to our common sense experience, and since it was little better as an explanation of what men saw, it remained an idea, only occasionally referred to, and later refuted by Aristotle's incorrect physics.

The earth at rest in the centre is not a dot, but a sphere. It was known to be a sphere to all ancient and medieval astronomers, from Plato's time on, and the proofs they adduced for the fact were those which are quoted now: the disappearance of ships over the horizon, the shape of the earth's shadow on the moon, and the appearance and disappearance of constellations as we move north and south on the surface of the earth. No scholar who knew even such rudimentary astronomy as he might pick up from one of the early medieval encyclopedias could ever have held the earth to be flat. Which is not to say that there were not 'flat-earthers' about in the Middle Ages; there were – and are now! But the earth is a sphere, and we must be at some point on its surface. The point on the sphere of the stars directly overhead is the zenith, and the circle limiting our vision, the edge of the earth's curve over which we cannot see, is the horizon. Let us put these on a new diagram, Fig. 2, and let us also put in the ecliptic and the tropics. These last represent the daily rotation of the sun at its furthest north and south points on the ecliptic, so let us draw in with a firm line those parts of the tropics which are above the horizon. These firm lines will then represent the daylight hours of the longest and shortest days. Twice a year, when the sun in its journey round the ecliptic crosses the equator, the day and night will be equal, and the crossing points are called the *equinoxes*; in the northern hemisphere the point where the sun crosses the equator on its way north is the spring, or vernal, equinox, and the other is the autumn equinox.

The whole starry sphere, like the sun, moon and planets, is going round from east to west each day; but since it moves slightly faster than the sun (or, more exactly, since the sun lags behind a bit), the constellations as it were catch the sun up, so that at one time of year a given constellation, say Orion, may be above the horizon during the daytime, and so be unseen, and later in the year it will have moved round and will come above the horizon at night, and we shall be able to see it. So, for example, Sirius, the Dog-star, the brightest star in the sky, is visible in winter in the northern hemisphere, but in summer is high in the sky in the daytime, and so invisible – which is why those days are the 'dog days', so notorious in ancient accounts of the behaviour of women, because then Sirius is with the sun, which is at its hottest.

The most conspicuous object in the night sky, when it is there, is the moon. Its motion is extremely complicated, and only three things need be noted now. First, its motion against the star-sphere, though apparently wandering, is always fairly close to the ecliptic. Second, the time between one new moon and the next is about 29½ days (the lunar or synodic month), while, third, the time it takes to go round the ecliptic is just over 27 days (the sidereal month). Fig. 3 shows why these months are of different lengths. When the moon is between the earth and the sun (though not in exactly the same plane, which would produce an eclipse), the moon's dark side is turned towards us, and then we cannot see it, and it is a new moon. At the same time, it is on a line joining the earth and some star – let us call that star S; this is position A in Fig. 3. When the moon and the earth have moved to position B, 27 and a bit days later, the moon is again in line with star S, the direction of which from the earth has not changed, since the stars are at such distances from us that their bearings are unaffected by the earth's motion in its orbit round the sun. That is, in position B,

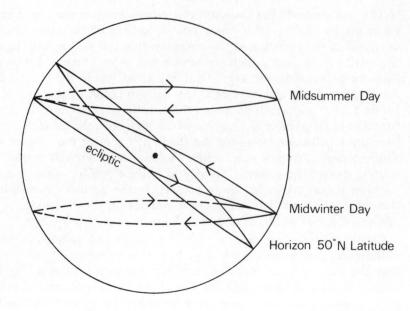

Fig. 2

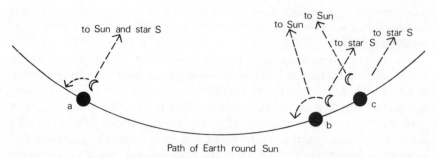

Fig. 3

the moon has been right round the sky, round the ecliptic, and that is one sidereal month. But the earth-moon system has to move on for a little more than two days before the moon is back in line with the sun, to give us another new moon, at the end of a lunar month (position C), because the position of the sun against the stars *is* changing, as we have seen.

The regular watcher of the night sky will soon distinguish the five planets visible to the naked eye. They shine with a sometimes brighter and always steadier light than the rest of the stars, and only twinkle slightly when low on the horizon. All of them move across the sphere of the fixed stars, with a rather irregular motion. They appear at times to stand still (in their 'stations') and even to move back for a while – to 'retrograde'. All travel within a few degrees of the ecliptic, at different rates, Mercury taking only 88 days to go right round, but Saturn taking nearly thirty years. The zone round the ecliptic, about 8½° on either side, in which the sun, moon and planets travel, is called the zodiac. Mercury, being so close to the sun, is a very difficult planet to spot, since it is only visible for about half an hour – before sunrise near the autumn equinox, and after sunset about the spring equinox – and it is rarely as bright as Sirius. Venus, in contrast, is the brightest object in the night sky after the moon. It can cast shadows, and is even visible sometimes in daylight. For part of the year it appears as a morning star, and as such the ancients knew it as Phosphoros (Greek) or Lucifer (Latin), both words meaning 'light-bringer'. At other times it is seen as Hesperus or Vesper, the evening star. Pythagoras is said to have identified the two as one planet, Venus. Mars shines with a reddish light, and because of its two-year period it is visible every night for about eighteen months, and then it disappears for four to six months. Its motion is the most irregular of all the planets' movements, as seen against the fixed stars, and its brightness varies greatly with its changing distance from the earth. It was this obviously varying distance which made the theory of concentric spheres so unsatis-factory – if all the spheres have the same centre, the distance of any planet cannot vary – but the irregularity of Mars' motion makes any geocentric scheme very complicated and difficult. Jupiter, taking nearly twelve years to complete its journey round the zodiac, is majestically bright – hence no doubt its association with the ruler of the Olympian gods. But the title, 'sun of the night', was given by Babylonians and Greeks to Saturn, which is no brighter than a fairly bright star, but which takes nearly thirty years to go round. Its slowness suggested age, and age no doubt wisdom and power, and it also suggested great remoteness, and so coldness and mystery. While the sun is bright and warm and life-giving, Saturn soon became associated with cold and death and malevolence. These five planets are the five known to astronomers and astrologers throughout the centuries before the development of the telescope.

That, then, was the system with which the astrologer dealt, a system built up from observations with the naked eye, observations which any man may make today who has the patience and a few simple instruments to measure angles and altitudes. That it was geocentric is not important: it must always be remembered that what is important to the astrologer is the *relative* positions of the earth, sun, moon and planets, and that these are the same, when expressed as angular relations seen from the earth, whether the system of cosmology we use is earth- or sun-centred. Our senses tell us that the earth is stationary, and that all else goes round it, and this was the system accepted by men throughout most of recorded history. The astrologer, said Ptolemy, should so understand the movements of the heavenly bodies that he can know 'the place and time of any configuration'; and certainly astrology as defined for this book could not exist before an accurate, or fairly accurate, mathematical system was devised which enabled men to plot such 'configurations' – that is, the relative positions of earth and planets against the background of the fixed stars. This gives us an earliest date for the beginning of astrology proper, so to speak. Somewhat surprisingly, to those who believe astrology to go back thousands of years before Christ, that date is about the end of the fifth or the beginning of the fourth century B.C. Before that, back to the times of the first intelligent men, no doubt, there was speculation about the influence of the heavens on the lives of men, and some prophesying from stellar omens. But this is a kind of 'proto-astrology', about which we can only make more or less informed guesses, and it does not come within the scope of this story. Most of what is written about it is four-fifths speculation, and some is very much more. The object of this book is to trace the history of mathematical astrology from Greek times, when it began, to the eighteenth century, to give some account of men's attitudes to it, and its place in the history of society and ideas. Whether it is a true science or art, or humbug, or something in between, it has been an important item in the mental furniture of Western man for twenty-three centuries, and its history is part of our history.

II

From the Beginnings to Manilius

Astrology is the interpretation and prognostication of events on earth, and of men's characters and dispositions, from the measurement and plotting of the movements and relative positions of the heavenly bodies, of the stars and planets, including among the latter the sun and moon. This may or may not imply belief in stellar 'influences'; it certainly implies constant and therefore usable relationships between configurations in the heavens and events on earth. Since astrology proper depends on the charting of the movements and positions of the planets, it could not arise until after the growth of mathematical astronomy. While many and fantastic claims have been made ever since antiquity for the vast age of Babylonian astronomy, it seems safe to say that some sort of mathematical, theoretical astronomy was only developed late in Mesopotamian history, from the fifth century B.C. on, and that the real development of the science was the achievement of the Greeks.[1]

Early Mesopotamian astronomy was purely descriptive, and the 'prehistoric' period lasted from about 1800 B.C. until the fifth century. Accurate and tabulated observations were probably not made before about 700 B.C., and then they mostly concerned the moon and eclipses, and not planetary movements. Indeed Ptolemy, in the second century A.D., while using old eclipse tables, complains of the lack of reliable planetary observations. Most of the mathematical astronomy that was developed in Mesopotamia by the end of the fourth century B.C. seems to have been concerned with the construction of ephemerides for the calculation of the difficult lunar calendar. Calendrial computation may be seen as the prime cause of the rise of scientific astronomy, whether the calendar was needed for religious or agricultural purposes (though the two are hardly separable in early times). Greek mathematical astronomy cannot be said to have really begun until the fourth century, with Eudoxus, and its great age was the third and second centuries B.C., from Aristarchus to Hipparchus. Ancient

---

[1] On this and what follows, see O. Neugebauer, *The Exact Sciences in Antiquity*, 2nd edn (Providence, Rhode Island, 1957) 97ff, and M. P. Nilsson, *Geschichte der griechischen Religion* (Munich, 1961) II, 268ff.

Egypt made only two contributions to the story of astronomy, since the science did not develop there: 'Egyptian astronomy', says Neugebauer,[2] 'remained through all its history on an exceedingly crude level which had practically no relations to the rapidly growing mathematical astronomy of the Hellenistic age'. The two contributions were a simple calendar, which in one form or another has lasted until the present, of twelve months of thirty days plus five or six extra days ('epagomenal' days) to make up the year; and the notion of twelve daylight and twelve night hours, which the Hellenistic astronomers made into the twenty-four equal, 'equinoctial', hours we still use.

So it seems that horoscopic astrology cannot be older than the fourth century B.C., and Neugebauer says categorically that 'the main structure of astrological theory is undoubtedly Hellenistic'.[3] The earliest truly astrological texts we possess are from Hellenistic Egypt, in Greek, from the late third and second centuries; the earliest more or less complete textbook is the poem in five books of the Roman poet Manilius, at the beginning of the first century A.D.; the earliest of the few known Babylonian horoscopes is dated 410 B.C., and the great mass of horoscopes preserved from ancient times, all Greek, belong to the first five centuries of our era. So the claims made by many astrologers for the great antiquity of their art must be taken with considerable scepticism. Astrology as defined here is a fairly recent and largely Greek creation. Which is odd. For it is commonly and rightly held that the classical Greeks had no star-cults, and indulged in no worship of gods or goddesses of the sun, moon or planets. So astrology was not indigenous to Greece, but must have been introduced. What sort of astrology could have been introduced, and when? Why did the non-starworshipping and rationalistic Greeks accept it so readily and develop it, and what did they do to it?

The science or art of horoscopic astrology was a late and Hellenistic creation, but it had, of course, a long prehistory; and two streams may be said to have mingled in the Greek schools, the Babylonian and the Egyptian. Egyptian ideas did not have to be imported. After the conquests of Alexander the Great, the Egypt of the Ptolemies was part of the Greek world, and Alexandria became and remained for centuries the intellectual capital of the ancient world. It was the Babylonian tradition that was introduced, and it was from the east that the very idea of such an art as astrology came into Greece. Not that the Greeks were wholly indifferent, or wholly scientific in their attitudes to the heavenly bodies. They would have been a strange people indeed had they not regarded the sun and moon as in some way

[2] Neugebauer, *op. cit.*, 80.
[3] *Ibid.*, 170.

12

divine. Farnell concluded 'that sun-worship had once been prevalent and powerful among the people of the pre-Hellenic culture, but that very few of the communities of the later historic period retained it as a potent factor of the state-religion, while at the same time the individual's perception of the great luminary was still one that may be termed religious'.[4] Wilamowitz is more emphatic: 'Sun-worship is not originally Hellenic. The gods of the Greeks, who loved and hated, helped men and harmed them, were of the earth, belonged to the earth, and appeared among men. In their ranks the Ὑπερίων (powers above) did not belong. Still less did the moon'.[5] After discussing star-myths, some of which, like those about Orion, were certainly derived from foreign sources, he says: 'All these had nothing to do with religion. It was first through astrology that the constellations had any influence on the fate of men, and even there they were fundamentally only σήματα (signs)'.[6] The clearest ancient authority on the subject is Aristophanes, who in his comedy, *Peace* (lines 406–413) distinguishes Greeks from barbarians by the fact that the barbarians worship the sun and moon as gods. The Greeks themselves believed that their astronomy was derived from Babylonia, and that astrology was brought into Greece by the 'Chaldaean' Berosus. What kind of astrology was it?

From the second millenium B.C. there was developed in Mesopotamia a vast bulk of omen-literature, which was collected and organised in the work known as the Enuma Anu Enlil, about 1000 B.C. The astronomy of these omens was purely descriptive, and all concern the nation as a whole, or the king and royal princes. None is concerned with the fate of individual men. A typical such omen reads: 'When the Moon occults Jupiter (*Sagmígar*), that year a king will die (or) an eclipse of the Moon and Sun will take place. A great king will die. When Jupiter enters the midst of the Moon there will be want in Aharrû. The king of Elam will be slain with the sword: in Subarti ...(?) will revolt. When Jupiter enters the midst of the Moon, the market of the land will be low. When Jupiter goes out from behind the Moon, there will be hostility in the land'.[7] These omens are taken from stars, sun, moon and planets, eclipses, clouds, thunder and earthquakes. They clearly presuppose that there is some relationship between what happens in the sky and what happens on earth, though they do not suggest that the relationship is one of cause and effect.

[4] L. R. Farnell, *The Cults of the Greek States* (Oxford, 1909) V, 419f.
[5] U. von Wilamowitz-Moellendorff, *Der Glaube der Hellenen* (Berlin, 1931) I, 257.
[6] *Ibid.*, 262.
[7] R. Campbell Thompson, *The Reports of the Magicians and Astrologers of Nineveh and Babylon* (London, 1900) II, 192, p. lxvii.

From the seventh century on exact observation becomes increasingly important, and still later arithmetical computation plays a part in this sort of proto-astrology. The names of the constellations, including those which lie along the ecliptic, are frequently used, but there is no sign of the zodiac as such. Many of the names were taken over by the Greeks, and the combined Greco-Babylonian description of the heavens was later given the name *sphaera graecanica*, to distinguish it from the *sphaera barbarica*, the non-Greek (the true meaning of 'barbaric') and usually Egyptian description. Alongside these omens there are a few which give predictions about a child according to the month of birth, but these may be derived from lists of lucky and unlucky months rather than from any astronomical data.

Among the constellations named in the omens are familiar ones like Aries and Leo and Scorpio, now known to everyone as zodiacal signs. But the zodiac of the astrologers is no older than astrology itself. The first divisions of the paths of the sun and moon through the heavens were made for calendrial purposes, as a way of measuring time. It is difficult for us now to imagine a time when 'the date' was not simply known, from looking at a calendar. But for many thousands of years men only knew what time of year it was by looking at the natural calendar of the sky, and dated the sowing of crops and all their activities by the risings and settings of the Pleiades or of Sirius or of some other easily recognisable star or star-group. The groupings of stars were of course quite arbitrary, and different peoples have different constellations, with different names, though some, such as Ursa Major (the Plough, or Big Dipper), are so clearly marked out in the sky as to be common to all. The sun's path round the ecliptic in the year seems first to have been divided simply into four, the four seasons, the dividing points being at the equinoxes and the tropics. The division of the path of the moon led to the naming of ·'lunar mansions', known in Greek and important in far eastern and Indian, and also in Arabic astrology. As early as the second millenium a number of constellations were listed as standing 'in the moon's path', and a list of eighteen contains the names of ten of the twelve we now call zodiacal signs. The twelve from Aries to Pisces seem to have emerged as standard form no earlier than the end of the fifth century B.C., and the first mention of twelve equal signs, as opposed to the constellations (of unequal extent in the heavens), was in 419 B.C.[8]

There was certainly some connection between this selection of twelve and the evolution of a lunar-solar calendar of twelve months of about thirty days, but it is quite unclear when or by whom this

[8] Rupert Gleadow, *The Origin of the Zodiac* (London, 1968) c.11.

time-measuring zodiac was linked with astrology. That it should be so linked was quite natural. The combination of the ideas of lucky and unlucky days and months, the importance of the birth date, and the movement of the sun round the ecliptic, would lead to it. The most obvious time and place for the connection to be made are the late fifth century and Babylonia, with its relations with Egypt affecting its astronomy. The general outline of the development of the idea of the zodiac is summed up by Gleadow: 'The zodiac grew up, and must have grown up, as a device for measuring time. Only later did it come to be used for divination, and later still for the analysis of character'.[9]

So around the end of the fifth and the beginning of the fourth century B.C. Babylonian astrology had probably reached the stage of putting together lists of lucky and unlucky days and months, the taking of omens (including those for individuals), and the course of the sun, moon and planets through the zodiac; though here, as often, it is very important to distinguish a belief in the value of signs in the heavens as prognosticators of earthly events, from that clear interpre-tation of plotted positions and movements which we know as horoscopic or, more properly, as genethlialogical astrology. The latter was probably just emerging at the end of the fifth century; and this is the most likely time for its introduction into Greece. That there was some contact between Classical Greece and Babylonian astronomy is evident from Democritus, Frag. 55A, which shows that he, towards the end of the fifth century, was acquainted with the Babylonian triad of Sun, Moon and Venus (Sin, Shamash and Ishtar); and a generation later, Eudoxus (according to Cicero, De Divinatione, II, 22) was repudiating the claim of the 'Chaldaeans' to be able to forecast a man's fate from the date of his birth. Slightly later still Theophrastus referred to the same claim, according to Proclus in his commentary on Plato's Timaeus (3.151 Diels). The earliest clear references to Babylonian astrology in Greek are in the Hippocratic medical work On Diets of about 400 B.C.

Now none of these sources is clearly referring to horoscopic or genethlialogical astrology: all could simply be talking about the kind of crude proto-astrology we have already described. The mention of the Hippocratic writings, however, leads us to a name we have already met: Berosus, who is clearly linked by the Roman writer Vitruvius (of the late first century B.C.) both with genethlialogical astrology and with Greece: 'It must be allowed that we can know what effects the twelve signs, and the sun, moon and five planets, have on the course of human life, from astrology and the calculations of the Chaldaeans.

---

[9] *Ibid.*, p. 206.

For the genethlialogical art is properly theirs, by which they are able to unfold past and future events from their astronomical calculations. And many have come from that race of the Chaldaeans to leave us their discoveries, which are full of acuteness and learning. The first was Berosus, who settled on the island of Cos and taught there, and after him the learned Antipater, and then Achinapolus, who however set out his genethlialogical calculations not from the date of birth but from that of conception' (Book VI, 2). Nothing further is known, incidentally, of either Antipater (whom there is no good reason to connect with the Stoic Antipater of Tarsus) or Achinapolus. The other relevant reference to Berosus in ancient authors[10] tell us that he was a priest of Bel and lived to be a hundred and sixteen years old; and Pliny quotes his authority for believing that the Babylonians had been observing the heavens and keeping records for 490,000 years! One might reasonably be forgiven if one rejected the whole story as fiction, but that there was a fairly widespread tradition that astrology was brought to Greece by Berosus, that there is evidence for his existence apart from his astrology, and that we know that astrology was not indigenous among the Greeks.

At least the association with Cos, and the date, probably the early fourth century, are plausible enough. Cos was the home of the Hippocratic school of medicine, and there were connections between astrology and medicine from very ancient times. And the time was ripe. The critiques of the old Olympian religion – of the anthropomorphic pantheon of Zeus and Hera, Ares and Aphrodite, Hermes and the rest – by the fifth century philosophers and Sophists had led to the attempt by the philosophers themselves, and notably Plato and Aristotle, to find more satisfactory gods in the heavens. In the *Laws* and the *Epinomis* especially, Plato argued for the divinity of the heavenly bodies, who were to be worshipped for the eternal mathematical beauty of their regular movements. Whether Plato was influenced by his somewhat dubious 'Chaldaean guest' or more by the Pythagoreans, who were inclined to the same sort of view of the stars and who had greatly influenced his cosmological dialogue, the *Timaeus*, is not of importance here. Pythagoreanism, Plato and Aristotle, and to some extent the Orphic religion (which came from the east, and also influenced Plato), all prepared the ground for the reception of astrological ideas. That astrology proper was late developing in Greece is evident from the fact that all later astrology fixes the vernal equinox at either 8° Aries or 0°, and not 15° as older astronomers like Eudoxus had done. The early fourth century, then, seems the most likely time

---

[10] Vitruvius, II.1, VIII.1; Seneca, *Quaest. Nat.*, III.29, 1; Pliny, *N.H.*, VII.123, 160 and 193; Censorinus, *De die natali*, xvii.

for the introduction of astrology into Greece, and Cos was probably at least one of the places where that introduction was effected. It is possibly not without significance that although the Greek states did not set up temples to the sun, moon or stars, Cos had a small shrine of Helios, the sun-god, and Hemera, the goddess of day.[11]

Why did the Greeks then take to astrology, so much so as to make it their own and create the art as we now know it? Only partly because they were at that time already turning from the old religious forms to more personal and sometimes mystical religions. There is no evidence of widespread popular astrology until much later, in the second century, and it was not the uneducated and superstitious who accepted and developed it. It was the philosophers, like Plato, who prepared the ground, and the Stoics – who were among the greatest logicians and physicists of their times – who most fully worked it into their system. It was the doctors and the scientists like Theophrastus who accepted it and developed its associations with medicine and plants and stones, and with the science of alchemy, which was then nearer to chemical technology than to the magical search for the philosophers' stone it much later became. Those who have admired the Greeks for their clear rationalism (and who have always ignored anything they saw as contrary to it as un-Hellenic, no matter whether the author was a Greek and the language Greek and the time Classical) have so pre-conditioned their own thinking as to misunderstand both astrology and its appeal to the Greek mind. Farnell wrote:[12] 'Let it also be here noted among the great negative gains of Greek religion, that the communities avoided star-worship, and that therefore in the days of its independence the Hellenic spirit was saved from the disease of astrology'. (Notice the curious 'liberal' assumption that it was the alien, autocratic rule of the Macedonians which turned the clear-headed Greeks into addle-pated astrologers and the like.) Even Cumont, after much of value on 'the new sidereal theology' of the philosophers, and on the Pythagorean 'system of numbers and geometrical figures designed to represent certain gods' being 'in accordance with astrological theories', even Cumont can write: 'The insatiable curiosity of the Greeks, then, did not ignore astrology, but their sober genius rejected its hazardous doctrines, and their keen critical sense was able to distinguish the scientific data observed by the Babylonians from the erroneous conclusions which they derived from them. It is to their everlasting honour that, amid the tangle of precise observations and superstitious fancies which made up the priestly lore of the East, they discovered and utilised the serious

[11] Farnell, *op. cit.*, 419.
[12] *Ibid.*, 420.

elements, while neglecting the rubbish'.[13] That statement is untrue both in its detail and in its totality; it could only have been written by one who had decided what was to be allowed as 'Greek' on *a priori* grounds. It is the 'Macarthyism' of the Classical scholar: too many Greeks indulged in un-Greek activities! George Sarton was much nearer the truth when he wrote: 'One might almost claim that Greek astrology was the fruit of Greek rationalism. At any rate, it received some kind of justification from the notion of cosmos, a cosmos which is so well arranged that no part is independent of the other parts and of the whole'; and 'the basic principle of astrology, a correspondence between stars and men, enabling the former to influence the latter, was not irrational'.[14] Neugebauer sums it up pithily: 'Compared with the background of religion, magic and mysticism, the fundamental doctrines of astrology are pure science'.[15]

The point, and it is a very important point indeed, is that astrology appealed to the educated Greeks precisely because they were rational, and because it was a rational system, or could be made to look like one. It is not an accident that the two greatest of the Greek astronomers, Hipparchus and Ptolemy, were both also astrologers, the latter the author of the most influential ancient textbook of astrology. Nor were the Greeks *necessarily* wrong about this; but right or wrong, they accepted astrology, and its acceptance as a learned and scientific study was the common, if not the normal, attitude to it down to the eighteenth century, and it is impossible to understand men like Kepler and Newton unless astrology is seen for what the Greeks made it, a rational attempt to map the state of the heavens and to interpret that map in the context of that 'cosmic sympathy'[16] which makes man an integral part of the universe. The scientific basis of astrology in antiquity is seen in the order in which the planets are named. In Plato and Aristotle we find what is known as the 'Egyptian' order: moon, sun, Mercury, Venus, Mars, Jupiter, Saturn; the older Babylonian order was moon, sun, Jupiter, Venus, Saturn, Mercury, Mars, an order which from the fifth century on was sometimes changed to moon, sun, Mars, Venus, Mercury, Saturn, Jupiter. But the order called 'Chaldaean', which was undoubtedly Greek and astronomical, derived from the planets' periods of rotation round the ecliptic, and hence their

---

[13] F. Cumont, *Astrology and Religion among the Greeks and Romans* (New York and London, 1912) 40ff and 53.

[14] G. Sarton, *A History of Science: Hellenistic Science and Culture in the Last Three Centuries B.C.* (Cambridge, Mass., and London, 1959) 165.

[15] *Op. cit.*, 171.

[16] The phrase is Greek: e.g., Ideler, *Physici et medici graeci minores* (Berlin, 1841) I, 396: χωρὶς γὰρ τῆς κοσμικῆς συμπαθείας τοῖς ἀνθρώποις οὐδὲν γίνεται: 'nothing happens to man outside, apart from, the cosmic sympathy'.

assumed distances from the earth, was moon, Mercury, Venus, sun, Mars, Jupiter, Saturn. It is this order, which becomes standard from the second century B.C., which is used in Greek astrology.

The learned Greeks of the fourth and third centuries received Babylonian astronomy and astrology together, and developed both – indeed, they used the same word, *astrologia*, for both. One of the first writers to distinguish the two words, *astronomia* (which is rare in the Classical period) and *astrologia*, was Isidore of Seville, in the seventh century A.D.[17] At almost any time in Latin, *astrologia* can mean either or both. But Isidore defines *astronomia* as dealing with 'the turning of the heavens, and the risings, settings and motions of the stars, and why they are called what they are', and then distinguishes what he calls physical astrology, which deals with 'the courses of the sun and moon, or the fixed seasons of the stars', from superstitious astrology, which is that which is 'pursued by the *mathematici*, who prophesy by the stars, and who distribute the twelve heavenly signs among the parts of the soul and body, and attempt to foretell the births and characters of men from the courses of the stars'. Now such a distribution of the twelve signs certainly was made in Egypt, in Alexandria; and many of the learned Greeks we are concerned with lived and worked in that great Greco-Egyptian city of the Hellenistic age. There they inherited some aspects of Egyptian thought which they incorporated into their astrological thinking, and which had a lasting influence on astrology. It is important, first, that ancient Egypt produced no astrology of its own. All the works directly or indirectly concerned with astrology as we know it were written by Hellenistic Greeks in the third century B.C. or later. Nor are there any astrological pictures from ancient Egypt, even though, as Gleadow says,[18] 'no culture has left more abundant monuments in record of its beliefs'; the two 'zodiacs' of Dendera, the two of Esna, the horoscope of Athribis and the coffin of Heter, all belong to the first two centuries A.D. Astrology was the creation of the Hellenistic Greeks; but many of the men who made it were Alexandrian Greeks, and the Egyptian influence was strong.

We have seen that one of the Egyptians' most important contributions to astronomy was the calendar, of twelve months of thirty days each, plus five 'epagomenal' days (six in leap years). They began their year with the heliacal rising of Sirius, which in dynastic times immediately preceded the flooding of the Nile, on which Egypt depended. The heliacal rising of a star or constellation occurs when the

---

[17] *Etymologiae*, III.27.
[18] *Op. cit.*, 182.

star is seen rising in the east just before sunrise; its heliacal setting is when it sets in the west immediately after sunset. By the end of the second millenium B.C., thirty-six constellations were associated with the calendar, each constellation's heliacal rising taken as the 'last hour of night' for ten days, when the next constellation had to be used. There are many lists of these thirty-six constellations from the Middle Kingdom on, and they vary a great deal in their names and order, as might be expected over a long period. The constellations so used are known as 'decans', though the origin of the name is obscure.[19] Now the risings of these decans during the night were used to divide the time of darkness into hours; and since in summer, at the time of Sirius' heliacal rising, twelve are seen to rise before dawn, the night hours were twelve. There were ten full daylight hours in the time of Seti I (about 1300 B.C.), decimal counting being the rule. Add to these an hour of twilight at each end of the day, and we have twelve day hours and twelve night hours, the length of the hour varying with the time of year. Twice a year, at the time of the equinoxes, day and night are equal in length, and all the hours are equal, and it was obviously more convenient for astronomers to use these equal, 'equinoctial' hours regularly, and so we got our twenty-four hour clock.

Now two constellations are easily and safely identifiable in the decan lists, Sirius and Orion; and Sirius was the leader. The interval between the heliacal setting and rising of Sirius, the period of its invisibility, was about seventy days; and the other constellations were probably chosen to have about the same period of invisibility. They thus all lie in a zone parallel to and south of the ecliptic – that is, in or near the zodiac. Now since the year is a little longer than 365 days, and not 360, the decanal calendar gradually got out of step with the actual year, which necessitated complicated alterations. When in Ptolemaic Egypt the calendar was reformed by the addition of a sixth epagomenal day in leap years, the Greco-Babylonian zodiac was already known, and it was a simple step to add the decans to the zodiac, so that they became ten-degree divisions of that circle. It is as such that they are shown round the edge of the circular zodiac at Dendera, in the time of the Roman emperor Tiberius. Once they became sections of the zodiac, they were absorbed into astrology.

One of the texts in connection with the decans belongs to what is known as the Hermetic literature, writings in Greek of Ptolemaic Egypt, which include one of the most important source-books of ancient astrology, the work attributed to Nechepso and Petosiris. But

---

[19] On the word, δεκανός, *decanus*, see A. E. Housman, *Manilii Astronomicon Liber Quartus* (London, 1920) ixff. On the astronomy of the decans, see Neugebauer, *op. cit.*, 81ff. 81ff.

first, why 'Hermetic'? One of the ancient Egyptians great gods was Thoth. He was originally associated with the moon, and hence became the god of time and time-measurement, and so of astronomy. Possibly because of this, or perhaps quite separately, he was also associated with writing, and so with all the arts and sciences which depend on writing, including medicine, astrology and alchemy. In the Egypt of the Ptolemies, in the course of the fourth century, the Greeks of Egypt identified the Egyptian gods with their own, so that Osiris became Dionysus, Horus Apollo, and so on. Hermes already possessed many of the attributes of Thoth, and we know from Aristoxenus of Tarentum that the identification Hermes-Thoth was made before the end of the fourth century. Now the Egyptian Greeks often applied the epithet *'megistos'* (greatest) to their gods, and sometimes used the Egyptian form of intensifying an adjective by repetition, and we find *megistos* so repeated in inscriptions. In some way we cannot now trace, the name of Hermes was so dignified, and in his case three adjectives were abbreviated to *'trismegistos'* (thrice greatest), and the form Hermes Trismegistos became a name in its own right. To Hermes Trismegistos were attributed works of all kinds, connected with many arts: 'The Hermetic literature presents us with the most varied forms: under the patronage of Hermes were put writings on astrology and astrological medicine, magical recipes, works on alchemy, small philosophical or theosophical treatises, questions of astronomy, physics, psychology, embryogeny, natural history (*Kyranides*) – in short, everything which, with the decline of rationalism, was taken to be science'.[20] All this literature is Greek, and there is no evidence that any of it preserves any of the ancient writings of the Egyptians themselves. Much of the earliest work in the corpus is on astrology, which must be later than the early fourth century, and most of it is second century or later.

Two of the most important of these astrological writings were the treatise known as the *Salmeschiniaka* (the *sch* is pronounced as in *school*), and the textbook of Nechepso-Petosiris; and fragments of many more lie buried in the appendices of the twelve volumes of the *Catalogus Codicum Astrologorum Graecorum*. Others have become known from Arabic writings of the ninth century and later, and a few in late Latin versions.[21] Only fragments of both works survive; the

---

[20] A.-J. Festugière, *La Révélation d'Hermès Trismégiste, L'Astrologie et les Sciences occultes*, I (Paris, 1944) 82.

[21] On the *Salmeschiniake* see W. Kroll in Pauly-Wissowa, Suppl. V, cols 843–6. For Nechepso-Petosoris, E. Riess, 'Nechepsonis et Petosiridis fragmenta magica', in *Philologus*, Suppl. VI (1892), 325–388. The *Catalogus Codicum Astrologorum Graecorum* was published at Brussels between 1898 and 1953 under many editors, chiefly Cumont and Boll. The Latin text of one important Hermetic astrological treatise had been published, with a long commentary, by W. Gundel: 'Neue astrologische Texte des Hermes

Salmeschiniaka is quoted by Nechepso-Petosiris, and the latter is quoted or referred to by almost all later astrologers. Both these works are Greek, and both belong to the middle of the second century B.C. Both works show evidence of ideas of Babylonian origin, and indeed the *Salmeschiniaka* may have been first a Babylonian work. It mentions the Babylonian god Nebu, and it deals with five-day intervals, which were Babylonian, as opposed to the Egyptian decans; and the name may be derived from the Babylonian word *salmi*, meaning 'pictures'. A five-day interval gives one seventy-two such pictures, and it is interesting that Pliny, nearly three centuries later, also refers to seventy-two pictures: 'They (that is, those who cannot cope with astronomy) are excused by the vastness of the universe, its immensity divided across its height into seventy-two signs, that is, likenesses of things and animals, into which the learned have divided the heavens'.[22] On the other hand, the pictures were probably Egyptian (Pliny puts the Pleiades in the tail of Taurus: but the *sphaera graecanica* had only the fore half of a bull in the sky, while the *sphaera barbarica*, which was basically Egyptian, had the whole animal); the decan names in the work are certainly Egyptian; it is included by later writers under the name of Hermes Trismegistos, and the papyrus fragments are Egyptian. So it looks as though in this work we can see the mingling of Babylonian and Egyptian Greek astrological traditions, in the second century B.C., in, probably, Alexandria.

Much more frequently quoted by later authors than the *Salmeschiniaka* is the work attributed by them to Nechepso and Petosiris. These two were assumed to be an ancient Egyptian Pharaoh and High Priest, which lent them the authority both of rank and antiquity. It was common (and still is to some extent) for astrological writers to claim great antiquity for their art; but there is no real doubt that the names have no historical connection with ancient Egyptian personages, or that the work was originally Greek, written in the second century B.C., or even between 80 and 60 B.C., as Riess thought. The book seems to have been a medley of verse and prose, and very long. It is difficult even in the pages of Riess' article to disentangle what was original to Nechepso-Petosiris; it becomes almost impossible in the works of later Greek writers of the second to eighth centuries A.D., who tend to refer to Nechepso and Petosiris, or simply to 'the ancients', whenever they feel the need for the authority of the centuries, which is much of the time. There was certainly much in the work which is commonplace in later writers, and a good deal, on comets, on eclipses in various signs,

---

Trismegistos', in *Abhandlungen der Bayerischen Akademie der Wissenschaften, Phil.-hist. Abteilung, Neue Folge*, Heft 12 (Munich, 1936).
[22] Pliny, *NH*, II.8110.

on good and bad times for action, and on the expected length of life, for example, which was probably ancient in the second century. Some of it, for example Riess' Fragment 12, sounds like 'updated' Babylonian omen-literature – brought up to date by being put into a zodiacal context: 'When Mercury is in Gemini at the time of the rising of Sirius, the rising (of the Nile flood) will be a proper one, there will be rejoicing among the people, and the king will be victorious'. It may be that the rule for the Lot of Fortune (that it stands to the Moon as the Ascendant to the Sun) was in Nechepso-Petosiris, and also the idea that the Ascendant at birth is where the Moon was at conception. It is impossible now to be clear about the origins of many of the ideas current in these early centuries of astrology. What is certain is that they were developed and gradually assimilated to a zodiacal system by the Hellenistic Greeks of Egypt, whether they were originally Egyptian or Babylonian ideas, or invented by the Greeks themselves.

Other evidence of early, relevant mixing of Babylonian and Egyptian thought is provided by astrological medicine. Berosus was said to have settled on the island of Cos, the home of Hippocratic medicine, and astrology early found its way into the Hippocratic corpus of medical writings. In Egypt, medicine was under the patronage of Thoth, as was astronomy; when, in the guise of Hermes Trismegistos, he collected astrology as well, he naturally gathered under his aegis astrological medicine, or *iatromathematica*, to give it its ancient Greek name. At some stage in the fourth and third centuries the parts of the human body had been allocated to signs of the zodiac, beginning at the top, with the head, and at the vernal equinox, with Aries, and working down the body and round the zodiac, ending with Pisces looking after the feet. This association of anatomy with the stars was most likely made by the Greeks themselves, under the influence of that idea of cosmic sympathy, of the oneness of the universe, including man, which played such an important part in Stoic thought. The idea of the universe as the macrocosm, and man as the microcosm, reflecting in his nature and structure that of the whole, is a Greek one, and largely Stoic. Now in the Hermetic corpus there are some writings concerned with what might be called homoeopathic medicine: the general idea was that the sign governing a particular part of the body was affected by a malevolent planet, or a planet in a bad aspect; and by sympathy, the part of the body was also affected, and was sick. It followed that the remedy was to increase the power of the sign, by using such plants and animals as were associated with it. Egyptian medicine already had a large and ancient stock of such semi-magical remedies, and the association with the stars was probably made under Babylonian influence. In Babylonia also, medicine was magical; the Greeks were the first to develop scientific medicine – it was indeed

23

their oldest empirical science. The Babylonians regarded the positions of the stars and planets as having favourable or unfavourable aspects, and medical charms and amulets were made or chosen to accord with favourable states of the heavens.

The association of plants with the heavenly bodies[23] probably grew out of astrological medicine. Plants were individually associated with signs of the zodiac, with the planets, with the decans, and even, though much more rarely, with fixed stars. Though most of the texts we have are from very much later, Pfister reckons that the material they contain points to the period between the second century B.C. and the first century A.D. as the time when the details were worked out. In the same way, Egyptian medical practice was responsible for the linking of certain animals with signs and planets. But the association of stones with signs of the zodiac is of dubious antiquity and presents many problems. Stones were early related to the planets, including the sun and moon in their number, and these relationships appear to have been derived from resemblances, mostly in colour, between the stones and the planets.[24] They were also associated with fixed stars, according to a treatise which exists only in a Latin version of the Arabic of Mesha'allah, the eighth century astrologer, but which the author claimed was derived from Hermes. Colours were associated with the planets from very ancient times in Babylonia, but the different colours attributed to the several planets differ widely in our authorities, the only common elements being red for Mars and gold for the sun. But there seems to be little connection between the stones attributed to signs or planets and colour. It seems more likely that the stones are derived from the association in Egypt of magic stones with days of the months and with the decans, and then later through the decans with the zodiac, and from that, still later, with the planets. Planetary metals were almost certainly derived from alchemy. The original home of alchemy was Hellenistic Alexandria, and the same Egyptian association of lucky and unlucky times – days or decans – with the stars led to the mingling of astrology and alchemy which was to have such a long history, and to the allocation of different metals to the several planets. Gold for the Sun, and silver for the Moon were obvious choices, and the association of quick-silver with Mercury, which already had just such a mobile character, lasted long enough to transfer the planet's name to the metal. Lead was given to Saturn: its weight and colour

---

[23] On this and for details, see F. Pfister, 'Pflanzenaberglaube', in *Pauly-Wissowa*, XIX.1446ff, esp. 1449ff on astrology; for lists of plants, see Festugiére, *op. cit.*, 139ff, Gleadow, *op. cit.*, 85f, and the Appendices to CCAG, e.g., VI.83; VII.253f; VIII.3.132, 153; VIII.4.260 etc.
[24] On planetary colours and minerals, see A. Bouché-Leclercq, *L'Astrologie grecque* (Paris, 1899) 313ff.

suited the slow, cold planet. Jupiter was originally given electrum (gold and silver alloy) but later and usually tin, Venus copper, and Mars, as befitted the god of war, iron.

Most of this sort of association, the mixture of different 'sciences' with astrology, took place in a confused and confusing way, with no general consensus of opinion, in those same third and second centuries B.C. in Egypt which saw the development of astrology itself. There is one further possible Egyptian contribution to the tradition. The zodiac as we know it, with its twelve signs, was the invention of the Babylonians. But there were and are other ways of dividing the circle to the ecliptic. The most important and longest lasting is into 'houses', which the ancients called, generally, τόποι, or in Latin loci. The name 'house' for such a division is confusing, since each planet has one or two signs of which it is the 'ruler', and these are called the 'houses' (οἶκοι or domi in the ancient languages – or domicilia) of the planets. But the τόποι, loci, developed into the modern 'houses', which govern different spheres of man's life, and which, since they are concerned with what happens in this world, mundus, are called 'mundane houses'. These may have originated in Egyptian divisions of the ecliptic.

The simplest division, and probably the oldest, is into four quadrants. The four points dividing the quadrants were called κέντρα or, in Latin, centra or cardines. They were: the point of the ecliptic which was rising above the horizon at the time in question; the point where the meridian (the arc of longitude passing through the observer's zenith) cuts the ecliptic; the point on the ecliptic which is setting; and the point directly opposite the second – that is, where the other half of the meridian cuts the other half of the ecliptic. The first was called the ὡροσκόπος, horoscopus, or ascendens, and is now known as the Ascendant, abbreviated to ASC. The second was the μεσουράνημα, the Midheaven, still known by its Latin name Medium Caeli, and abbreviated to MC. The third was the δύσις or δυνόν, the occasus, or setting-point; and the fourth was the ὑπόγειον, still, like the second, called by its Latin name, Imum Caeli, the IMC.

For the ancient Egyptians, the sun and stars are strong and young in the east, rise to their greatest power in the midheaven, and decline into age and weakness in the west. Hence if the quadrants are related to human life, it is natural that the first, from the horoscope to the MC, should govern a man's youth, the next from the MC to the setting point his manhood, and so on round the circle. This is simply stated in a Hermetic astrological work, a late compendium of older material, some of which survives in a Latin translation: 'Chapter XXIV: On the four quarters of the figure, and how you can know of the four ages of man in nativities. The beginning of the four is the horoscope. Now

25

from the first degree of the ascendant to the degree of the *Medium Caeli* is called the eastern, masculine quarter; and this quarter signifies the first age of life. The second quarter is feminine, and is called meridional; that is, from the degree of the *Medium Caeli* to the degree of the setting point. This is the southern and meridional quadrant. This signifies the middle age, which follows youth; for in middle age a man shows what he can do. The third quarter is from the degree of the setting point to the degree of the IMC, which is opposite the MC. It is a masculine quarter and signifies old age. The last is from the degree of the IMC to the ascendant, and this is feminine and is the northern quadrant; it signifies extreme and decrepit old age and death'.[25] Early astrology probably worked simply in terms of these quadrants, and traces of this can be seen in the same Hermetic treatise, for example in Chapter XXVI: 'If the Moon is in the ascendant, and Venus in the setting quarter, and Mars in the MC, then the child will be born of a slave mother or of one of low degree ...' etc. Or again: 'If the Sun and Saturn are in the ascendant, and Jupiter in the MC, and the Moon and Mars either following or in the setting quarter ...' But the later twelve-house division is found in the same chapter, as in the formula: 'If the Moon is in the ascendant and Jupiter and Mars are in the eleventh (house) ...'

The next step was to divide each of these quadrants into two, so that each cardinal point had two houses, one on each side of it, one having risen just before it, the other just after it. This system of eight houses, the *octatopos*, was to live on in various forms. To each of the eight was allocated some sphere of human life, such as marriage, sickness, children, riches, and so on. There is considerable difference among ancient astrologers as to exactly what is attributed to each house, and which is the more important, the ascendant or the MC. The step from eight houses to twelve (the number influenced no doubt by the twelveness of the zodiacal signs) may have arisen from giving a sphere of influence to the cardinal points themselves, and then giving them an equal space in the ecliptic circle. It may have happened the more easily since the old diagrams were generally not circles at all, but squares, as indeed they continued to be for centuries. In Figure 4 the square is simply divided by its diagonals into four Quadrants or quarters. In Fig. 5 the square formed by joining the mid points of the sides is added, so that each cardinal point now has two sections, one on each side, and the eight sections of the *octatopos* result. Twelve sections are achieved by inserting the inner square shown in Fig. 6, and there are our twelve houses, each allocated a particular sphere of life. It is very important to notice that these twelve sections or houses are

25 See Note 21, Gundel.

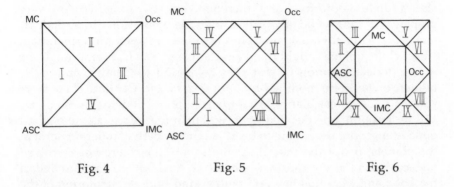

Fig. 4   Fig. 5   Fig. 6

independent of the zodiac. Their position round the ecliptic is fixed by the degree of the ecliptic rising over the horizon, the ascendant. The sign of the zodiac which will be in that position will depend on the time and place. The twelve mundane houses, then, are a sort of fixed framework within which the zodiac revolves, in a clockwise direction.

Two other elements of the birth-chart were introduced or developed at this same time from the mixing of the Babylonian, Egyptian and Greek traditions. One is the doctrine of the *dodecatemoria*, the other that of the Lots (κλῆροι, *sortes*), and in particular the Lot of Fortune (Τυχή, Fortuna, the sign for which was often ⊕). As to the dodecatemoria, the ancients are thoroughly confused and confusing; the clarity introduced by the logical mind of Housman, for all its plausibility, is his own, as he confesses:[26] 'The materials are dispersed and fragmentary, and the order and sequence which I here bestow upon them are conjectural; but this history, true or no, will explain the variety of the evidence and harmonise its discord. I advise no one to read Mr Bouché Leclercq's account of the matter, *L'astrol. grecque* pp. 299–303, unless he wants to be confused and misled'. Alas, though the misleading is Bouché-Leclercq's – he conflates and simplifies without enough reference to datable sources – the confusion was that of the ancients themselves.

As to the word itself, *dodecatemorion*, it clearly has something to do with twelve parts (*dodeca* is the Greek for twelve, and a *morion* is a part), so that any twelfth part might be called a dodecatemorion. Consequently, in the Babylonian tradition, the signs of the zodiac themselves, as twelfth parts of the ecliptic, were sometimes called dodecatemoria. Now each thirty degree sign could be divided into twelve parts of 2½°, and each part allotted to a sign, in the same order

[26] Housman's *Manilius*, Book II (London, 1912) xxii.

as they are arranged in around the zodiac. Each of these 2½° parts was also a dodecatemorion, and therefore was by some writers very properly if long-windedly called a 'dodecatemorion of a dodeca-temorion'. This obviously mutiplies the possibilities for interpretation, since while a planet might be in a certain sign, say Cancer, it might be in the dodecatemorion of that sign belonging to Gemini, and so its influence would be modified by both Cancer and Gemini. There were various rules for calculating what the sign of the dodecatemorion was, and because the one decided upon was then referred to as the planet's dodecatemorion, they came to be called, improperly, 'dodecatemoria of the planets' or 'of the moon'. At the same time, there were evolved dodecatemoria of the cardinal points (the ASC, MC and so on) and of the Lots; and Manilius has yet another kind of dodecatemorion of the planets, in which each 2½° part of each sign is allotted in ½° steps to the five planets in the order Saturn, Jupiter, Mars, Venus, Mercury. All this looks clearer than the sources in fact are, and some of the confusion, involving single degrees or half degrees of signs, possibly arose from the grafting on to the Babylonian-Greek zodiac of some of the Egyptian lore of lucky and unlucky days and times, each having its *chronocrator*, the 'ruler of the time'.

The Lot of Fortune as we know it in our sources is certainly the invention of Hellenistic Egypt, but it may ultimately be derived from an older Babylonian 'place of the moon', the great god Sin. The moon was very important in Babylonian astronomy and astrology, and their calendar was lunar. The involvement of the moon in all the various methods of calculating the position of the lot of Fortune, plus the fact that it is sometimes referred to as 'the horoscope of the moon', suggests an early connection with Babylonia. The moon was commonly regarded as having power over man's physical constitution, while the sun was responsible for his psychical make-up – though ancient writers occasionally reversed these roles. Now the goddess Fortune, *Tyche*, became in Hellenistic times, with the breakdown of the older religion, almost the most important of the gods. Men felt, in the post Alexandrian world, that more and more of their lives was ruled by chance, luck, *Tyche*. And, as Bouché-Leclercq remarks, 'her sex, her Protean nature and her capriciousness all brought her closer and closer to the moon'.[27] So a place in the circle was found for her which depended on the moon, the sun, and, since all positions ultimately depended on it, the *horoscopus*, the ascendant. The means of calculating the position of the Lot of Fortune are variously described by different authorities, some of whom seem not to be at all clear about what they are doing. Its general importance – it ranks with the

[27] *Op. cit.*, 289.

ascendant itself – was however admitted by all, even by Ptolemy, who mentions no other Lots, but who sums up the basic principle of its computation by saying that the Lot of Fortune should have the same relation to the moon as the ascendant to the sun, 'that it may be as it were the *horoscopus* of the moon' (*Tetrabiblos*, III, 10). The other Lots most commonly used were the Lot of Daimon, the Lot of Necessity, and the Lot of Eros, though there were probably other Lots in these early centuries, which left traces in later horoscopes. There may also have been confusion between Lots and houses, *loci*, as Neugebauer and van Hoesen suggest,[28] which would not be surprising, since the *loci* often bore the same names, Necessity, Daimon, Eros and so on.

We may now sum up the position of Hellenistic astrology in the time of Hipparchus, astronomer and astrologer, in the mid second century B.C., omitting details, since on details the sources are frequently, indeed most often, contradictory, as astrology was still in the early stages of its evolution. The main lines are, however, fairly clear. The birth-chart, which has for long been called (strictly speaking, improperly), the horoscope, gave as accurate a picture as was possible of the state of the heavens at the moment of birth, setting the sun, moon and five planets against the circle of the zodiac. This moving circle was then itself set within a fixed framework of eight, or more often twelve *loci*, or houses, each one governing some sphere of the life of man, so that the influence of the planets could be evaluated. This relationship of the zodiac to the circle of the houses was fixed by the *horoscopus*, the ascendant, the degree of the zodiac which was rising over the horizon at the moment of birth, which marked the first house. Interpretation was then further complicated by the addition of dodecatemoria and various Lots, among which by far the most important was the Lot of Fortune. The fixed stars played almost no part in all this, apart from those constellations which gave their names to the signs of the zodiac. There is an occasional mention of *paranatellonta*, or *synanatellonta*, stars which rise at the same time as a given sign, and of major stars like Regulus or Sirius, but they appear to be of little or no significance at this stage. The mathematics and the astronomy behind all this was very crude, and in particular the methods of calculating the divisions of the houses were clumsy and approximate; it was not until the invention of spherical trigonometry, probably not before the time of Ptolemy, that more accurate division became possible.

---

[28] O. Neugebauer and H. B. van Hoesen, *Greek Horoscopes* (Philadelphia, 1959), commentaries on horoscopes Nos 95 and 137, pp. 36 and 41f.

III

From Manilius to Vettius Valens

Manilius takes the story of astrology to Rome, where it had arrived at least two centuries earlier; it is referred to both by Ennius and Plautus, who wrote at the end of the third and the beginning of the second century B.C., and the first expulsion of the astrologers from the city had been in 139 B.C. But before we consider people's attitudes to astrology, especially those of the philosophers, and the reactions of the state and the growing Christian Church, let us continue the account of the evolution of astrology itself, beginning with the poem of Manilius.

Nothing is known of the life of the author, and even the name has occasioned much discussion and doubt, though the commonly accepted form Manilius has been most cogently argued for and will be used in this book. The exact dates of the writing of the five extant books of the poem are also the subject of much argument, though there is no doubt that the poem as a whole belongs to the period between 9 A.D. and the early years of the reign of Tiberius, say 15 A.D. As we now have it, the poem is in five books, the last possibly somewhat mutilated, as Housman thought, and having large gaps. The work is probably unfinished: in Book II Manilius promises an account of the planetary influences, which we never get, and twice in the work he promises to gather it all together, but never does; and it is certainly impossible to cast a horoscope or fully interpret one from Manilius' work, though it clearly sets out to be an astrological textbook. It may seem a little odd to the modern reader that anyone should want to write a textbook in verse, but there are two points to remember. First, hexameter verse had been the vehicle for the greatest Latin philosophical work of the preceding hundred years, the *De Rerum Natura* of Lucretius, and the only astronomy the Romans had in Latin was in verse translation, of the astronomical poem of the Greek Aratus, of the third century B.C. And second, Manilius was undoubtedly writing for the circle of *litterati* of the court, and verse was the proper didactic medium for such people. Indeed, the difficulty of expressing mathematical and astronomical ideas in Latin hexameters was for them one of the great attractions of the work, and one of which Manilius was fully conscious and – not wholly justifiably – proud.

The first book is an introduction to elementary astronomy, a *sphaera*, as it was called – just sufficient description of the heavens to enable the student to follow the astrological matter to come. It covers in part the ground of the last section of the first chapter of this book, describing the circles of the tropics and equator, the arctic and antarctic, the horizon and the meridian, and also the Milky Way. It includes this last not as relevant to astrology, but because Manilius is copying an older *sphaera*, a description of the heavens, and much of the book is taken up with lists of the fixed stars in their constellations – not always accurately placed, since Manilius' astronomy reflects the state of the science before the time of Hipparchus, a century and a half before his own time. Lines 263–274 list the signs of the zodiac, though the position of the zodiac itself is not described until four hundred lines later:

> First Aries shining in his golden fleece
> Wonders to see the back of Taurus rise,
> Taurus who calls, with lowered head, the Twins,
> Whom Cancer follows; Leo follows him,
> Then Virgo; Libra next, day equalling night,
> Draws on the Scorpion with its blazing star,
> Whose tail the Half-horse aims at with his bow,
> Ever about to loose his arrow swift.
> Then comes the narrow curve of Capricorn,
> And after him Aquarius pours from his urn
> Waters the following Fishes greedily use,
> Which Aries touches, last of all the signs.

The order of the signs, moving round the zodiac in an anticlockwise, east-west direction, and beginning with the vernal equinox, was Aries, Taurus, Gemini, Cancer, Leo, Virgo, Libra, Scorpio, Sagittarius, Capricorn, Aquarius and Pisces, to give them the Latin names by which they are commonly known, and which are familiar to all those who read their 'horoscopes'. They are usually denoted by symbols, which vary a good deal in older authorities, and are not found at all before Byzantine times; the common forms today are, in the same order: ♈ ♉ ♊ ♋ ♌ ♍ ♎ ♏ ♐ ♑ ♒ ♓. Manilius' lines 805–812 list the planets, in the Chaldaean order we have already met: Saturn, Jupiter, Mars, Sun, Venus, Mercury, Moon. These also have their symbols, again of recent origin, except those for the sun and moon, though that for the sun seems to have changed at the Renaissance: the older form was ⊘ and the post-Renaissance form ☉; the others are Saturn ♄, Jupiter ♃, Mars ♂, Venus ♀, Mercury ☿, and Moon ☾. The book ends with a lengthy section on comets, and their importance as portents, with historical examples, but we shall leave comets for a later chapter. The last thirty-five lines of Book V (which looks unfinished) possibly also belong to the *sphaera* of Book I, where they certainly more naturally fit. They classify the fixed stars according to their magnitude.

The other four Books deal with astrology; for detailed summaries the reader is referred to the editions of Housman and Goold.[1] We shall here be concerned only to illustrate Manilius' own thought and the confused and evolving state of astrology at this time, from those passages where he differs from many other ancient authorities. In his fourth book, as occasionally in odd passages elsewhere, he indulges in some philosophical generalities. He was writing for the educated Roman gentleman of the Augustan literary society, a gentleman with considerable acquaintance with Greek philosophy, especially, perhaps, that of the Stoic school. Near the beginning of the book (lines 14ff) Manilius wrote:

> The fates rule the world, and all things are established by a settled law; each long age is marked with its settled chances. At our birth we begin to die, and our end depends upon our beginning. Hence flow wealth and power, and poverty, too often found; hence all are given their skills and characters, their faults and virtues, their losses and their gains. No one can renounce what he is given, or possess what he is not given, nor can he grasp by his prayers the fortunes denied him or escape that which presses on him: each must bear his own lot.

These fine phrases are the commonplace of the Stoics, and there is no doubt that the Stoicism accepted by many educated Romans, especially in the form in which it was cast by Posidonius, who adapted it to some extent to suit Roman ideas, made easier the acceptance of Greek astrology. Not that all Stoics did believe in astrology; but their creed, insisting that fate ruled all things, and that a common law and 'sympathy' bound everything in the universe into one whole, clearly allowed for divination, the perception of the workings of that law, of fate, through signs, including signs in the heavens. For, as Manilius says later (lines 883–896):

> Nature is nowhere concealed: we see it all clearly, and hold the universe in our grasp. We, being part of the universe, see it as our begetter, and, being its children, reach to the stars. Surely no

---

[1] A. E. Housman, *M. Manilii Astronomicon liber primus* (London, 1903). The other books were published as follows: Book II in 1912, Book III in 1916, Book IV in 1920 and Book V in 1930. G. P. Goold's edition and translation in the Loeb Classical Library appeared in 1977. It contains (pp. xvi–cv) a comprehensive guide to the poem.

one doubts that some divinity dwells in our breasts, and our souls return to the heavens, and come from there; and that just as the universe is constructed out of the four elements of air and fire and earth and water, the whole being a lodging for the governing Mind within, so we too possess bodies of earthly substance and spirits nourished by the blood, and a mind which governs all and controls every man. Is it so strange if men can understand the universe, seeing that there is a universe within themselves, and each is in small image a likeness of god?

This is that cosmic sympathy so dear to the Stoics, which made man an image of the universe, a microcosm; an idea that was to have a very long history, with ramifications in many fields besides astrology.

A little more than the first quarter of Book I, which runs to nearly a thousand lines, is taken up with the classification of the signs of the zodiac according to their natures and qualities, as masculine and feminine, human or bestial, simple or multiform, and so on. The gender of the signs, as Housman remarks, 'is founded not on sex but on the Pythagorean fantasy that odd numbers are male and even numbers female', so that the feminine group, since we start from Aries as first, 'is led by a female Bull, providentially amputated at the shoulders'. In three places Manilius is either unique or at any rate different from most ancient astrologers: he classifies Aries, Leo and Sagittarius as running, Gemini, Virgo and Aquarius as standing, Taurus, Libra and Capricorn as sitting, and Cancer, Scorpio and Pisces as lying down. This classification is different from a similar one in Ptolemy, in that Ptolemy's is obviously based on the nature of the signs, while Manilius bases his on the posture of the signs in pictorial representation. Again, Manilius lists four signs as 'maimed' (Housman's word: the Latin has *fraudata ... amissis ... membris*, diminished by the loss of some parts), Scorpio, Taurus, Cancer and Sagittarius. Lists of such signs in other astrologers are generally longer, though Vettius Valens names only two. Scorpio was maimed by the loss of his claws, which went to make the constellation Libra; Taurus limps on a doubled-up leg, Cancer has no eyes, and Sagittarius but one (in the pictures, that is). In the allocation of signs to seasons, the ancient astrologers differ: most begin the seasons with the tropical signs, spring with Aries, summer with Cancer, autumn with Libra and winter with Capricorn; but occasionally they are put as the ends of the seasons, and Manilius sets them in the middle of his groups of three, so that Pisces, Aries and Taurus belong to spring, and so on.

He then deals with what are technically known as *aspects*; that is, the geometrical relations of the signs. A modern textbook defines aspects thus: '*Astronomically*, aspects are certain angular distances made at the centre of the earth between a line from one planet and a line from another. These are measured in degrees along the ecliptic'.[2] For 'planet' read 'sign' and this will do for the ancients. We shall have much more to do with aspects when we come to Ptolemy, and one example must suffice here. Since there are 360° in a complete circle, three lines can be drawn from the centre to the circumference 120° apart, the three points on the circumference making an equilateral triangle (Fig. 7). As there are twelve signs of the zodiac, it can be seen that four such triangles, known in antiquity as trigons (the Greek for 'triangle' is τρίγωνον, transliterated into Latin as *trigonum*), can be inscribed in the zodiac, each linking three signs as a group, which modern astrologers usually call a 'triplicity' but sometimes a trigon, like the ancients (Fig. 8). So one can also inscribe squares (with an angle of 90° at the centre) or hexagons (with a 60° angle), or draw lines across the circle horizontally or vertically, to get other aspects, the most obvious of which is direct opposition.

With regard to the aspects, the only point in which Manilius differs from others is in his estimate of the trigon as being much more important and powerful than the square; most others make them equal in power, but opposite in effect.

There follow twenty lines linking the signs with the twelve great gods and goddesses, six of each. The list given by Manilius is:

Aries: Minerva	Libra: Volcanus
Taurus: Venus	Scorpio: Mars
Gemini: Apollo	Sagittarius: Diana
Cancer: Mercury	Capricorn: Vesta
Leo: Jupiter	Aquarius: Juno
Virgo: Ceres	Pisces: Neptune

It will be noticed that by this arrangement, gods face goddesses across the zodiac. There is other evidence, both literary and monumental, for the attribution of the same signs to the same gods, and two things should be remarked here. First, that there is no connection between the allocation of gods or goddesses to signs and the gender of the signs; and second that this has nothing to do with the system of planetary 'houses', according to which, for example, Gemini is in the house of Mercury.

After this digression, Manilius goes on with the relations between signs, describing those signs which 'see' and 'hear' one another (in which classification there are minor differences between the various

2 M. E. Hone, *The Modern Textbook of Astrology*, 4th edn (London, 1968) 180.

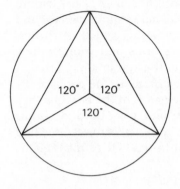

Fig. 7

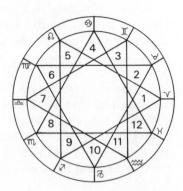

Fig. 8

authorities), and those which 'love' and 'lie in ambush for' one another: with these last it is perhaps better to stick to Manilius's Latin terms, and call them *amantia* and *insidiantia*. It is here worth quoting Housman's note in full, for the joy of his English:

> The *amantia* and *insidiantia* are apparently unknown except to Manilius, who arranges them as follows. From the point or μεσεμβόλημα between the first masculine sign Aries and the first feminine sign Taurus, there is drawn a diameter of the circle; and across the wall thus built the masculine signs play Pyramus to a series of treacherous or apathetic Thisbes. Each pays court to that feminine sign which is equidistant with himself from the dividing point, and she, if a northern sign, repays him with trickery, if a southern, with indifference. The scheme therefore is the following.
>
> Aries loves Taurus, who tricks him.
> Gemini loves Pisces.
> Leo loves Capricornus.
> Libra loves Scorpius.
> Sagittarius loves Virgo, who tricks him.
> Aquarius loves Cancer, who tricks him.

On the enmities between signs, Manilius is again alone among our ancient authors, as he is on what Housman describes as 'the less fertile and attractive topic of friendship'.

There is more on the signs, on their 'characters' and effects on men's arts and professions and interests in Book IV. Between ten and eighteen lines are given to each of the signs in order, beginning with Aries; as an example, we may take what he writes of Gemini (152ff):

A softer inclination and gentler way of life comes from Gemini, through various kinds of singing, and harmonious voices, and slender pipes, and words fitted to the natural sound of strings. Work itself is pleasure to them. War's arms and trumpet they wish far from them, and bitter old age; they go lovingly through life in peace and perpetual youth. They discover the paths of the stars, and by understanding the mathematics of the heavens they complete the whole circle of the sky and pass beyond simple knowledge of the constellations. Nature is subject to their intelligence and at their service in all things. Of so many gains are Gemini said to be productive.

Much of this can be seen to tie up with the fact that Apollo, the god of the Muses, was said to dwell in this sign (Book II, 440), and much of it accords with what other astrologers say. Most later astrologers, however, make the planets responsible for most of it, not the signs. In all of this, Manilius is drawing on sources now lost, and is using them carelessly enough to get some of his details wrong – or perhaps his sources made the mistakes, and he did not spot them. It is one of the characteristics both of astrological writers and even more of the scribes who copied their work that they did not always fully understand what they were doing, and their mathematics was generally weak.

On the quadrants, Manilius is very much in accord with other astrologers, and makes the same mistake as many of them in assuming that they cut the zodiac into four equal parts, and seeming to imply that the Medium Caelum is directly over the observer's head, and the Imum Caeli beneath his feet. Now the place of each of the four cardinal points is fixed as regards the observer; the zodiac moves through them. They are, it will be remembered, the points where the observer's horizon and meridian cut the zodiac, and the horizon and meridian are stationary lines; the zodiac, of course, is turning round the observer every twenty-four hours. If the zodiac were on, or parallel to, the equator the signs would rise and set at a constant rate and the cardinal points *would* divide the zodiac into four equal parts. But the zodiac is inclined to the equator at an angle of about 23½°, and the consequence is the signs rise at different rates, and the quadrants are not equal. Since the division into *loci*, mundane houses, depends on this first location of the cardinal points, ancient authorities are confused about that division. Older methods of computation were arithmetical and clumsy, and though fairly accurate for Babylon or Alexandria, were, when taken over and applied to other places in other latitudes, inaccurate.

Manilius' order of importance of the four cardinal points is his own, but there is so much disagreement among early astrologers that it is

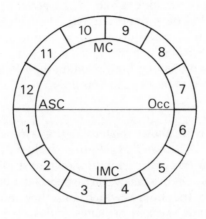

Fig. 9

clear that the doctrine had not yet been settled. The same is true of the allocation of functions, areas of life, to the houses. These are the twelve divisions forming that fixed framework with the cardinal points within which the zodiac revolves. They are generally numbered from the ascendant, the *horoscopus*, round in an anticlockwise direction (Fig. 9).

Manilius' account of the houses, which he calls *loca templa, sedes* or *partes*, is given here for comparison with later sources. He does not number them, nor does he deal with them in order round the circle. He first takes those not in any aspect, that is, not standing in any of the recognised geometrical relationships, with respect to the ascendant: that is, numbers 2, 6, 8 and 12, which are either next to the ascendant or five places away. Of these Manilius says (II, 864ff):

The one which has risen third from the highest heaven (i.e. third from the MC, counting back – No. 12) is an unfortunate place, hostile to future affairs, and over-productive of evil; nor is it alone, for equal to it is the one which shines with its star opposite, next to the setting point (the *occasus* – No. 6). And last this one seem to excel (that is, that the sixth house may not be better than the twelfth), each moves equally subject to a cardinal point (both are what the Greeks called ἀποκλίματα, setting after, by modern astrologers called *cadent*) and spreads the same ruin. Each is a gate of labour (*porta laboris*); one is for climbing, the other for falling. No better fate attends the one above the setting point (No. 8) or the one below the ascendant (No. 2): one (8)

37

rushes down, the other is backward and retarded, and each either trembles at its imminent end, being so close to a cardinal point, or is about to lose support and fail. They are rightly known to be the abodes of Typhon (Typhon, or Typhoeus, was one of the Titans who rebelled against Zeus and were defeated and punished, Typhon by having Etna piled on top of him; this name for these two houses is peculiar to Manilius).

He next deals with those related to the ascendant by trigon or hexagon, numbers 3, 5, 9 and 11. He first deals with the last of these, next to the MC on the east, 'which follows next after the summit of heaven' (which the Greeks called ἐπαναφορά, rising after, now called *succedent*). This is the house which in other authorities is called ἀγαθὸς δαίμων, *bonus daemon*, or *bonus genius*, 'the good spirit', and which Manilius calls *Fors*, or *Fortuna felix* (the text is doubtful at this point). Jupiter dwells here and, as Housman says, 'Manilius loads it with praises, and forgets in his enthusiasm to tell us what it presides over'. He then deals with the one diametrically opposite, No. 5, next on the west to the IMC, which is called *Daemonie* (Manilius confesses he cannot find a Latin name for it) and presides over health and sickness. We are then told about the other two opposites, Nos 9 and 3; the first, next to the MC on the west, where the sun lives, is called *Deus*, God, and looks after the affairs of the body, and the other, next on the east to the IMC, is called *Dea*, Goddess, and is the house of the moon. It is not clear from the text what the function of this 3rd house is; as it stands the text says that it 'shines with a yellow light and rules over deaths' – *fuluumque nitet mortisque gubernat* (line 912), but the first three words are all doubtful, especially *mortis*, which is a highly irregular accusative plural; and in any case Manilius himself puts death under the seventh house. (Goold reads, 'fratrumque vices mortesque', and translates 'it controls fortunes and fates of births'; but it's an odd translation of vices mortesque, and where did fortune come from?)

The last four houses form a square, since they are the four containing the cardinal points. Manilius starts from that containing the MC, which is Venus' home, and which looks after marriage; it is often simply called *Fortuna*, and is No. 10. Opposite is No. 4, with the IMC. It is called *Daemonium*, and there Saturn dwells. Being where it is, and having Saturn as its tutelary god, 'it acts as a father exercising its powers over the fortunes of fathers and of old men' (lines 934–5). The other pair of opposites is Nos 1 and 7, the first containing the ascendant, the other the *occasus*, or setting point. The first house is the abode of Mercury, and presides over the fate of children and the desires of parents; the seventh is called *Ditis ianua*, the door of the underworld, and presides over death, as it does over the end of the day, and also over constancy and the keeping of promises. Two points should be noticed with regard to what Manilius says about the planets and these houses. First, they are not the planetary houses properly so called, about which Manilius says nothing anywhere; and second, that Mars has apparently no house to dwell in at all.

So much for the 'mundane houses'. Manilius' doctrine of the Lots, or *sortes*, is in his third book. He is alone in having twelve such Lots, numbered in the same direction as the houses, and starting with the Lot of Fortune as number 1. Other ancient astrologers deal in terms of anything from one to seven such Lots; the only point on which they all agree is the importance attaching to the Lot of Fortune. On the other hand there are more than twelve names for Lots in the ancient texts, and it may be that Manilius found his circle of twelve in his source-books – it is extremely unlikely that he invented it, since he is obviously following other authorities, often with less than complete understanding. Since Manilius' Lots are numbered in order, it clearly suffices to know where to put the first, and the rest follow.

Now the position of the Lot of Fortune is determined with relation to that of the *horoscopus*, the ascendant: the Lot of Fortune must be as far from the moon as the ascendant is from the sun. So the calculation of its position involves those of the sun, moon and ascendant. And this implies knowing where the ascendant is. Given that the time of birth is known, where is the *horoscopus* – what degree of what sign was rising over the eastern horizon at that moment? The answer to this question depends on the rising times of the signs, and these rising times depend in turn on the latitude of the birthplace, because of the obliquity of the ecliptic (the zodiac) to the equator. Manilius here displays the modesty of his understanding. He rejects, early in the book, what he calls 'the vulgar method of calculation', which assumes that each sign takes exactly two hours to rise – because, as he says explicitly (line 225), 'the circle of the signs lies in an oblique circle' (a point he had ignored in Book II when discussing the cardinal points). Then two hundred or so lines later he describes a third way of working out the position of the ascendant, which is with a minor variation precisely that same vulgar and erroneous method. As Housman says, 'Alas, alas! This alternative method of yours, my poor Marcus, is none other than the vulgar method which in 218–24 you said you knew, and which in 225–46 you exposed as false. The wolf, to whom in his proper shape you denied admittance, has come back disguised as your mother the goose, and her gosling has opened the door to him'. The details of the calculations are complicated, and we shall leave them until we come to Ptolemy and his *Tetrabiblos*; suffice it here to say that earlier writers are few of them clearer or better than Manilius.

A further inconsistency between this book and the previous Book II lies in Manilius' attribution to each of his twelve Lots certain areas of human life, as for example civil life to the third, and money and prosperity to the sixth. But, to quote Housman again, 'liars need not have long memories if they address themselves only to fools, who have short ones; an astrological poet writing his third book may safely forget his second, because an astrological reader will never remember it. But the impious and attentive sceptic will not fail to remark that some of the goods now packed in these compartments have already been stowed elsewhere'. Marriage is indeed here assigned to the fifth Lot; it has already been given to the setting point in II 839 and to the tenth house in II 925, and these three places cannot all be the same.

Passing on to further division of the zodiac itself, we come to the decans, on the Egyptian origins of which something has already been said in Chapter II. Here yet again Manilius preserves what must be an older tradition, in allocating each decan, each 10° third of each sign, to the *signs* in order; most other, and all later astrologers attribute them to the planets. So, for Manilius, the first ten degrees of Aries belong to Aries, the second ten to Taurus, and the third to Gemini; the first decan of Taurus is Cancer's, the second Leo's, and the third Virgo's; and so on round the circle. Manilius himself gets the first two decans of Pisces wrong, allocating them to Aries and Taurus instead of Capricorn and Aquarius. He does not say precisely what the effect of all this is, but presumably the effect of the sign is modified by the decan: if the birth lay in, say, the second decan of Gemini, the effects of Gemini were modified by the influence of Scorpio; if in the third decan of Scorpio, then Pisces modifies the influence of Scorpio itself.

The next smaller division is into dodecatemoria, on which Manilius is confused and confusing. The only point in which he stands alone is in producing dodecatemoria which are only half a degree. Each is therefore one fifth of the 2½° dodecatemorion, and the five in each of the 2½° units are then allocated to the five planets (excluding the sun and moon, that is) in order. They are called dodecatemoria presumably, as Housman suggests, because each planet then possesses twelve of them in each sign. To add to the complications, Manilius treats of the degrees of the zodiac individually, in Book IV, listing those degrees of each sign which, because they are too hot or too cold, too wet or too dry, are *partes damnandae*, harmful degrees. Something over a hundred (the text is doubtful) out of the three hundred and sixty are such. Although other astrologers have similar lists of individual degrees and their effects or their links with planets, there is no agreement between them, and Housman says of Manilius' scheme,

'I have found no counterpart anywhere else, and I have discovered no plan or principle at the bottom of it'.[3] Manilius apologises profusely (lines 430ff) for the necessity he is under to put so many numbers into verse, and goes on obviously enjoying his own dexterity in doing so.

The way in which we are having to leap from book to book in order to get some sort of logical order into the exposition of Manilius' ideas shows how lacking in coherent organisation his work is. The second half of the third book is concerned with two topics: the ways in which the divisions of time composing man's life – years, months, days, hours – are influenced by the heavens; and the methods by which we may know how long our lives are going to be. As to the first, Manilius expounds two, mutually incompatible, systems. The first starts from the sun's sign, the second from the ascendant. The common and peculiar element is that in both systems the influence in question, over years and months and so on, is attributed to the signs of the zodiac, whereas Ptolemy and most later astrologers ascribe this influence to the planets. There is little doubt that Manilius' system is the older. It was possibly the system of an astrologer friend of Cicero, Nigidius Figulus, the first truly Roman astrologer we know of.[4] There is a reference to it in a satire of Persius (V 45ff), who may have been drawing on Nigidius, as did his contemporary Lucan in the *Pharsalia* (I 649–65). Manilius may have got his ideas directly from Nechepso-Petosiris, since the idea is certainly Egyptian, derived from an earlier level of ideas in which periods of time were governed by star-groups unrelated to the zodiac. A half-way stage between the position of Manilius and that of Ptolemy is found in Paulus Alexandrinus – two centuries later than Ptolemy, but such was the confusion among astrologers that old elements of the system were preserved in some, and changed in others, and it is practically impossible to set a date to any particular doctrine's invention or introduction. Paulus describes a system of 'time-rulers', χρονοκράτορες, very similar to the second method of Manilius, but then goes on to ascribe the influence to the planets in the signs.

The same process of evolution may be seen in the matter of forecasting the length of life. Manilius ascribes the prime influence to the signs (though he also allots some power to the houses, and is alone in doing so). Many other ancient writers do the same, all apparently following Nechepso-Petosiris in this principle, though not in the

---

[3] Book V, p. xii.
[4] The fragments, which tell us virtually nothing about Nigidius Figulus' system, were published by A. Swoboda, *P. Nigidii Figuli Operum Reliquiae* (Vienna/Prague, 1899; reprinted Amsterdam, 1964) 106–128. Swoboda's detailed disquisition on Nigidius' astrological writings is on pp. 35–61 (in Latin).

crudity of the older practice, which dealt simply in terms of quadrants and degrees of the equator. Later astrologers, like Ptolemy again, ascribe the influence to the planets. The overall picture is one of broad evolution from ideas of the influence of fixed stars and star-groups in general, to that of certain particular star-groups which lie in the path of the sun and moon, and hence to the signs of the zodiac, and then to the paramount influence of the planets in the signs. It is, of course, precisely this last that Manilius promises to deal with, and never does. What he does treat of at the end of Book IV is the effect of lunar eclipses in each of the signs; which doctrine Manilius probably also got from Nechepso-Petosiris, though there is little of it in other and later astrologers.

A lot of this fourth book is devoted to astrological geography, the lands and regions of the earth allotted to the several zodiacal signs. There are many such lists in our sources, and it is possible to put them into some sort of rough chronological order by considering the geographical scope of each list. The earliest are concerned only with the Near East and India (known of through trade up the Red Sea and Persian Gulf, as well as through Alexander's conquests), while the later lists extend to the north and west. There is very little agreement between these lists, and no good reason to go into details here. But the reason for this kind of astrological geography is stated clearly enough by Manilius in lines 807–817:

> So the whole earth lies divided between the stars, from which are to be drawn the rights proper to each; for they enjoy the same communication with one another as the signs between themselves, and as they (the signs) join together or in hatred separate, at one time diametrically opposed, at another joined in a trigon, by different causes directed to various influences, so lands are related to lands, cities to cities, shores to shores, and kingdoms set against kingdoms. So will each man have to avoid or choose a place for himself and, according to the stars, mutual trust is to be hoped for or dangers to be feared, as his genes (race, family) has . come down from the high heavens to earth.

So far we have hardly mentioned the fifth book, which deals with the stars and constellations which rise at the same time as the various signs of the zodiac, or their decans, or even their separate degrees. The technical words for such stars are συναvατέλλοντα and παραvατέλλοντα, paranatellonta being the usual word for them in later sources and the one we shall use here. It seems most likely that lists of paranatellonta were first drawn up in order that men might be able to tell the time at night when the signs of the zodiac were themselves not visible; like the zodiac itself, and the decans, they were originally time-measurers. Plato's pupil Eudoxus made a list of them, which was used in the early third century B.C. by Aratus in his *Phaenomena*, a poetic description of the heavens. Hipparchus made a more accurate list a century later, and no doubt there were many more. It was difficult to make an exact list, since the rising times of the signs were themselves only approximate, and clearly, since these last vary with the latitude of the observer, so too should tables of paranatellonta. It would therefore be necessary to specify for what latitude the table was drawn up. In fact, the ancients dealt not with latitudes, but with *climata*, or 'climes'. Each *clima*, clime, was defined by the ratio of the longest to the shortest day. For example, at Alexandria the longest day was fourteen equinoctial hours, the shortest ten, and the ratio was 7:5, while at Babylon the ratio was 3:2. Based on these two cities, two systems of *climata* were developed, in each case seven climes being listed, and the two systems were constantly confused. Later, with more accurate trigonometrical methods, a system of climes beginning with the equator where the days are always the same length, and increasing the length of the longest day in half-hour steps, was developed; Ptolemy, in his astronomical work, the *Almagest*, lists eleven such climes, of which the presumed habitable seven became standard for most later writers. So a table of paranatellonta could be made up for a given clime, and used to tell the hour of the night when the signs of the zodiac were hidden.

At some stage these paranatellonta began to be used for astrological purposes also. Later authorities say that this was first done by Teucer of Babylon, who probably lived in the first century A.D., but it must have begun much earlier. A link was probably established, in Egypt, between these time-reckoning lists and lists of fixed stars and their influence on men's lives; and then between these and accounts of the effects of the decans and separate degrees of the zodiacal signs. Something of this early confused state can be seen in the Hermetic treatise we have already referred to in Chapter 2.[5] Chapter XXV of that work deals with 'the fixed stars, and in what degrees of the signs they rise', and contains a very long list indeed, with such items as: 'Between the twenty-sixth and twenty-seventh degrees of Aries, Aelurus (the Cat) rises, and it makes men fearful, and unwilling to accept responsibility, and foolish'. The name of the star-group *Aelurus* is from the *sphaera barbarica*, the Egyptian description of the heavens. But it is not only the fixed stars that are mentioned in the list: for example, 'when the twentieth degree of Aries is the *horoscopus*, it makes men immodest'. Teucer of Babylon did make such a list, and

---

[5] Pp. 20–21 and note 21.

there are fragments of others extant, but there is only so much agreement between them as might be expected to be derived from the similar inferences made from the names of the constellations.

As an example from Manilius' list, we may take lines 118–127 of Book V:

> With the twenty-seventh degree of Aries the Hyades will rise. Those born at this time do not enjoy peace or quiet, but they seek crowds of people and the bustle of affairs. They like noisy social unrest, and want the Gracchi holding forth from the platform, leading revolutions; they enjoy civil strife, and add fuel to the fires of disquiet. They (that is, the Hyades) stir up dirty hordes of filthy peasants; and they begat the faithful swineherd of Odysseus. These are the characters the Hyades produce as they rise.

This sort of treatment of paranatellonta belongs to an early stage in the evolution of astrology; the fixed stars play a decreasingly important part in the art as it develops. In modern astrological practice only a few important fixed stars actually occupying particular degrees of the signs themselves are taken into account in the interpretation of a natal chart.

So the general picture which emerges from Manilius' five books is of astrology in the early stages of its growth from crude beginnings with quadrants and various influences from the stars to more precise use of the signs of the zodiac, and more and more complicated subdivision into different sorts of dodecatemoria, down to half-degrees of signs. The actual interpretation of the influences and their effects varies greatly from writer to writer, and there is as yet no standard practice among astrologers, no general agreement, though some lines are beginning to be discernible. We know nothing of what Manilius believed about the influence of the planets, since either he did not write about it at all or what he wrote has been lost. It would not be safe to argue that because he gives so much influence to the signs and parts of signs, and to the fixed stars, the planets must have been pretty unimportant; since as we have seen, Manilius is quite happy to allocate the same field of influence to a number of different parts of the heavenly machinery.

That the planets were important and were becoming more so is evident from the fragmentary sources we have telling us of astrology in the time between Manilius and Vettius Valens, and from Vettius Valens himself. Mention has already been made of Nigidius Figulus, who worked in the mid- first century B.C. That was, of course, before Manilius; but Manilius was drawing on sources much older than his own time and, as is evident from his mistakes, he was not a practising astrologer. Nigidius was; and we are told by Lucan in the *Pharsalia* (I 649–665) that he consulted the skies for guidance on the outbreak of the civil war between Caesar and Pompey, just before morning twilight in late November 50 B.C.[6] What Nigidius did was describe the positions of the planets and pronounce his verdict: the state of the heavens forecast great dangers and disasters for Rome. He told his audience that the sun was not in Leo, nor was Saturn in the tenth *locus* – either would have made things worse, presumably; but Mars was in Scorpio, and above the horizon, the only planet to be seen; Jupiter was in the sixth *locus*, Venus dim and obscured, and Mercury stationary. It appears that all this is astronomically impossible for that time, and it may be that either Lucan has got it wrong, or he or Nigidius 'cooked' it to make it look black for Rome. The details do not matter; but it can be seen that what interests Nigidius is the positions of the planets and their relations to the *loci*.

The same emphasis on planetary positions is found in the horoscopes collected together by Neugebauer and van Hoesen.[7] Their book contains all the Greek horoscopes they could find in the papyrus sources together with those they gleaned from literary sources such as Vettius Valens and the appendices to Cumont's Catalogues.[8] Those from the papyri are scattered fairly evenly over the first four centuries A.D.; those from literary sources, which make up the great majority, because of the collection of Vettius Valens, mostly belong to the second century (from about 100 to 188 A.D.). The literary horoscopes are all used as illustrative examples by their authors, and are clearly all drawn from collections of horoscopes made in these early centuries – all are obviously genuine natal charts, and can be dated accurately, for the most part, from the astronomical data they present. Almost all of them are simply lists of the planetary positions, with a few references to the positions of the *horoscopus* (the ascendant) and the Lot of Fortune. All four cardinal points are mentioned in only one horoscope, one of the earliest literary examples; the Medium Caeli is only regularly included from the late fourth century on. Fixed stars are very rarely mentioned at all, and paranatellonta only once, in the second century. Very few of the horoscopes contain any recognisable astrological material besides the factual data on which interpretation could be based, and very few indeed make any kind of predictions. The positions of the planets are obviously computed from 'handy tables' such as those later made by Ptolemy, and are often only approximate –

---

[6] The astronomy and astrology of these lines is dealt with by R. J. Getty, 'The Astrology of P. Nigidius Figulus (Lucan I 649–65)', in *Classical Quarterly*, XXXV (1941) 17–22.
[7] O. Neugebauer and H. B. van Hoesen, *Greek Horoscopes* (Philadelphia, 1959).
[8] See Chapter II, note 21.

indeed, frequently only the sign, without any degrees, is given. The order of enumeration of the planets varies in the papyri, but in the literary sources regularly follows the sequence Sun, Moon, Saturn, Jupiter, Mars, Venus, Mercury, followed by the *horoscopus*.

These horoscopes provide us with ample evidence of the wide-spread interest in the practice of astrology in these first two centuries of our era. They are drawn up for individual citizens as well as for emperors and governors, and astrology is clearly becoming popular, at least in the Greek cities of Hellenistic Egypt and the Near East. They also show us yet again how fluid was the state of astrology at that time: the few examples that contain some astrological material display features which are sometimes unique, and of no lasting significance. There was obviously no standard practice, no 'Bible' of astrology: any theorist was free to develop his own ideas and to borrow from wherever he chose. One such second century theorist, according to his editor[9] was 'a notably independent personality' since his theory was 'held together by a principle foreign to all the rest' of his contemporaries, 'that the portions of the heavens measured in the zodiac which are governed by the various planets are determined by the sizes of their epicycles'. The epicycles were the circles which carried the planets in the geometric model of the universe of contemporary astronomy. He lists the spheres of influence of those portions of the zodiac in a manner all his own. That of the *horoscopus* governs the life and psychic character of the subject; that of the Sun, fathers and their affairs, matters of ruling, and of perception; that of the Moon, mothers and their business, and the body; and so on. He also preserves an account of the older division of the zodiac into eight *loci*, the *octatopos*. This, and the linking of the Sun with the soul, and of the Moon with the body, brings this fragmentary treatise into close relation with the Hermetic work referred to earlier.[10] It is clear that Egypt, and probably that means Alexandria, was still the home of astrology, and astrology was still, as it was to remain until its virtual disappearance from the western scene in the sixth century, very much a Greek science.

Vettius Valens is a Latin name, but the man came from Antioch, travelled widely, and came to rest in Egypt, in Alexandria, where he wrote, in Greek, his *Anthology* of astrology.[11] It is a long work, in difficult, crabbed Greek, and the text as published by Kroll is anything but reliable. Of the book Neugebauer and van Hoesen wrote: 'In spite of the great extent of astrological doctrine contained in the *Anthology*,

---

[9] F. E. Robbins, 'A New Astrological Treatise: Michigan Papyrus No. 1', in *Classical Philology*, XXII (1927) 1ff.
[10] Chapter II, p. 21 and note 21.
[11] *Vettii Valentis Anthologiarum Libri*, ed. W. Kroll (Berlin, 1908).

one receives the impression that the development of the theory had not yet reached its climax in the second century A.D. when both Vettius Valens and Ptolemy wrote their compendia. And both authors were satisfied by using simple arithmetical schemes, e.g. for the rising times, which belong to a period of astronomical theory which had been long surpassed at that time. The cliché which is so popular in histories of astronomy about the stimulating influence of astrology on exact astronomy is nowhere borne out where we are able to control the details.'[12] There is no need for full summary of the *Anthology* here (it is tedious enough in the original!) simply to demonstrate again the truth of what Neugebauer and van Hoesen say. But a few points are of interest. At the beginning of his second book, Vettius Valens lists the four trigons, and links them both with the planets and with the four elements of later Greek philosophy and medicine: the three signs Aries, Leo and Sagittarius are attributed first to the Sun, secondly to Jupiter and Saturn, and to the element of Fire; the trigon Taurus, Virgo and Capricorn belongs to the Moon, and Venus and Mars, and to the element of Earth; Gemini, Libra and Aquarius are Saturn's, with Mercury and Jupiter, and Air; and the last trigon, Cancer, Scorpio and Pisces go to Mars, with Venus and the Moon, and Water.

In Chapter XV of the same book, after a number of chapters setting out details of the *loci*, τόποι, we are given a short list of the twelve, telling us the names of the nine with 'private' names, as it were: the others are the Lot of Fortune, the *horoscopus*, and the Medium Caeli. 'The one called θεός, god, signifies the affairs of fathers, that called θεά, goddess, the affairs of mothers; the ἀγαθὸς δαίμων, the "good spirit", concerns children; ἀγαθὴ τύχη, "good fortune", looks after marriage (as well it might!), κακὸς δαίμων, the "bad spirit", sufferings, and κακὴ τύχη, "bad fortune", distress; the Lot of Fortune and the *horoscopus*, the ascendant, deal with life and the life of man; δαίμων, *daemon*, or "spirit", signifies matters of thought, the M.C. matters of action; ἔρως, *Eros*, love, concerns desires, and ἀνάγκη, Necessity, concerns enmities.' Later, in Chapter XII of Book IV, there is another much more detailed list of *loci*. It is not clear whether these are the same τόποι, or *loci* – Valens nowhere uses οἶκοι, houses – or different ones, and the confusion is typical; but it looks as though what follows is a list of the 'mundane houses', and the previous list was of the *sortes*, the Lots, like Manilius'. 'Let the *loci* begin from the *horoscopus*,' he says, 'which rules life, governorship, the body and the spirit. The second governs a man's life and is the gate of Hades; it rules the shadow (or possibly shade), giving and taking and sharing, intercourse with women, commerce and business and inheritance, and is the *locus* of testaments. The third is that of brothers, of life abroad, of kingship and power, friends and kinsmen, of profits and of slaves. The fourth, of reputation, of children, wives, private affairs, old persons, business, the city (in the ancient, not the modern, sense), the house and possessions, of permanence and change, including change of place, of dangers and death and distress, and of mystical matters. The fifth, the *locus* of children, is that of friendship and community, of freedom and of all good works. The sixth, of slaves, of injury, enmity, suffering and weakness. (The seventh is missing from the text; it is the locus at the cardinal point of the *occasus*, the setting, and its role may have been similar to that described by Manilius, looking after the end of life, and oaths and good faith, and so on, since these things are missing from Valens' list.) The eighth is the *locus* of death and inheritance, of idleness and of weak judgment. The ninth, of friendship, of life abroad, and foreign profit, of god and the king and the ruler, of astronomy (though ἀστρονομία should very likely be read as οἰκονομία, administration) and decrees of ordinances, of epiphanies of the gods, of prophecy, and of participation in mysteries and hidden matters. The tenth is the *locus* of affairs, and reputation, of progress, of wife and children, and of change and new matters. The eleventh, of friends, of hopes, gifts, and the children of freedom. The twelfth, of foreigners, of enmity, of slaves, of distress and dangers, and judgments, and of sufferings, death and weakness.' The general masculine and somewhat xenophobic basis of all this may be noted, as well as the confused and considerable overlap of the *loci*, and it may all be compared with Manilius' account to reinforce the impression of fluidity, not to say confusion, of astrological ideas at this time.

One new note is struck in the *Anthology*, however. Or at least, if it is not new, it is here sounded clearly for the first time in our literature, though by no means for the last. Astrology has now become, if not a secret art, at least one jealously guarded by its practitioners. In Chapter XI of the first book Vettius Valens writes: 'I adjure you, most honoured brother, and all those being initiated into this systematic art, learning of the starry bowl of the heavens, and the zodiac, and the Sun and Moon and the five planets, and also of foreknowledge and holy Necessity, to keep all these things hidden, and not to share them with the uninstructed, except those who are worthy and able to guard and receive them rightly.' It is an adjuration repeated elsewhere in the *Anthology*, as in the Proemium to Book VII: 'Now concerning all these things and this book, an oath should be required of all who receive them, to accept what they read guardedly and as if it belonged to the mysteries.' (The mysteries were the religious secrets of sects such as the Mithraists or the Orphics, carefully guarded by the initiates.) Some reasons for this secrecy will soon become apparent; it may not be taken as evidence that astrology was from the beginning some sort of arcane knowledge disclosed only to initiates, and derived from far-off Egyptian priests. It was not; though it was a Greco-Egyptian art, as is evident from the Alexandrian provenance of most of our early sources, and from the authorities used and quoted by Vettius Valens. Of the ninety-three source references in Kroll's index, only two are to *Chaldaei*, Babylonian authorities; ten are to Critodemus, of whom not only is nothing known for certain, but what little is known is contradictory: he is referred to by Pliny, which means he must be at latest a contemporary (that is, not later than 79 A.D.), but the passages in Valens which are derived from him are probably to be dated, by the horoscopes they include, to the end of the first century. Eight references are to the work *On the Ascendant* of Hypsicles, of whom again nothing is known; and the rest are in ones and twos, apart from 'the ancients' – except those to Nechepso-Petosiris, who are referred to no less than forty-two times. Since 'the ancients', οἱ παλαιοί, probably refers to the same authorities, over half the source references in Vettius Valens are to these Egyptian books.

Astrology was always, for the Romans as for later ages, a foreign, an eastern art. There is no evidence for any indigenous Roman astrology. With all their superstitious predilection for divination, the Romans never indulged in star-gazing. Their divination, like their religion, was firmly earth-bound, as befitted their farmers' common sense. Astrology, together with Greek philosophical ideas and Greek literary models, was introduced into Rome in the early second century B.C., the time when Romans first soldiered among the Greek cities of southern Italy and came into contact with the civilisation of Hellenistic Greece. Nor did astrology ever gain any firm hold among the intelligentsia: references to astrology in Roman literature are few, considering the extent of that literature. It came into Rome with Greek slaves and teachers, and was at first regarded with great suspicion, as were all new things Greek. Typical, no doubt, of the reaction of the old republican Roman gentry was that of Cato, who wrote, when outlining the characteristics of the good bailiff:[13] 'Let him harbour no sponger or diviner or soothsayer, nor let him want to listen to the counsels of any astrologer (*chaldaeum*).' The counsels of the astrologer would have concerned, doubtless, the right (in the astrological sense) time to plant or prune or reap or put the bull to the cow; a curiously uncertain way, Cato obviously thought, to run a farm. Some twenty years later, in 139 B.C., when there was considerable unrest among the lower classes and

13 Cato, *De agri cultura*, 5.4.

especially among the large immigrant slave population, an edict of Cornelius, the *praetor peregrinus*, expelled astrologers from Rome and Roman Italy. At this time the Stoics, whose philosophy was just being introduced into educated Roman circles, were largely opposed to astrology, under the influence of Panaetius of Rhodes, whom Cicero mentions[14] as having 'rejected the predictions of the astrologers', as did the Stoic astronomer Scylax of Halicarnassus. But between this time and the death of Julius Caesar in 44 B.C., as Cramer says,[15] 'the majority of Rome's upper class had been converted.' One of the chief causes was the teaching of Posidonius, the Stoic philosopher and teacher and friend of Cicero, who had such a great influence on many Roman minds.

There were then as there are now, at least two kinds of astrologers, and two kinds of astrology. On the one hand there were the 'quacks', the popular hawkers of horoscopes, on a level with the soothsayers and fairground magicians who plagued the Roman mob and who, being all 'easterners' and foreigners, were so suspected in times of civil disturbance. On the other hand, there were the 'scientific' astrologers, also Greeks, and usually from Alexandria, who developed the theory and practice of the art at the intellectual level of the educated Roman. To this latter kind of astrology there were throughout Roman history two attitudes, one of acceptance – though generally only of a 'soft' astrology: few Romans accepted a hard fatalism – and one of qualified rejection: qualified by a greater or less willingness to allow some influence of the stars on the lives of men. Epicureans like Lucretius, with their atheistic materialism and their desire to rid man of all superstitious fears, were bound to be opposed to astrology, and so were Academic sceptics like Cicero and eclectics like Pliny.

The attitude of the state was always ambivalent. The emperors, from Augustus on, nearly all had their court astrologers, some of them, like Tiberius' friend Thrasyllus, of very great influence. The theory of astrology was never proscribed and anyone was free to dabble in it or argue about it; the practice, however, was limited. Augustus' decree of 11 A.D. made illegal the holding of any private or secret consultation with 'diviners', and the predicting of anyone's death. This decree was invoked at least twenty times in the next hundred years or so to bring charges of treason against individuals suspected of plotting the

---

14 *De Divinatione*, II.42.
15 F. H. Cramer, *Astrology in Roman Law and Politics* (Philadelphia, 1954) 80. Cramer's book is a summary of Roman history from the second century to the end of the Principate, with all the gossip included, in which everything touching on the stars and star-worship, magic and superstition, is more or less indiscriminately included, and in which there is much guesswork and 'probable inference'. Nevertheless it does assemble most of the not very numerous firm facts.

emperor's death. But although court astrologers contrived to have great power, those not in favour with the emperor, and the horde of popular horoscope sellers in general, suffered frequent persecution. Six times in the first century they were banished from Rome and Italy, always at times when political unrest made the possibility of the 'support of the stars' for rebels dangerous for the authorities. As Cramer says,[16] once the senatorial order had accepted scientific astrology, as did Crassus and Pompey and Caesar himself, 'the time was past when governmental curbs of astrologers breathed contempt of this "science" as such. On the other hand, the argument that astrological promises of success might encourage subversive elements had become all the more valid during the decades of ferocious civil strife from the days of Marius to those of Octavianus (90–30 B.C.). With the advent of monarchic government another motive was added: to keep in times of tension from political opponents that very information about the future which the rulers themselves considered reliable.' It was no doubt this hostile attitude of the authorities, and the dangers attendant on becoming involved with any prominent political figure as patron, especially the emperor himself, and possibly also the scepticism of many of the abler intellectuals, which made astrologers keep themselves and their art to themselves.

The Stoic philosopher and teacher Panaetius was one of those who argued against astrology. Cicero, in the *De Divinatione* (II 42), tells us that Panaetius was the only one of the Stoics to reject the claims of the astrologers. He flourished in the second half of the second century B.C., a period when astrology was developing rapidly in the Greek world. There were at this time a number of 'schools', or sects, of Greek philosophy, including Sceptics and Cynics (who naturally rejected astrology, as they did almost everything else); the successors of Plato in the Academy, now heavily tinged with ideas from other schools; and those of Aristotle in the Lyceum, the Peripatetics. The two most important sects, in terms of later influence on men's thoughts about themselves and the world, were the Epicureans and the Stoics. Epicurus' philosophy, best known through the poem of the Latin writer Lucretius, *De Rerum Natura*, was materialist and atheist, with the avowed intention of freeing men from superstition of all kinds and so allowing him to attain to peace of mind, free from vain fears. Epicureanism was by its nature bound to be unsympathetic to astrology, except perhaps an astrology of a hard, fatalistic and scientific kind such as did not in fact exist. Astrology was then, as ever, too tied up with the aspirations and emotions of men, with their religious feelings, for the Epicurean to accept it.

---

[16] Cramer, *op. cit.*, 236.

The Stoics were also technically materialist, but their materialism was not simple and hard like that of the Epicureans, who admitted the existence of nothing except the atoms and the void. The Stoics admitted no distinction between matter and spirit; it might be said that they 'spiritized' matter as much as they materialized spirit. They inherited the four elements, earth, air, fire and water, and a fifth, also probably from Aristotle, the ether, finer than the other four. For the Stoic, the soul was material, but of a fine matter that could inter-penetrate the body, and such that after death it could rejoin the etherial regions of the heavens. For him, Fate ruled everything, and it was the part of the wise man to move with, rather than against, Fate, and so achieve that freedom from care which was the common aim of Stoic and Epicurean alike. All things in the universe obeyed the same law of Fate, so that the 'cosmic sympathy' was natural to Stoic thought, and indeed they were the first to assume that the same physical laws would apply to heavenly bodies as to earthly ones, as opposed to Aristotle's view that the laws of the sublunary world were different from those of the celestial. Manilius' famous line,

fata regunt orbem, certa stant omnia lege

(the fates rule the world, all things are established by a settled law), is pure Stoicism. And Stoicism was thus naturally inclined to accept astrology. It – Stoicism – was also a creed suited to the Romans. Whereas the Epicureans advised the wise man to withdraw from the distractions and dangers of political life, the Stoics emphasised his duty to his state, his commitment to politics.

If Zeno, Chrysippus and Panaetius made Greek Stoicism, it was Posidonius who gave it the form in which it became part of the Roman tradition. He was a great admirer of Rome, and the teacher of many young Romans, including Cicero; and his Stoicism became an impor-tant part of the Roman intellectual life. Much is sometimes made of the 'Stoic opposition' under the early emperors, though in view of the fact that all those who opposed what they saw as an un-Roman tyranny were brought up on tales of Brutus and Mucius Scaevola and the old Roman heroes – Stoic sages before Stoicism – it is perhaps difficult to say whether it was opposition because it was Stoic or Stoic because it was opposition. Certainly one of the greatest of the Roman Stoics, Seneca, was no opponent of the emperor, even if he was sentenced to death by his old pupil Nero.

Now we know that Posidonius was favourably inclined towards astrology from Cicero. In the *De Divinatione* (I 130) he says that Posidonius thought 'that there are in nature certain signs of future events'; and according to St Augustine, quoting probably from the lost

De Fato, Cicero referred to Posidonius as 'much given to astrology'.[17] It was Posidonian Stoicism which the Romans inherited; but the practical scepticism which seems to have been typical of the Romans prevented many intellectuals, even Stoics, from fully accepting the ideas of 'the Chaldaeans'. Seneca, in his *Quaestiones Naturales* (II 32), argues that since everything in nature moves according to the same laws of fate, all things may be signs for him who can read them – though he is careful to point out that not all the signs can in practice be read, since we do not yet know enough about them and their laws. Now the observations of the Chaldaeans, he says, take into account the powers of the five stars (that is, the planets); but surely all those thousands of stars do not shine for nothing? 'What else is it which introduces such great errors into the work of those skilled in casting natal charts except that they allot so few stars to us, when all those that shine above us lay claim to part of us? It may be that those which are lower in the heavens direct their power upon us more closely, but surely those too that either are fixed or because their motion is equal to that of the sky appear fixed, are not without some lordship over us?' This is obviously both anti- and pro-astrology: at the least it leaves room for the astrologer, especially one who makes much use of the fixed stars.

In the early third century A.D., Plotinus erected the last great philosophical structure of antiquity, Neo-Platonism; so called because it was a development of Platonism, with much of Aristotle, and much that was pure Plotinus. His works, all in the form of shortish essays, were gathered together by his pupil and disciple Porphyry – not, alas, in chronological order of writing – into groups of nine, whence they are known as the *Enneads, ennea* being the Greek for nine. In two essays, a very early one (Enn. III 1) and a very late one (II 3), Plotinus attacked astrology. His basic objection was that the soul, the true self of man, in proper Platonic style, is above the physical world and therefore outside its laws. In the earlier treatise he argues first that astrology takes away what is properly ours, and 'leaves us as stones rolled along, not as men acting of ourselves and according to our own natures.' Secondly, if the stars are signs, and it is then to be argued that they are therefore causes of those things they signify, then all such signs are causes – birds and entrails and other omens. Again, he says that according to the astrologers, inferences can be made concerning the fortunes of others from one man's birth-chart – parents or children, wives or husbands – but what about *their* proper birth-charts? Further, at a given moment a man and an animal might

17 St Augustine, *De Civ. Dei*, V.2.

be born: do they therefore have the same destiny? And lastly, how can the stars, who are gods, cause evil, and how can they be better or worse depending on their relative positions in the heavens?

Now it is a striking fact that many of these same arguments are deployed by Plotinus' great contemporary, Origen, one of the greatest of the Greek Fathers. A detailed comparison of the long passage quoted from Origen by Eusebius[18] with the essay of Plotinus shows clearly that they were drawing on a common source of ideas. That can only really have been Ammonius Saccas, their common master in the school at Alexandria. There is more in Origen than in Plotinus, however, and one short passage is interesting and important enough to be quoted: 'There is a theorem around which demonstrates that the zodiacal circle moves like the planets from west to east, one degree in a hundred years, and this in a long time alters the positions of the twelve signs, so that the calculated sign and the actual sign are different; and the prognostications, they say, are found not from the actual sign but from the calculated sign of the zodiac; which cannot really be understood at all.' This is a problem, concerning the precession of the equinoxes, to which we shall have to give some attention later. The point is that the equinoctial points, the points where the ecliptic crosses the equator, are not fixed; what is called 'the first point of Aries', when the sun is on the equator on its way north, is in fact today no longer in Aries but in Pisces. So Origen is absolutely right, for the sign of the zodiac Aries, if one starts Aries at 'the first point of Aries', the vernal equinox, does not correspond with the sign actually in the sky, which is Pisces.

Origen takes us for the first time into a Christian context. He and Plotinus, if they are representing the arguments of Ammonius Saccas, really represent the philosophers' views of the mid-second century. By then the Christian Church was, of course, over a hundred years old, and was spreading across the Roman Empire from its beginnings in the Near East. It was still a Greek church. The common tongue of the eastern Mediterranean, and of most of the traders, craftsmen and professional classes, was the Koinê, which word is simply the Greek for 'common'. Greek, this late common language, was the tongue also of all the Jews of the Dispersion – to whom the Gospel was first preached. The books of the New Testament were all written in Greek. Latin was the language of the western half of the Empire, stretching from present Romania and Italy north and west, and including North Africa west of Cyrenaica. But western cities like Marseilles (an ancient Greek colony anyway and always an 'international' city) and Arles,

---

[18] *Eusebii Pamphili Evangelicae Praeparationis Libri XV*, edited and translated by E. H. Gifford (Oxford, 1903). The passage is in Book V, c.XI; the quotation is at 294d.

centres of trade and commerce, had large Greek-speaking communities. While it is not true that Christianity was restricted to the lower social classes, as is so often asserted, it had certainly not yet made any considerable inroads into the governing classes of the Roman Empire. The *Octavius* of Minucius Felix, the first Latin apologetic work deliberately aimed at the educated Romans, was probably written at the very end of the second century. Even as late as the middle of the fourth century, Augustine in Latin North Africa had a pagan father.

If we look for the attitude of the early Church, of the first two centuries or so, to astrology, we find very little evidence indeed of any 'attitude'. There is no mention of astrology or astrologers, or even of divination in general, in any of the early councils of the Church: they are mostly concerned with matters of discipline and of relations with pagans, and sometimes with heresy. The so-called 'Apostolic Constitutions', which are possibly as late as the fourth century, prohibit association with those dealing in incantations, divination, soothsaying and so forth, but do not explicitly mention astrology. A late Arabic version of the decrees of the Council of Nicaea, in 325, does include a prohibition of astrology, but it is the only source for that council which does. The first clear condemnation comes in the decrees of the Council of Laodicaea, in 364 or 367, which somewhat curiously made an apparent distinction between *mathematici* and *astrologi* (perhaps the first are the 'scientific' astrologers and the second, the 'quacks'). However, we might expect the Church to be opposed to astrology as a pagan form of divination, another superstition, and one that diminished if it did not deny the freedom of man. There are at least two pieces of evidence that this was so.

Epiphanius, in his book *De Mensuris et Ponderibus*, chapter XV, tells the story of Aquila, dating from about 120 A.D.:[19] 'Now Aquila lived in Jerusalem, and noticed that the disciples of those who had themselves heard the apostles, in their great faith, worked miracles of healing and other wonders, and being much stirred in spirit by this, embraced the Christian faith himself, and after a little time sought and was admitted to baptism. But since he did not change from his previous way of life, that is, from believing in the vanity of astrology (the Greek here has ἀστρονομία, *astronomia*, but it is astrology which is meant; the two words, *astronomia* and *astrologia*, are still interchangeable), in which he was very exactly learned; but every day he consulted the position of his own birth-chart: he was questioned by the masters and reproved on this account, but he not only did not correct his ways, but rather contentiously opposed them, and sought

---

[19] Migne, *Patrologiae Cursus Completus, Series Graeca*, XLIII.262.

to establish what is not to be established, namely fate and all that follows from it; he was therefore thrown back out of the Church, as being unsuited for salvation.' The other piece of evidence comes from the acid pen of the great African Tertullian, from the forty-third chapter of his *Apologeticum*: 'I freely admit that there may be some who can rightly complain of the uselessness of Christians. First among them will be the pimps and panders and procurers, and then cut-throats and poisoners and magicians, and also soothsayers and diviners and astrologers.'

Tertullian was writing at the end of the second century. It was about the middle of that century that Ptolemy wrote the *Tetrabiblos*, with which we are concerned in the next chapter. Although it had very great influence on medieval and later astrology, that book itself only marks a stage in the long evolution of the art from its beginnings in Babylonia and Egypt. Ancient systems of time-reckoning produced the ideas of the zodiac and its signs, and the decans, and these were then used to assist in the interpretation of heavenly signs for earthly events. The primitive astrology thus produced was refined by the Greeks, with their astronomical and philosophical ideas – especially perhaps Pythagoreanism with its number-symbolism, and Stoicism with the ideas of cosmic sympathy and the universal rule of Fate – to bring about the confusion of systems and parts of systems found in the early sources, with dodecatemoria and single degrees, *loci* and Lots, planetary aspects and characters, genders and spheres of influence, the four elements and stones and metals and plants – all the apparatus we have seen gathering about astrology in these first chapters. Much of this was systematised by Ptolemy, though his was by no means the last word.

IV

Alexandria to Byzantium:
Ptolemy and Later Greek Astrology

'Of the ways of foretelling the future through astronomy (*astronomia*), two are among the most important and the most powerful: one, which is first both logically and practically, is that by which we learn about the ever-altering configurations, produced by their movements, of the sun and moon and stars in relation to one another and to the earth; the second is that by which we enquire into the changes produced in the world through the particular natural states of those configurations. The first has its own proper theory and method, desirable in itself even if it does not achieve the results given by its combination with the second; and it has already been systematically and scientifically set out (as best I could) in its own treatise (*syntaxis* – the *Almagest*). Of the second, which is not so self-sufficient, we shall give an account (*logos*) in this book in a way that is philosophically fitting.'

So 'the most divine Ptolemy' begins his *Tetrabiblos*.[1] He is most widely known today as a scientist, as geographer and astronomer, but for many centuries he was also the most famous of Greek astrologers. It is only very recently that anyone has thought it odd that a great scientific astronomer should also be an authority in matters astrological. Ptolemy regarded the two as complementary, and although astrology is 'not so self-sufficient', since it depends on astronomy for its factual basis, he promises to give of it a genuinely philosophical account. It is the other part of the science of the heavens, which renders the whole useful. The *Almagest* is Part I: Part II is the *Tetrabiblos*.

This famous textbook, which gathered commentaries about it right from its first publication, Ptolemy wrote about the middle of the second century A.D., most likely in Alexandria, the cultural and scientific capital of the age. The city of Alexander the Great[2] was

---

[1] *Claudii Ptolemaei Opera*, III.1, *Apotelesmatica*, ed. F. Boll and E. Boer (Leipzig, 1954); or with an English translation in the Loeb Classical Library, *Ptolemy, Tetrabiblos*, ed. and tr. F. E. Robbins, 1940 (latest reprint bound on its own, 1980). Reference in the text are to the Boll-Boer edition; translations by the author.

[2] For what follows see E. Brescia, *Alexandria ad Aegyptum* (Bergamo, 1922).

founded by the young conqueror – he was then twenty-four! – in 332 B.C., nine years before his death. A good harbour on the Mediterranean was formed by joining the island of Pharos to the shore of the bay: the light on the island eventually gave its name to all such lighthouses. On the south side, the city had a port on Lake Mareotis; the lake was connected by a canal with an eastern branch of the Nile, which gave Alexandria good access to the hinterland. It remained a Greek city until its conquest by the Khalif, Umar in 641, and continued to be the chief maritime city of the Levant until the fourteenth century. To say that it was a Greek city is, however, a little misleading. It was founded as a Greek colony in Egypt, but it was always from its foundation a mixed city, with an 'international' population. It was, at its height, a large city of about half a million inhabitants, of all sorts. For it was not only a port, but a manufacturing centre, of glass and metalwork (from which alchemy takes its origins), of paper, of scents and incense, and of weaving, especially of carpets. It had a reputation, for culture and also for extravagance and luxury, similar to that of fifteenth century Florence or nineteenth century Paris. There were fine buildings in Alexandria, many erected by Roman emperors: Antoninus Pius, for example, contemporary with Ptolemy, built the Gates of the Sun and of the Moon. Perhaps the historically most important buildings were the Museum and the Library. They were probably built by the first two successor-kings of Egypt – successors, that is, to Alexander: their dynastic name was Ptolemy, which misled some medieval Latin writers into calling our Ptolemy, the scientist, *rex Aegyptorum*, king of the Egyptians. 'Museum' did not then mean a home for a collection of monuments of the past. The word is merely the Latin form of the Greek for 'home, or temple, of the Muses', and the Muses were the goddesses of the arts; so the Museum was the home or temple of the arts and sciences. It was in fact a sort of research institute, where scholars were maintained by the state, and all kinds of scholarship, literary, philosophical and scientific, were practised and encouraged there for about five hundred years.

Not that Alexandria was the only centre for learning, or of philosophy, in those centuries. Athens continued to be the home of philosophy until Justinian closed the pagan schools in 529; and philosophy flourished also in other places, notably in Rhodes and in Syria. It was part of the intellectual background of all educated men, and well to the foreground for many. A number of philosophers from Aristotle on wrote short 'evangelical' tracts, proclaiming the good news of the value of philosophical contemplation in a troubled world, and exhorting men to its practice. It was one such protreptic work, the *Hortensius* of Cicero, which converted the young Augustine to the study of philosophy in the fourth century. Philosophy included what the ancients called 'physics', a rational account of the physical universe; and just as in our own time most educated people have some ideas of atoms and molecules, and even of more fundamental particles, and of the theory of evolution, so in Ptolemy's day the cultured man had an eclectic philosophy drawn from many schools, which made up a general picture of himself and his world. The parts of this picture of most importance to the understanding of astrology are the doctrine of the four elements and the four qualities, and the notion of the unity of the universe. Behind such philosophical ideas as these, as behind the development of astrology itself, lay the Greeks' belief that this is a rational universe, that we can give a reasoned account of it and understand its workings: that it is an ordered structure, a *cosmos*. The Greek word meant 'order', and since good order was for the Greek beautiful, the verb formed from *cosmos* meant to make beautiful, to adorn – hence 'cosmetic'! Throughout the story of astrology, through whatever dark and muddling ways it winds, we must remember that it would never have emerged from the slough of superstition in which it was begotten, and into which it so often seems about to disappear, it would not even now exhibit the same two antique faces, of rationality and of magic, if the Greeks and above all Ptolemy had not caught it and bound it to the framework of their own rationalist vision of the world.

The four elements are older than philosophy. In the sixth century beginnings of philosophy, Thales selected water as the 'stuff' of the universe, Anaximenes air, and Heraclitus fire; and both the latter produced the other elements out of their 'first matter'. Fire, air, earth and water: air, water and earth represent the three commonest examples of the three states of matter we are familiar with – gaseous, liquid and solid. And fire is obviously different: it seems to come out of solids, it is usually killed by water, and it is a source of light and heat. A fifth element was added by the Pythagoreans, the aether, a sort of heavenly fire. They possibly added it because their philosophy was based on number, on mathematics, and there are five regular solids, one for each element: the cube for earth, the pyramid for fire, the octahedron for air, the icosahedron for water, and the dodecahedron for aether. More important, the Pythagoreans extended and 'canon-ised', as it were, another very ancient doctrine, that of the 'opposites' – one-many, limited-unlimited, odd-even, male-female, and so on – which runs right through Greek philosophy and Greek medicine. It was Zeno of Elea who took two pairs of these opposites, hot and cold, and wet and dry, and made all else from them; and Aristotle who married the two doctrines and made his four 'simple bodies' (*Physics* 192 etc.) fire, air, water and earth, from, in turn, the hot and the dry, the hot and the wet, the cold and the wet, and the cold and the dry (*De*

Gen. et Corrup., II). The Stoics took this over, and some of them simplified the equivalences to fire – hot, air – cold, water – wet, and earth – dry. The elements, the qualities and the opposites passed into the general background of late Classical thought, especially in medicine. And it was the Stoics who made widely accepted the other great doctrine, of the oneness of the cosmos, including man. All things, they said, are held together by the same cosmic force, or *logos*, reason, including man, so that Epictetus, who was an ex-slave from Nero's bodyguard, could write (II, 10.2): 'Consider then what you are distinguished from by your reason: you are distinguished from the wild beasts, you are distinguished from your flocks. You are because of it a citizen of the world and a part of it (πολίτης τοῦ κόσμου καὶ μέρος αὐτοῦ).' Because all things are one, and all are governed by the same natural law, or *logos*, we can understand it all, and also each part affects the whole and is affected by it.

It is the outstanding mark of Ptolemy's astrology that it is informed by the philosophical and scientific spirit of his age. He aims to give an account (*logos* again) of astrology which is systematic and which fits in with contemporary philosophical ideas. The details of his system, which do not differ in any great respect from those of his predecessors – for Ptolemy was not so much a discoverer or innovator as a collector and systematiser – are less important than his methods. Sometimes what he has to say on a particular topic is less noteworthy than what he has not said; for though he was not an inventor of new doctrines, he ordered his material according to his own ideas and did not blindly follow his sources. These he seldom mentions at all, and never by name. Quite likely 'the ancient', of chapter 11 of Book III, is Nechepso-Petosiris; the Egyptians are referred to several times, in particular as having 'completely united medicine and astronomical prediction' (I.3); and in I.21 the Egyptian and Chaldaean systems of 'terms' are distinguished. In the same chapter Ptolemy refers to an 'ancient manuscript' he had come across, much damaged, he says, but does not tell us where it came from or who may have written it. It is probable that the introductory chapters to the whole work, and possibly those on astrological ethnography, are derived from the Stoic Posidonius. Several times Ptolemy refers to 'those who have written on these things'; but always he makes up his own mind, and explains his principles. It is what he does with his material that matters.

In I.iii.18 Ptolemy says that the Egyptians 'completely united medicine with astronomical prediction' (συνῆψαν πανταχῆ τῷ δι' ἀστρονομίας προγνωστικῷ τὴν ἰατρικήν). But the link was ancient, and forged in Greece. The old magical medicine of Babylon and Egypt already dealt in terms of lucky and unlucky days, and possibly also of lucky and unlucky states of the moon and stars, before Berosus came to Cos. The moon and stars and magic and medicine have gone together throughout history: there is still more than a little of the magician in the modern physician, and some people still believe that the phases of the moon affect their health. Medicine as an empirical science was the creation of the Greeks; and since they had made a science of astrology, as part of astronomy, it was not surprising that they should accept and develop the ancient links between the two. It was probably the Sicilian school which established them on what appeared to be a sound philosophical basis. Sicily had been colonised from Greece, along with southern Italy: it was the Magna Graecia of the ancients. One of the greatest Sicilians was the mid-fifth century philosopher Empedocles, and it was most likely under his influence that the idea was developed that man's body was made up of the four elements and the four qualities, held, in good health, in a proper balance, or harmony. The idea of harmony seems to have been one of the bases of all Greek thought, and the notion of the balance of opposites in man's nature was soon part of Greek medical thinking. The late fifth century Hippocratic treatise 'On the Nature of Man'[3] spends the first seven chapters on the 'humours' and their relation to the seasons: chapter 4 says: 'The body of man has in itself blood, phlegm, yellow bile and black bile; these make up the nature of his body, and through these he feels pain or enjoys health;' the mixture has to be exactly harmonious to produce perfect health. Chapters 6 and 7 associate the four qualities with the humours, and these with the seasons, as follows: blood is warm and moist, and associated with spring (and, later, with childhood); yellow bile is warm and dry, and goes with summer (youth); black bile is cold and dry, going with autumn (maturity), and phlegm is cold and wet, like winter (old age).[4]

The Hippocratic writings had already more than hinted at *iatroma-thematica*, as astrological medicine was called. An early collection of medical maxims, 'Airs, Waters, Places', firmly asserts (I.8) that 'astronomy' is of the greatest assistance to medicine. We have already seen that the various parts of the body had been placed under the influence and protection of the different signs of the zodiac. The planets had similar and parallel responsibilities; several lists exist in the literature, more or less agreeing in detail, and Ptolemy gives his in III.13.4f: 'The natures of the planets produce the forms and causes of the symptoms, since of the most important parts of man, Saturn is lord of the right

---

[3] 'The Nature of Man' in vol. IV of the Loeb Classical Library *Hippocrates*, tr. W. H. S. Jones, 1931.
[4] For the later development of this humoral theory, its associations with astrology, and its ramifications in the history of art, see the fascinating *Saturn and Melancholy* by R. Klibansky, E. Panofsky and F. Saxl (London, 1964).

ear, the spleen, the bladder, phlegm and the bones; Jupiter of touch, the lungs, the arteries and the seed; Mars of the left ear, the kidneys, the veins and the genitals; the sun of sight, the brain, the heart, the sinews (or possibly, by the mid-second century, the nerves – νεῦρον in the Greek), and all on the right side; Venus of smell, the liver and muscles; Mercury of speech and thought, and the tongue, the bile and the buttocks; and the moon of taste and of drinking, the mouth, the belly, the womb and all on the left side.' Clearly the relationships of the planets and the signs, and the aspects of the planets, could make quite a difference to the patient's chances of recovery from sickness or injury, whatever the drugs used. And the drugs themselves, the plants used, were also affected by the movements of the heavens.

Gathering certain flowers or herbs at particular times in the moon's cycle, or under special stars, was an older practice than astrology, but here again it was assimilated, and the zodiacal signs and the planets gathered each their own flower or plant, or several, since there were many more useful plants than there were signs and planets. Nor did those who made the lists always know why they were doing it or even what plants they were listing: one, for example, says 'Mercury's plant is the *pentadactylum*, or the *pentapetalum*, or the *eupatorium*, or the *anthropocheir*, or the *pentaphyllum*, or the *pseudoselinum*.' The first, second and fifth are all the same plant, the creeping cinquefoil, which is also given as Mercury's plant in three other lists at least. In other lists mullein is given to Mercury, and *pseudoselinum* is probably wild parsley. There are many lists[5] and all very different not only in the plants they name, but in the fullness of their information; some are bare names, and others give some medical reasons for their choices, though these reasons seem to bear no more than a chance relationship to the parts of the body governed by the attached signs or planets. Sometimes the connexion is magical: the cinquefoil is said by one authority to be good for fevers, for the joints, the spleen and the stomach, and to stop toothache. This seems to indicate little connexion with Mercury: but we are also told that to touch the mouth with the root produces good orators, and there is the link. It is not perhaps surprising to find the heliotrope associated with the sun; and it was probably because Saturn was 'the sun of the night' that it was sometimes listed under that planet. The sun's plant was more commonly the polygonum (bistort), which was apparently an aphrodisiac, the root of which was good for the eyes; and Saturn's was often the asphodel, which among other virtues possessed those of removing fear of demons and easing the troubles of teething. The peony went with the moon. The moon and magic were always associated, and the

5 See Chapter II, p. 24 and note.

peony was anciently a magical plant: 'It had to be dug up at night, lest woodpeckers should peck out one's eyes; and like the mandrake, the groan it gave on leaving the ground was fatal to all hearers. The seeds were a protection against witchcraft, and the roots, even if only hung round the neck, a remedy for the falling sickness'.[6]

Most of these plant-lists are to be found in the writings of authors later – sometimes much later – than Ptolemy. Since they all copied freely from one another, and astrology was always a conservative art, and plant magic is very ancient, we may safely assume the assimilation of much of this into Greek astrology by the second century. It had not, however, become sufficiently rationalised, nor sufficiently grounded in 'physics', for Ptolemy to use it, and he does not mention plants. But medicine he is certain about. In Chapter 3 of Book I it is cited as one of the important benefits of 'astronomy' that it is used in the 'iatromathematical systems' of the Egyptians, so that (§19) 'through astronomy they may know the qualities of the underlying temperaments, and the symptoms which will occur because of the circumstances, and the proper causes of these; since without the knowledge of these remedies would for the most part fail, because the same ones are not suitable for all bodies and all afflictions.' In the thirteenth chapter of Book III he explains why it is important to observe the east and west especially carefully, and note which signs are 'afflicted' by malevolent planets in bad aspects, because (§4) 'the parts of the individual sign of the zodiac which surround the part of the horizon which is afflicted will show the part of the body which the cause will affect, and whether the indicated part can suffer a wound or a disease or both; and the natures of the planets produce the forms and causes of the symptoms.'

It is the nature of the planets which is the cause; for Ptolemy this is the 'physical', or philosophical, explanation for *iatromathematica*. For example, Saturn is said (I.4.3) 'chiefly to possess the quality of cooling and by cooling gently drying, most likely because he is furthest away both from the warmth of the sun and from the exhalations of moisture about the earth.' Consequently (III.13.6) 'in general Saturn makes men cold-bellied and over-full of phlegm, and subject to discharges, emaciated, weakly, jaundiced, liable to dysentery, and coughing, and bringing up phlegm, and colic, and elephantiasis; and women he also makes liable to afflictions of the womb (or hysterical: the Greek ὑστερικάς means both, the two being connected in ancient medicine).' Now here, in the cooling and drying, the warmth and moisture, and the phlegm – though not, be it noticed, melancholy (black bile), which Ptolemy attributes to Mars – we have the four qualities and the

---

6 A. M. Coats, *The Treasury of Flowers* (London, 1975) p. 8.

humours. The Aristotelian-Stoic background is clearly shown in the second chapter of the work: 'It could easily and very clearly be demonstrated to anyone that a certain power from the (outer) ether-like and invisible nature is distributed over and penetrates all the wholly changeable substance round the earth; of the primary sub-lunar elements, fire and air are surrounded and changed by the movements of the ether, and themselves surround and change all the rest, earth and water and the plants and animals in them.' Changes in the qualities of the elements, their balance, produce the sub-lunary changes, and these are mediated and affected by the heavenly bodies, by the sun particularly, and the moon, but also by the planets and the rest of the stars. Consequently their relative positions, or aspects, affect the results on earth; as is known to farmers and herdsmen, and sailors, and others who observe the sky in the course of their work. And this is all very philosophical and rational.

Which is what Ptolemy undertook to be in giving his account of this part of astronomy. That is why and how he can select from his sources what he is going to use and what he will leave out. Sometimes the omissions are explicit. At the beginning of I.22, for example, after the long chapter on 'terms', in which he discusses the relative merits of the Chaldaean and Egyptian systems and decides between the two, he says: 'Some have distinguished even finer divisions of the rulerships than these, calling them 'places' (τόποι) and 'degrees' (μοῖραι); they suppose the 'place' to be the dodecatemorion of a dodecatemorion (i.e. the twelfth part of a sign, the twelfth part of the zodiac), that is two and a half degrees, and give the lordship over each to the signs in turn. Others, according to some other sorts of irrational arrangements, (ἀλόγως, without *logos*), assign each degree from the beginning to each of the planets, following the Chaldaean arrangement of the terms. These, as having only a plausible and not a physical (but a baseless) explanation (*logos*), we shall leave out.' In the following chapter Ptolemy deals briefly (in twenty-three lines!) with 'faces' and 'chariots' and 'the like': all begun with 'they say'. 'They' differed a great deal over these curious divisions: at least the idea of 'faces' suggested by Ptolemy – a planet is in its proper 'face' if its house and those of the sun and moon stand in the same relation as itself and those two luminaries – and that of the fourth century Paulus Alexandrinus, who equates the 'faces' with the decans, so that Mars is in its proper 'face' in the first ten degrees of Aries, and so on, are completely different. It was clearly something Ptolemy did not wish to be concerned with. Again, after his outline of what he is going to cover in the last two books, he says: 'Of each of these subjects we shall make a summary sketch, setting out the actual practical methods of investigation with a bare outline of their active powers, as we have promised; and the superstitious nonsense of many, for which plausible reasons cannot be given, we shall pass over, going straight to the primary physical causes. What can, however, be properly comprehended we shall investigate, not by means of lots or numbers (where no account of causes can be given) but through the proper observing of the configurations of the stars with relation to their houses.'

This is the nearest Ptolemy comes to hinting at the intrusion of numerological magic into astrology, though it was clearly a temptation for the quack. Numbers are, of course, magical; very curious things can be done with numbers, as every non-mathematician and some mathematicians know. The Greeks did not invent mathematics, though they did discover their own, and made very great advances in the field. Kitto writes:[7] 'Mathematics are perhaps the most character-istic of all the Greek discoveries, and the one that excited them most.' He then describes some mathematical games that whiled away his own quiet hours, and says, 'it was with great delight that I disclosed to myself a whole system of numerical behaviour of which my math-ematical teachers had left me (I am glad to say) in complete ignorance ... They had never told me, and I had never suspected, that Numbers play these grave and beautiful games with each other, from everlasting to everlasting, independently (apparently) of time, space and the human mind. It was an impressive peep into a new and perfect universe. Then I knew how the Pythagoreans felt when they made these same discoveries ... The ultimate and simplifying Truth that the Ionians were trying to find in a physical Something was really Number.' The Pythagoreans made number games philosophically respectable, and the great authority of Plato raised mathematics into theological realms. But at the lowest level, numbers remained magical. And it was easier to play these games in Greek, for the Greeks used their letters as numbers, so that alpha, beta, gamma etc. were written for 1, 2, 3 and so on. This meant that a name was also a number: the name of Plato, Platōn in Greek, could be added up to 1261 – and that again added to make 10, which was surely significant! It was easy to combine this sort of symbolism with a list of the planets, or a diagram of the zodiac, or both, to produce some very simple rules to achieve certain results without bothering too much with the complications of astrology. Many such devices survive in the literature: to find a man's zodiacal sign, for example, add together the letters of his and his mother' names (for a woman take her own and her father's names) and then count round the zodiac, starting of course from Aries. Six of the signs are then good, three – Cancer, Scorpio and Capricorn – are bad,

[7] H. D. F. Kitto, *The Greeks* (Harmondsworth, 1951) pp. 190–1.

and the remaining three, Libra, Taurus and Sagittarius, are in between. Or to discover which will die first, a man or his wife, add the syllables of their names, and count round the zodiac, beginning this time from Capricorn, until you land on either Leo, which indicates that the man will die first, or Virgo, which marks the wife as doomed.

Ptolemy will have none of this; it is all *alogon*, unaccountable, irrational. The result of his philosophically critical requirement is that his work is more restrained, and generally simpler, than that of other Greek astrologers. Four short chapters (14–17) of Book I deal with the aspects and other relations between the signs, including the lack of any relationship, or disjunction. Ptolemy only recognises four aspects properly so called: opposition, trine, quartile and sextile, all of which can be measured in whole signs. In opposition, signs are separated by six signs, in trine by four, in quartile by three and in sextile by two; or, more accurately, the angles between them include those numbers of signs. Conjunction is not mentioned, since it cannot apply to signs, only to planets. Ptolemy gives a curious mathematical explanation why these four aspects are significant, but goes on to explain that trine and sextile are harmonious aspects because the signs concerned are all the same, all masculine or all feminine; and quartile and opposition are bad because they relate differing signs.

Comets are dealt with very summarily in the *Tetrabiblos*. Apart from four lines in II.14.10, where they are said to signify droughts and winds, there is only one paragraph in II.10, which is very general and does not go into the details of classification and interpretation found in other writers. Hephaistion of Thebes, for example, who wrote a three-book *Apotelesmatica* early in the fifth century,[8] quotes Ptolemy verbatim, the whole of II.10, but then goes on for nearly two pages of Pingree's text describing the different kinds of comets and their effects, drawing on 'Nechepso-Petosiris'. After Ptolemy's words Hephaistion goes on: 'Of comets, one is called Hippeus (the Knight) and is the sacred star of Venus; it is the same size as the full moon, moves very swiftly, and has a bright tail streaming behind it. It is borne backwards through the zodiac by the cosmos. It indicates the swift fall of kings and tyrants, and brings about changes in the affairs of those countries towards which its tail points.' Seven such descriptions are given, one comet for each of the planets, and Hephaistion concludes the chapter: 'Those called Locides and Pogoniae, with the rest, occur outside the zodiac in the northern part of the sky.'[9] There was a great deal of argument in antiquity over whether comets could occur outside the zodiac or not, and what difference there was

---

[8] Ed. David Pingree, *Hephaestionis Thebani Apotelesmaticorum Libri Tres*, I (Leipzig, 1973).
[9] Pingree, *op. cit.*, 74–96.

between northern and southern comets. Most authorities regarded comets as sub-lunary; it was a reasonable view, when everything above the moon was thought to be eternally unchanging, and when comets were grouped together with 'shooting stars', or meteorites. It had the authority of Aristotle behind it, who in his *Meteorologica* spends two chapters discussing theories of their nature and origin, in the course of which he says: 'We may regard as a proof that their constitution is fiery the fact that their appearance in any number is a sign of coming wind and drought.'[10]

Not only is Ptolemy usually briefer and simpler than others, but he frequently gives some reason for his statements, where other astrologers just say 'Saturn is exalted in Libra' and leave it at that. Ptolemy gives a 'physical' explanation of exaltations and depressions, so that Venus, which is moist by nature (I.4.6) is exalted in Pisces, 'in which sign the beginning of the moist spring is signified', and depressed in Virgo, the sign of dry autumn. Occasionally his 'explaining' leads him into some awkward wriggling. Chapter 6 of Book I is 'Of masculine and feminine planets': 'Again, since the primary kinds of natures are two, male and female, and of the powers we have already set out that of the moist substance is especially feminine (for generally there is more of this part in all females, and more of the others in males), tradition reasonably has it that the Moon and Venus are feminine, because they have a larger share of the moist, and the Sun, Saturn, Jupiter and Mars are masculine, and Mercury is common to both kinds, since he is equally productive of the dry and the moist substance.' So indeed Mercury is described at the end of Chapter 4. When we come to the next chapter, on the 'sects' of the sun and moon, the diurnal and nocturnal planets, we are told that the day is more masculine because it is hotter and active, and the night feminine as being moist and restful. Tradition, again, reasonably tells us that the Moon and Venus are feminine and therefore nocturnal, and the Sun and Jupiter, as masculine, are diurnal; and Mercury is common, as before. What has happened to Saturn and Mars? They should, by the same argument, both be diurnal. But tradition, alas, knew nothing of Ptolemy's reasoning, and divided them; so Ptolemy finds a reason: 'tradition also assigns to each of the sects the two planets of a destructive nature, but not this time as having the same physical causes, but for opposite ones. For similar stars being associated with those of a good constitution increase their power to do good, but if those which are not suited to the natures of the destructive planets are mixed with them, then much of their power to do harm is broken. Therefore

10 Aristotle, *Meteorologica*, trans. H. D. P. Lee, Loeb Classical Library, 1952, 55.

tradition assigned Saturn, which is cold, to the warmth of the day, and Mars, being dry, to the moisture of the night; so each of them achieves due proportion because of the mixture and becomes a fitting member of the sect which provides the right mixing.' A curious – and curiously Greek – argument: it seems that these two powerfully malevolent planets themselves seek a 'due proportion', the proper mixture, even to their own detriment.

However, the basic rationality of Ptolemy, the orderliness of his thought, is shown in the planning and setting out of the whole work. It is set out as a system. Book I is concerned with the mechanics of astrology, which is then divided into two parts: 'catholic', or universal astrology, treated in Book II, and individual astrology, or geneth-lialogy, which takes up Books III and IV. These two books are further divided into three parts, the first concerned with events before birth, the second with the time of the birth itself, and the third with what comes after birth. The last section takes up the whole of Book IV. Each book has an introduction telling the reader the proposed order of presentation, and in III.4 Ptolemy provides a detailed 'table of contents' for the last two books. He does his best to make his account of this part of astronomy 'philosophically fitting'.

The philosophy to which his astrology is suited is, not surprisingly, Stoicism. Not surprisingly, because Stoicism was the most successful, the most accepted, philosophy at the time: it was immensely adapt-able, and it was complete – it provided a workable system of ethics based on a physics which was not only highly advanced but made sense.[11] The aim of the Stoic was to achieve a state of self-sufficiency, αὐτάρκεια, so that nothing should be able to trouble his fundamental peace of mind. The way in which he could reach this state was by 'living in accordance with Nature', which implied knowing what Nature was and how it worked. The basis of the Stoic position is the oneness of nature, of the universe, including gods and men. It is neither materialist nor spiritual, or perhaps it is both. It could be said to materialise mind, since for Stoicism minds are of the same stuff as the whole physical world; but it could equally be said to spiritualise matter. Since mind and matter, men and gods and things, are all of the same stuff, all work according to the same laws, to the same Law, which can be called Fate. In contradistinction to Aristotle, who thought that there were two kinds of physics, one for the sublunary world, and one for the heavens ('natural motions' in the two regions were quite different), the Stoics invented astrophysics, for they

---

[11] See S. Sambursky, *Physics of the Stoics* (London, 1959). Chapter III of that book is an illuminating consideration of the problems of Fate and determinism, 'the possible' and free will.

believed, as we do, that the same physical laws applied throughout the universe. Not that we are not free; we may always choose to act in this way or that, or not at all. So we may choose to act in accordance with those laws, with Fate, or not. Whether we do live according to Nature or not makes no difference to what happens: what is bound to happen will happen anyway. But it makes a great difference to the quality of our lives. We can go our own way, and conflict with Nature, and suffer disappointment and pain and grief; or we can walk with Fate, and achieve peace. And we have already seen that since all things are one and the same stuff and work in the same way, there is a cosmic sympathy which makes sense of divination, and therefore of astrology.

It was the Stoic teacher of Cicero, Posidonius, who rationalised divination most accommodatingly for the late Classical mind, and on whom Ptolemy probably drew most heavily for his *apologia* in his opening chapters. In his Prologue he says that 'most chance events of great importance clearly display their cause (αἰτίαν) as coming from the heavens surrounding us', and astrology, the second and useful part of astronomy, investigates τὰς ἀποτελουμένας μεταβολάς, 'the changes produced' in what they, the heavens, surround. This explicit idea of causation is reinforced in Chapter 2: the aspects of the planets are there said to cause changes (ἀπεργάζονται), and the temperament of each man is determined by the state of the heavens at his birth. There are of course other causes at work (συναιτίαι) such as heredity and environment and upbringing, which are very important and must be taken into account, but the causes derived from the surrounding heavens are the most important and powerful. The same doctrine of causes is reiterated at the beginning of the next chapter, which sets out the benefits astrology can confer – a chapter which is essentially Stoic in its arguments. This causation is not restricted to the planets: the chapter on the fixed stars (I.9) tells of their natures 'with reference to the active power of each'; the same phrase is used in the following chapter where the modifying effects of the seasons are considered. When we come to universal astrology in Book II we find that the basic causation of ethnic differences is 'climatic' (in both the Greek and the English senses) and through the 'humours'; but national differences are derived from the characters of the planets, as masculine, diurnal and so forth. 'The first and most powerful cause' (ἡ πρώτη καὶ ἰοχυροτάτη αἰτία) of the general conditions of countries and cities lies in the eclipses of the sun and moon and the movement of the stars at the time (II.5), and Chapter 8 tells us how to calculate which stars are helping to cause any event. The whole chapter on 'rulerships' (οἰκοδεσποτίαι) is concerned with the active, causative powers of the planets. And so far as the individual is concerned, III.1.1 makes the position quite clear: 'The cause of events both in general and with respect to each individual is the movement of the planets, sun and moon'.

So the answer to the question, was Ptolemy's astrology 'hard' or 'soft', were the movements of the heavenly bodies causes of tempera- ments and events or only signs, must be that it was 'hard': or at least, that it was fatalistic in a Stoic sense. It is an important reservation. The Stoic's somewhat ambivalent position is made clear by Ptolemy in I.3.6ff: 'We should not think of all these things happening to men as if they followed their heavenly cause by some original and irrevocable divine ordinance, decreeing exactly what has been laid down for each man, bound by necessity to happen to him, no other cause whatever being able to counteract it. Rather we must think that while the movement of the heavenly bodies is eternally completed according to a divine and immutable fate, the change of earthly things happens according to a natural and mutable fate, drawing its primary causes from above according to chance and natural consequence. And also, while some things happen to men through very general circumstances and not according to the individual's own natural endowments – as when because of great and inescapable changes in the heavens men die in great numbers by fire or plague or flood (for the lesser cause always gives way to the greater and stronger) – other things happen because of small and chance antipathies in the heavens, according to each individual's nature and peculiar temperament. So we ought to listen to the astrologer (genethlialogos) when he says that to such and such a temperament, with such and such a particular condition of the heavens, such and such will happen as a result. If what is going to happen to a man is not known, or if being known it does not receive treatment to inhibit it, it is bound to follow the sequence dictated by its original nature; whereas if it is foreknown and is provided with a remedy (the remedy being what it is because of natural laws and fate together) it either does not happen at all or is considerably modified'. So our fate, foretold by the stars, which are part of the working of the eternal law, is natural and mutable, and the foreknowledge provided by the astrologer helps us to cope with it.

Ptolemy says that we ought to listen to the astrologer. One would have expected an astrologer to say, 'You ought to listen to us when we say ...'; and there is other evidence in the Tetrabiblos to suggest that Ptolemy was not himself a practitioner of the art. The book is not in any sense a practical handbook: it would be very difficult to draw up a natal chart and interpret it from what Ptolemy wrote. He was led to make a rational summary of this part of astronomy by the logic of his thought as a philosopher and scientist. So he drew on all the sources he could find, including his battered old manuscript: and he did not always fully understand his sources – indeed he occasionally misunderstood what he read. He may be forgiven for some of the confusion; for example, for not being entirely clear what a τόπος, *topos*, was. The word means 'place', and it is used in various ways to different divisions of the zodiac by different authors. How did Ptolemy himself divide the ecliptic?

First, and obviously, into the twelve signs of the zodiac. That is, into the twelve thirty-degree divisions bearing the names of the old constellations Aries, Taurus and so on; incidentally, Ptolemy always refers to the sign we know as Libra by its older name, the Claws (of the Scorpion, that is: Χηλαί in Greek). He was, of course, well aware of the precession of the equinoxes, which had been discovered by Hipparchus three hundred years earlier: that what is still called 'the first point of Aries' moves to the west at a rate of about ½ of a second of arc each day, or right round the equator in 25,800 years. The result is that the vernal equinox, the first point just referred to, where the sun crosses the equator moving north, is now actually in the constellation Pisces. Ptolemy, like most astrologers, works with a fixed zodiac, not a natural one: the thirty degrees beginning from the vernal equinox are the sign Aries, whatever the constellation which is actually there. He usually calls these divisions *dodecatemoria*, often *zodia* (ζῴδια), and occasionally simply signs (σημεῖα) or 'parts of the zodiac'. He firmly accepts (I.10) the first point of Aries as the beginning of the circle (recognising that a circle has no natural beginning) and explains in chapter 22 why the fixed zodiac is used: 'The beginnings of the signs and of the terms it is very reasonable to take from the solstitial and equinoctial signs, both because our authorities make this clear, and especially because from what we have already said we see that the signs' natures and powers and associations take their cause from the solstitial and equinoctial starting-places and not from any other sign. For if other starting-places are assumed, we shall be compelled either never to use the natures of the signs as indicating the future or, if we do use them, to be wrong: for the divisions of the zodiac which cause the signs' powers (i.e. the thirty-degree units beginning with the solstices and equinoxes) move on and are changed.'

He also divides the zodiac into quadrants (τεταρτημόρια), each beginning with one of the 'angles', or κέντρα, the Ascendant, the *Medium Caeli*, the Setting point, and the *Imum Caeli*. In III.11 the MC is said to be quartile to the ASC, and chapter 2 of the same book suggests that the MC is known separately from the ASC and can be used instead of it in particular circumstances; but nowhere in the *Tetrabiblos* does Ptolemy describe how to find them, nor worry about or mention the problem of the inequality of the quadrants caused by the obliquity of the ecliptic. In fact all this is dealt with in the

Almagest, as part of the other branch of astronomy (II.7–9); but the astrologer not prepared to study that difficult work would get little help in avoiding confusion or worse from the *Tetrabiblos*.

Now *dodecatemorion* does not always mean 'sign'. Strictly it simply means, in Ptolemy, a twelfth part, and consequently it is most often used of the most frequently referred to twelfth parts, the signs of the zodiac. But in III.11, a long chapter on length of life, one of the important 'places' (τόποι) is 'the *dodecatemorion* about the horoscope', defined as the five degrees before the ASC and the twenty-five degrees after. These thirty degrees clearly do not constitute a sign; they are a 'place', a *topos*, which nowadays would be called the first 'house'. 'House', οἶκος, is never used by Ptolemy of such a division, nor indeed by any other Greek astrologer; the word is kept for the 'houses of the planets'. Aries and Scorpio, for example, are the houses of Mars. Generally, Ptolemy uses *topoi*, 'places', to refer to the mundane houses; sometimes he calls them *dodecatemoria*, and frequently *zodia*, which we translate as signs. To add to the confusion, *topos* is used in two other ways: in I.22 *topos* is defined as 'the *dodecatemorion* of a *dodecatemorion*, that is two and a half degrees' – a division Ptolemy rejects: and the term is nowhere else used in this sense. But the word does simply mean 'place', and is used in both the literal and metaphorical senses of the English word. It can also mean 'topic', and there are one or two places in the *Tetrabiblos* where it may be used in that sense. *Topos* is translated pretty haphazardly in the Loeb edition, as 'place, house, region and topic', with little understanding – and consequent confusion.

That there should have been such confusion in Ptolemy's time is a reflection of the still unsettled state of the art of astrology. Imprecision of language is the inevitable result of lack of clarity of ideas. Nevertheless, there is no doubt that Ptolemy did divide the zodiac into houses, each concerned with particular aspects of human life, which were later generally called *topoi*; and that this division was based, like that into quadrants, on the ascendant. The late fifth century commentary on Paulus Alexandrinus, attributed to Heliodorus, makes it plain: 'As in the beginning Paulus divided the zodiac into 12 parts and made the beginning of that division Aries, so now he cuts the whole circumference of the zodiac into 12 parts, not calling them by the names of the signs, but the first, taking the first point on the horizon according to the time of birth, he calls the horoscope ... and we begin from the horoscope, because it is the foundation and ground of the other eleven houses (*topoi*); for unless this one is found, it is impossible to set up the rest'.[12] Since Ptolemy usually deals in whole

---

[12] *Heliodori, ut dicitur, in Paulum Alexandrinum Commentarium*, ed. E. Boer (Leipzig, 1962); c.23, 62–63.

signs, one house is equivalent to one sign – which sign depends on the time of birth – and so he can use 'sign' of this sort of 'twelfth part' also.

We have already seen that Ptolemy rejects the 2½° *dodecatemorion*, and the consideration of separate degrees; nor is there in the *Tetrabiblos* any mention of the decans. He does, however, spend a whole long chapter (I.21) on the 'terms', ὅρια. This he does without definition or explanation: it is simply taken for granted that the reader knows what it is all about. The only other place terms that are considered is in the curious appendix to the whole, IV.10. He begins, 'with regard to the terms, there are two main systems in use: the first is the Egyptian, which is based on the lordships of the planets' houses, and the other is the Chaldaean, based on the rulerships of the triplicities.' Each sign of the zodiac is divided into five unequal sections, and each section then allocated to one of the five planets (excluding, that is, the sun and the moon, which have no terms). The obvious areas of potential differences are, how many degrees for each term in each sign, and to what planet should each term be assigned? The Chaldaean system, which Ptolemy describes briefly but rejects in favour of the Egyptians', has at least the merits, as he himself admits, of simplicity and plausibility. It is based on the triplicities: Aries, Leo and Sagittarius; Taurus, Virgo and Capricorn; Gemini, Libra and Aquarius; and Cancer, Scorpio and Pisces. The ruler of the first is Jupiter; of the second, Venus; of the third, Saturn by day and Mercury by night; and of the last, Mars. Each sign is then divided into five terms of eight, seven, six, five and four degrees – thirty in all. The planets are then taken in the order of their rulerships – Jupiter, Venus, Saturn, Mercury, Mars – and assigned to the terms in order, in each sign; in each triplicity the first, 8°, term is given to the ruling planet, and then the same order of planets is preserved.

It is a simple system, being clearly 'artificial' and arithmetical; which is exactly why Ptolemy preferred the Egyptian system, because it at least appeared to have some sort of reasoning behind it. He says it is based on the lordships of the planetary houses, and then accuses it of inconsistency, because sometimes 'they assign the first terms to the lords of the houses, and sometimes to the lords of the triplicities, and sometimes also to the lords of the exaltations', and even this they do not do properly. Why, for example, do they give the first place in Capricorn to Mercury, when Mercury has no relation of rulership to that sign? Secondly, he says, the numbers of degrees in the terms do not seem to follow any system.[13] 'For (§5) the number totalled for each

---

[13] It is at this point, p. 92, that the Loeb translator loses contact with his author to some extent, largely because he seems to have relied on Bouché-Leclercq, who is himself more confused than Ptolemy.

planet from all the signs (in proportion to which they say the planets' periods are distributed) rests on no fitting or acceptable reasoning.' There may be variations in detail, he says, but the totals remain the same: they are in fact, 57 for Saturn, 79 for Jupiter, 66 for Mars, 82 for Venus and 76 for Mercury – a grand total of 360°. (These very figures are given as planetary 'periods' by Vettius Valens.) And the system he 'accuses' the Egyptians of actually using is the Egyptian system as described by Paulus Alexandrinus,[14] who gives a table identical to that of Ptolemy.

Ptolemy himself then goes on with a passage of curious difficulty, the understanding of which depends on knowing what 'rising times' are. They are defined by Neugebauer and van Hoesen[15] as indicating 'how many degrees of the equator cross the horizon of a given locality simultaneously with the consecutive zodiacal signs'. So the rising time of a given sign is the number of degrees of the equator which rise at the same time. For anyone on the equator, the rising time of any point, say, 30°, ♈, is its Right Ascension; in this case the ancients spoke of the *sphaera recta*. As one moves further north or south from the equator, the rising times vary, and this is the *sphaera obliqua*, and one can indeed talk of Oblique Ascension. At the equator the rising times of all the signs are equal; at the Pole, the same six signs are above the horizon all the time. Fig. 10a below shows the situation as the first point of Aries is about to rise over the horizon at latitude 45°; in 10b the equator has turned enough to bring the whole 30° of Aries above the horizon, and the amount of the equator that has risen at the same time is shown by a heavier line. In 10c and d we are looking at the other side of the sphere and watching Aries set. Since Aries is directly opposite to Libra in the zodiac, it can be seen that the rising time of Aries is the setting time of Libra and *vice versa*. The correct working out of the rising times of the signs involves spherical trigonometry; it is done by Ptolemy in the *Almagest*, and the results are set out in Tables in II.8.

The passage in the *Tetrabiblos* (I.21.6–7) is as follows: 'Now some try to produce a persuasive and rationalistic argument about the terms, that the rising times of each planet in every clime make up together the same sum; but that is false. For they follow the common practice, which being based on evenly increasing rising times does not even come close to the truth, and according to which on the parallel running through lower Egypt they want the sign of Virgo and also of Libra to rise in 38°20' and that of Leo and Scorpio in 35°, while it is shown in the tables that the latter rise in more than 35° and Virgo and

---

[14] *Pauli Alexandrini Elementa Apotelesmatica*, ed. E. Boer (Leipzig, 1958) 11ff.
[15] Neugebauer and van Hoesen, *op. cit.*, 11.

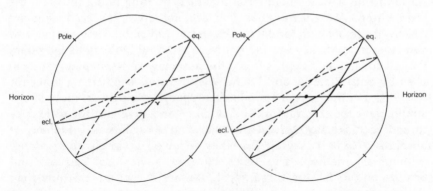

Fig. 10a   Fig. 10b

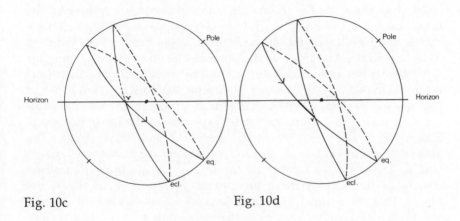

Fig. 10c   Fig. 10d

Libra in less'. In fact, the rising time given for Leo and Scorpio in Ptolemy's tables is 35°36' for the clime of 'Lower Egypt', and that for Virgo and Libra is 34°47'; the times for Meroe, in Upper Egypt, are 32°44' and 31°20' respectively – they will become relevant in a moment.

Ptolemy's criticism is that the rising times do not add up to the totals for the terms, and the authorities have the wrong rising times anyway. It is true that the rising times are wrong, compared with those of the *Almagest*. But the picture changes when we look at the tables for rising times compiled for the seven climes, on two different systems, A and B, by Neugebauer and van Hoesen.[16] Although Paulus

16 *Ibid.*, 4.

Alexandrinus says explicitly (c.3) that he is quoting rising times for the third clime, Alexandria, those he actually gives for each sign are exactly those set out for Meroe in Upper Egypt by Neugebauer and van Hoesen; and they are the figures quoted by Ptolemy as Egyptian, though for Lower Egypt. Clearly the authority (? Nechepso-Petosiris) used by both Ptolemy and Paulus Alexandrinus used rising times for Meroe and either gave them mistakenly for Alexandria or, more likely, simply gave the column for the first clime and gave also the difference to add to make up each of the following six columns – Ptolemy is absolutely right in saying that they followed a simple (but wrong) arithmetical method. The times Ptolemy quotes, 35° for Leo and Scorpio and 38°20' for Virgo and Libra, are in fact more wrong than Ptolemy realised.

If we add up all the rising times for each of the planets – that is, for the two signs which each planet rules – we get totals which are far larger than those for the terms: for Mars, for example, adding up the times for Aries and Scorpio, Mars' two houses, we get 388. But if we divide this by six, we get (to the nearest whole number) 65, which is nearly the same. And if we do the same for the other planets, using the figures from the same first column, we get the following totals, all the result of division by six: Saturn 59, Jupiter 59, Mars 65, Venus 76 and Mercury 81. Curiously, we can get a closer approximation to the term-totals by taking the figures of the first column on the other system, B: Saturn 57, Jupiter 62, Mars 66, Venus 73 and Mercury 78. The anomalies are obviously Jupiter and Venus, but the similarities are too striking for us not to accept that the term-totals are indeed based on the rising times; that these are probably Upper Egypt times, not Lower; that the rising times totals have all to be divided by six; and that Jupiter and Venus have more than their proper share. We can also be fairly sure that Ptolemy did not really understand all this; nor, *a fortiori*, did Paulus Alexandrinus.

But how did such a complicated system arise? And what *are* 'terms'? The Greek word is ὄρια, *horia*, which means limits or boundaries; the Latin word used by Firmicus Maternus is *fines*, and by others, *termini*, both being simply translations of the Greek. They are the limits within which a planet exercises 'lordship', οἰκοδεσποτεῖα. Now in ancient Egypt the heavenly bodies ruled over times, days and months and so on. And we have seen[17] that there were once seventy-two divisions of the sky: seventy-two five-day segments of the Egyptian year of 360 days. Supposing that the planets were originally assigned 'limits' within each of these seventy-two divisions, when the twelve-sign

[17] See Chapter II, p. 22.

zodiac took over, the totals would have to be divided by six. The original allocation probably included the sun and moon as well as the five planets, and certainly the old Egyptian scheme was linked to ideas on the length of life an individual was granted by his 'time-lord', *chronocrator*. Now Paulus Alexandrinus tells us that the total number of terms was made equal to the 360 degrees of the zodiac; and that the sun and the moon are not included in the scheme because they are lords of all times. If the sun is in a good position, it grants 120 years, and if the moon is favourable, she gives 108. The sun's 120 divided by six gives us roughly the difference between the rising times total and the term-total for Jupiter, and it looks as though the terms originally assigned to the sun were given to Jupiter, and enough of the moon's to Venus to make up the 360. The association of Jupiter with the sun and of Venus with the moon is common enough to explain this re-allocation without positing any particular optimism among those who made up the system – both Jupiter and Venus are beneficent planets.

At the end of this section, Ptolemy gives an account of his battered ancient manuscript, and the system it describes, and sets out his own table of terms, which is slightly different in detail from the Egyptian, but gives the same totals to each of the planets. None of this is given the sort of philosophical explanation which Ptolemy provides elsewhere. So aspects are explained in I.14, and in the following chapter he gives reasons for the terms 'commanding' and 'obeying': 'In the same way those signs are called "commanding" and "obeying" which are equidistant from the same equinoctial sign, whichever it is, because they have equal rising times and are on equal parallels. Of these, those which are on the summer semicircle are called "commanding" and those on the winter semicircle "obeying", because when the sun is in the former it makes the day longer than the night, and when it is in the latter, it makes the day shorter'. The 'summer semicircle' is that half of the zodiac which is north of the equator, containing Aries, Taurus, Gemini, Cancer, Leo and Virgo: the six signs that would be permanently above the horizon for anyone at the north pole. That Ptolemy (and all other ancient authorities) should not mention the fact that in the southern hemisphere the converse would hold, and the signs change roles, is not surprising: for them, as for many centuries after, the inhabited world, the *oikoumene* (hence 'oecumenical' for 'world-wide'), lay wholly in the northern temperate zone.

The planetary houses are explained in terms of their natures and positions. Having assigned to the sun and moon Leo and Cancer, because they are the most northerly of the signs, and therefore closer to our zenith and 'most productive of heat and warmth', and Leo is masculine like the sun and Cancer feminine like the moon, Saturn, for example, 'which is by nature colder and opposed to heat, and has the highest and largest of the orbits', acquires 'the signs diametrically opposed to Cancer and Leo, that is Capricorn and Aquarius', because they are cold and wintery signs, and what is more, since they are in opposition to the sun in Cancer and Leo, their aspect is 'inconsistent with beneficence'. So for the rest of the planets: Jupiter's houses are Sagittarius and Pisces, Mars' houses are Scorpio and Aries,[18] Venus' are Libra and Taurus, and Mercury's, as befits the planet nearest to the sun, the houses next to the luminaries', Gemini and Virgo. The same sort of logic applies to the 'exaltations' and 'depressions' of the planets: the sun is exalted in Aries, when it is increasing in strength, and depressed in Libra, and Saturn again is the opposite of the sun, depressed in Aries and exalted in Libra. And so on, though the explanations have to be 'stretched' a bit occasionally: for example, Venus is exalted in Pisces because she is moist by nature and it is in Pisces that 'the beginning of the moist spring is presignified', where the 'pre-' is what is important, since in I.10 it is Aries which signifies spring.

When he comes to genethlialogy in Book III, Ptolemy is well aware of the claims of conception to be treated as more important than birth, for the calculation of the natal chart (chapter 1). When the time of conception is accurately known, he says, we should use it. But usually it is not known, whereas the birth time is observable, if not easily measured accurately in those days before good mechanical clocks, as he recognises at the beginning of the next chapter. So the use of the birth-time has to be justified. The former, the time of conception, may be called the source, or origin, or first beginning, the ἀρχή, but the latter, the time of birth, is also a beginning, the καταρχή. 'The first might be called the coming into being of a human seed, the second the coming into being of a man.' At birth, he says, the child takes on most of the characteristics, which it did not have in the womb, which are proper to human nature. This may reflect both some knowledge of embryology, a fairly advanced part of Greek medical science, and something of that Neo-platonist 'journey of the soul' through the spheres we shall meet in Macrobius and others. In any case, he argues, the configuration of the heavens at birth has a similar causative function to that of the configuration at conception, since the two are similar. This unexplained assumption is probably derived from his

---

[18] Mars is 'destructive and unharmonious', and these signs are quartile to the luminaries: Aries is quartile to Cancer, the moon's house, and Scorpio to Leo, the sun's. It is however perfectly true, as Robbins says in his note on p. 81 of the Loeb text, that Aries is also in trine with Leo and Scorpio in trine with Cancer, and these are good aspects. But Aries and Scorpio are here said to be of a similar nature to Mars, that is, dry, though this is the only place where they are so described, and it is not really consistent with what is said of them elsewhere.

Egyptian sources; for example, Nechepso-Petosiris is probably the authority for the belief that the ASC at birth is the sign of the moon at the time of conception. This belief has an air of plausibility: since the moon runs through all the signs of the zodiac in four weeks, and the length of pregnancy varies a good deal, a reasonable conception date can generally be found, with the moon in the same sign as the ASC is in at birth.

There is behind much of what Ptolemy says a great deal that is of social historical interest, as indeed there is in other astrological writings.[19] A long chapter (III.14) on 'the quality of the soul', or as we might say, the mental character, caused or produced by the planets in different combinations and aspects, is followed by one on 'diseases of the soul', or mental disorders. The 'more moderate diseases', he says, have already been dealt with in chapter 14: they include such afflictions as stupidity, extravagance, avarice, lewdness and so on. These Ptolemy describes as extreme patterns of behaviour, those which fall short of or exceed the mean. But chapter 15 is concerned with those which affect the whole nature, both the active, intellectual parts and the affective, passive part, and might be called pathological, νοσηματώδη. The perversion of the intellectual part produces epilepsy and various kinds of insanity; but if Jupiter or Venus, the benign planets, have any influence, these afflictions are curable. If Jupiter is the good influence, they can be cured by medical means such as diet or drugs; but if Venus is at work, through oracular responses or by the help of the gods. The perversion of the passive part of the soul affects the character most apparently in regard to matters of sex, and here it is obvious that Ptolemy has a 'modern' (though not contemporary) attitude to 'perversion', which includes both male and female homosexuality.

The title of the fifth chapter of Book IV is rather coyly translated in the Loeb edition as 'Of Marriage'; but the Greek simply says, 'of combinations', that is, of men and women, and though much of the chapter is taken up with 'lawful connexions', other kinds of union are also dealt with. The virtues of a good wife are dignity, industriousness, and managerial ability; it is a bonus if Venus makes her also beautiful and charming, or Mercury bestows intelligence. Husbands should also be dignified and industrious, and practical; the corresponding bonus is to be neat and handsome. And thrift is a virtue in both husband and wife. It is a fascinating chapter which shows that Ptolemy and his contemporaries would have found little to be surprised at in the 'agony columns' of our press (sex magazines included).

---

[19] See for example Franz Cumont's *L'Egypt des astrologues* (Brussels, 1937).

The longish chapter 7 of the same book is concerned with friends and enemies; and the last eight lines with slaves. Some manuscripts, possibly correctly, make this a separate chapter. It merely tells us that the relevant part of the zodiac to consult is the twelfth house, of the Evil Daemon; and it is all Ptolemy has to say on slaves. Paulus Alexandrinus, two centuries later, does no more than mention slaves under the twelfth house. But Firmicus Maternus, a near contemporary of Paulus, spends eight pages on slaves, including a chapter on their offspring. Hephaistion, at the beginning of the fifth century, wrote three books on astrology, the first two derived largely from Ptolemy and Dorotheus of Sidon (a century earlier than Ptolemy), the last wholly from Dorotheus. In Book II he quotes the chapter of Ptolemy entire; and he has an extra chapter of eight lines which refers to a Lot of Slaves, a κλῆρος, which is found by counting from Mercury to the moon, and then taking the same angular distance from the horoscope. He also gives an alternative method, counting from the same planet to the Lot of Fortune. But in Book III he has a chapter on the manumission of slaves, and a long one on runaways, both derived from Dorotheus. Heliodorus' commentary on Paulus, written at the end of the fifth century, reverts to brevity, but also mentions the Lot, with another method of counting, from Mars. There was, it seems, the now familiar confusion among astrologers as to how to calculate the Lots.

Now the Alexandrians Ptolemy and Paulus seem to regard slavery with much less concern than some other authors, and less than one might have expected of ancient writers. But this in fact merely reflects the difference between Egypt and most of the rest of the Empire in the matter of slavery. Large scale slavery was unknown in Egypt. Agricultural land was the king's, and most manufacturing industries were state monopolies; so peasants and workers, who could not afford to own slaves themselves, provided a pool of cheap labour for those who needed it. The only forms of slavery introduced by the Greeks were domestic – the middle and upper class Greeks could not have existed without their household slaves. It is significant that in Ptolemy's time, when slaves were at their most expensive throughout the Empire, they only fetched half the normal prices in Egypt;[20] local demand was low, since they were really only needed for domestic purposes, and the export of native slaves was prohibited. Rostovtzeff puts it briefly:[21] 'In sum, slavery, as an economic factor, was of far less importance in Ptolemaic Egypt than in other parts of the Hellenistic world.'

[20] A. H. M. Jones, 'Slavery in the Ancient World', *Economic History Review*, 2nd Series, 9 (1956) 185–199.
[21] M. Rostovtzeff, *Social and Economic History of the Hellenistic World* (Oxford, 1941) 322.

On the dangers of travel, and the many ways in which men can die, Ptolemy might be disturbing, even frightening, were it not that our own age can more than match Ptolemy's catalogue at most points. In a time of air disasters and road deaths astrologers are once again much exercised by the questions of the right and wrong times to travel. The list of dangers that might beset the traveller if the planets were against him included shipwreck and piracy, deserts and cliffs and earth-quakes, running out of provisions, wild beasts, serpents and other poisonous creatures, highway robbers and 'dangerous accusations' – a perennial hazard of foreign travel, it seems, – and the best he could hope for would be a profitless voyage. In the account of the ways in which a man might meet his end there is no mention of old age! It is true that under 'natural deaths', a term embracing death by every conceivable illness, 'cardiac affections' are listed as caused by Jupiter; but one would have expected old age to come under Saturn. There is a terrifying picture suggested by the list of 'violent deaths'; they include being trampled by a mob, the noose, wild beasts again (including those in the arena!), 'in prison', poisonous bites, poison and 'feminine plots', death 'through women or as a murderer of women', drowning, being crushed in the collapse of a building, fall from a height, being killed in civil faction or war, being killed by pirates, robbers, criminals, generals and kings, decapitation, crucifixion and burning, cautery and the surgeon's knife; and at worst, one could lie unburied.

In this chapter (IV.9) there occur some of the very rare mentions of fixed stars. If Saturn is in the neighbourhood of Argo, it indicates shipwreck; if Mars is 'in the Gorgon of Perseus', death by decapitation or mutilation; if the same planet is at the MC or IMC, 'particularly in Cepheus or Andromeda', crucifixion is forecast. The power of the fixed stars (the Greek word is ἀπλανεῖς, which simply means 'not-wandering' and avoids the notion of being 'fixed' to something; the Latin *fixae* can mean just 'firm, unmoving') is dealt with in I.9, where three lists are given of those in or near, north of and south of the zodiac, and each star is likened to one of the planets in its effects. Very similar lists are given by most ancient astrological writers, and the attributions to the planets are fairly constant in all. These lists include the constellations in the older eighteen-house zodiac of the Babylon-ians, in which Taurus was split into the Pleiades, the Hyades and Orion, the southern and northern Fish were separate, and Cetus, Perseus and Auriga were included. Not much use, however, is made of the fixed stars (except perhaps Regulus, in Leo) by any Greek astrologers, and very little indeed by Ptolemy, who makes no mention of one of their chief connexions with astrology, the 'lunar mansions'.

The phrase merely means the lodging places, resting places, of the moon; they are sometimes called stopping places, *stationes*, 'stations'.

They are probably the main reason for the survival of interest in the fixed stars. Like other features in this early astrology, they originally had nothing much to do with it, but were assimilated. They became more important later in Arabic astrology, mainly because the Islamic calendar was and is lunar, and the mansions belong to what might be called a lunar tradition going back, in all probability to Babylon, which also had a lunar calendar.

Here once again we find the mingling of the three traditions, Babylonian, Greek and Egyptian. The Babylonians contributed the stars, the constellations and groups associated with the moon; the Greeks the lists of days, hemerologies, fit or unfit for this or that activity, though these might have been as well derived from Egypt: many primitive peoples have such lists of lucky and unlucky days, often linked with the moon, since in times without calendars the only way of knowing which day was which was by reference to the heavens, especially the phases of the moon. And the Egyptians' contributions were the pictorial symbolism and the involvement of the gods, and hence, later, of the planets.

That the lunar mansions were originally Babylonian is fairly clear.[22] They are behind the second century list of fixed stars of Maximus of Tyre; the Arabic lists of mansions of Alchandri (ninth century) and Abenragel (eleventh century) go back to seventh century sources, and a very similar Coptic list, with Greek names, must be earlier, since Coptic was 'dead' by then; they were known in Vedic India, and all seem to betray Greek origins. But they are lunar, not solar, and the Babylonians had by the sixth century B.C. a list of seventeen 'constellations which stand in the way of the moon', and an eighteen-group zodiac probably linked with it; and their calendar was lunar. The twenty-eight mansion scheme was derived via Egyptian magic by the linking of the lists of lucky and unlucky days of the lunar month with the hemerologies and with the zodiac.

As far back as Hesiod, in the mid-eighth century B.C., the Greeks had lists of days of the month when it was or was not propitious to carry out certain activities. The last section of his poem, *Works and Days* (lines 765–828) mentions sixteen of the thirty days of the month and what should or should not be done on each; the fifteenth alone is a wholly bad day, and the fourteen not mentioned are 'changeable or neutral'. But Hesiod also warns the reader that 'the same day is at one

---

[22] S. Weinstock, 'Lunar Mansions and Early Calendars', *Journal of Hellenic Studies*, LXIX (1949) 48ff; *cf.* also *CCAG*, IX.1, 138ff; I. E. Svenberg, *De latinske Lunaria* (Goteborg, 1936); *Lunaria et Zodiologia latina, Studia Graeca et Latina Gothoburgensia*, XVI (Goteborg, 1963); Philip Yampolsky, 'The origin of the Twenty-eight Lunar Mansions', *Osiris*, IX (1950) 62–83.

time a mother, at another, a step-mother', and very few men know which. He does not link the days individually with gods, though Zeus (Jupiter to the Romans) has overall control, but merely numbers them, 'first, fourth and seventh', and so on, with a 'sixth from the middle' which suggests reference to the phases of the moon: 'sixth from the middle' presumably means sixth from the full moon. All this is presumably from a native Boeotian Greek tradition, and there are Orphic hemerologies from about the same period. But by the time of Herodotus, in the fifth century, the Greeks were fathering all their ideas on the Egyptians: 'And these are other discoveries of the Egyptians, to which of the gods each month and day belongs, and what will happen to each man according to his (birth) day, and how he will die and what sort of a man he will be. And these things those of the Greeks who are poets make use of.' (II.82) So according to Herodotus the attribution of the days to gods is Egyptian; but Babylonian hemerologies from the tenth century on do the same, so it was perhaps common, and the Greeks were the exception.

The Orphic list quoted by Weinstock has animal symbols of the phases of the moon, and twenty-eight such symbols, most of them animal, are found in Egypt. The figure twenty-eight occurs in magical papyri also: it is four times seven, and lunar, which is enough to make it a magic number. The symbols were easily linked with similar symbols of divinities, without as yet any connexion with the stars. The process was then probably as described by Weinstock:[23] the 'constellations standing in the way, the path, of the moon' were systematised as twenty-eight, and this series and that of the animal symbols and days converged. Out of this came the mansions of the moon, with the same pictorial symbolism, tied now to the star-groups, as in the Arabic lists. By the second century A.D. they had been assimilated into zodiacal astrology, but with only the most tenuous connexion, through the association of first days, then mansions and thence star-groups, with gods, and hence with planets. And this was done in Greek, probably again in Alexandria.

Ptolemy, as has been said, makes no mention of these lunar mansions, though they were certainly known in his day, not even in his outline of the effects of the fixed stars in the zodiac. There is, however, a hint of them in IV.10.20: when writing of the 'time-lords', the *chronocratores*, the one for the month, he says, is found by counting round the zodiac at *twenty-eight* days per sign, and the one for the day by counting at two and a third days (that is, one twelfth of twenty-eight) a sign: that is, the whole zodiac equals one month of

---

[23] *Op. cit.*, 65.

twenty-eight days. And with regard to 'ingresses', or transits, (§21), the moon is the planet which is important to the consideration of a day. The combination of the association of the moon with the day and the use of a twenty-eight day lunar month is surely an echo of the mansion system.

This last chapter of the work is a curious one. Its matter is not included in the 'list of contents' in III.4, and is different from that of most of the rest of the *Tetrabiblos*; there are also some small inconsistencies of detail and of terminology. But the style is undoubtedly Ptolemy's, and there is no reason why the chapter should not be an appendix added by Ptolemy himself; it looks like an afterthought added because of its importance, possibly from another source. It describes its own subject at the beginning as being 'the divisions of times': it is about the governance of sections of time, the influences brought to bear on particular 'bits' of time. It is closely linked with III.11, which deals with the complicated matter of determining the expected length of a man's life. Bouché-Leclercq is perhaps overstating things when he writes: 'The calculation of the length of life, with an indication of the kind of death ordained by the stars, is the chief task of astrology, the operation judged most difficult by practitioners, most dangerous and damnable by its enemies.'[24] Certainly it is the part that kings and governors and those in authority have sought to repress or at least control; but there is and was a lot more to astrology. But that the topic was of great importance is shown by the length of Ptolemy's chapter and the number of illustrations he gives to help the reader understand an immensely complex procedure. This is very unusual, since Ptolemy tends to avoid details of practice, and consequently needs and uses few illustrations. There were many different methods of finding out the expectation of life in Greek astrology, some very crude and simple, and some, like Ptolemy's, both bafflingly complicated and flexible enough in their possibilities to provide almost any answer.[25]

The system was probably based on Nechepso-Petosiris, since 'the ancient' is quoted at the beginning; and it is the system Ptolemy says he finds most agreeable and according to nature. It depends on finding what he calls the ἀφετικὸς τόπος, the 'aphetic place or house': 'the house which sends a man out into the world' perhaps, or it may be 'the house sending its influence out on to the subject' – what Ptolemy really meant by the word we can only guess. The Latin

---

[24] *L'astrologie grecque*, 404.
[25] The reader who is interested in all the details will find the Loeb translation fairly literal – though the text is in some places certainly corrupt – but will get little help from the footnotes, based as they are on Bouché-Leclercq.

writers use a number of terms for it, the commonest being *prorogator* and *significator*. The five aphetic houses in order of preference, of power, are: the *Medium Caeli*, the Ascendant, the eleventh house, that of the Good Daimon, the Setting point, and the ninth house, that of 'the god'. Then the actual 'sender forth', the αφέτης, is, for a daytime birth, in order of preference again, the house where the sun is, if it is in an aphetic house; the moon's house, under the same condition; the house of the planet which has the most rulerships over the house where the sun is, or the house of the preceding syzygy (full or new moon), or over the ascendant; and in the last resort, if none of these bodies is suitable, the ascendant itself. For night-time births, the order is the moon's house, then the sun's, and then the planet's which rules over the moon's house, or the syzygy, or the Lot of Fortune; and as long-stops, the Lot of Fortune if the preceding syzygy was a full moon, the ascendant if it was new. The lunar astrology of the night-time births, with its use of the Lot of Fortune, the 'horoscope of the moon', must eventually hark back to Babylon.

Having found the beginning (some simpler systems just take the ascendant as a starting-point, without any complications), we have to find the end, and this is where the complications really set in. The ultimate limit is set by the occident, the setting-point; and then there are all the complex ways in which the luminaries and the planets and their aspects may interfere and shorten or lengthen the expectation. Ptolemy's method involves measuring intervals in degrees of the zodiac and then converting these into degrees of Right Ascension (that is, along the equator), and those into years. To do this accurately we need his tables in the *Almagest*, which is no doubt why he preferred this method, and why other astrologers with less understanding of spherical trigonometry stuck to simpler arithmetical methods.

The appendix, IV.10, also uses aphetic houses, or prorogators. But first it makes some general points about 'times': 'Just as in all genethlialogical matters a greater destiny takes precedence over particulars, that greater destiny being about the countries of the subjects, to which the general enquiries about births are naturally subordinated (such as the form of the body and so on), so also anyone making a scientific enquiry must always grasp the first and more powerful cause, so as not to call one born in Ethiopia, let us say, white-skinned and straight-haired, and a German or Gaul black and curly-haired, without realising it, simply in accordance with the indications of their births; or call the latter (the Germans and the Gauls) gentle in character and fond of discussion and contemplation, and those born in Greece savage and uneducated' (§§2–3). One gets a distinct feeling that here Ptolemy's prejudices are showing. At any rate the point is that one should first grasp the universal conditions of destiny, and then join with them the particular modifying conditions.

So when we are dealing with the 'divisions of times' the actual ages of the subjects must be taken into account, so that we do not predict unsuitable things, assigning 'to a baby business dealings or marriage or other adult affairs, or to a very old man begetting children or other such belonging to younger men.' One might well wonder how old 'very old' has to be, and doubt Ptolemy's knowledge of biology – or the world! Some indication of how old is given in his list of 'the ages of man' and their allocation to the planets: for there are, in the general sense, seven ages of man corresponding to the seven planets, 'beginning with the first age and the first sphere from us, that is, the moon's, and ending with the last of the ages and the furthest of the planetary spheres, that of Saturn.'

These seven ages of man became commonplaces, and are familiar to readers of Shakespeare from Jaques' speech in 'As You Like It'. The moon rules over infancy, up to the fourth year, when Mercury takes over for the age of childhood, to fourteen, the age, as Ptolemy says, of the schoolboy. From fourteen to twenty-two Venus is in charge, the age of the lover. The fourth age, young manhood, lasts nineteen years, and is the sun's, the age of ambition. Mars has fifteen years of manhood, when a sense of mortality and urgency seizes a man; and Jupiter has twelve years of old age and retirement. Shakespeare's picture of the rest of life, Saturn's portion, is no less depressing than Ptolemy's:

> Last scene of all,
> That ends this strange eventful history,
> Is second childishness and mere oblivion:
> Sans teeth, sans eyes, sans taste, sans everything.

The periods thus allotted to the planets are: Moon, four years; Mercury, ten; Venus, eight; Sun, nineteen; Mars, fifteen; and Jupiter, twelve. No specific period is given for Saturn in this context, since all that is left after the age of sixty-eight belongs to the cold planet; but other sources for these same 'periods' give Saturn thirty years.

These periods have puzzled many commentators; Neugebauer and van Hoesen merely quote them as minimal periods, following Vettius Valens and Firmicus Maternus, without comment; and Bouché-Leclercq, having given plausible explanations for the sums allotted to Saturn, Jupiter and the Sun (the two planets' sidereal periods, and the Metonic cycle), says (p. 409) that the ten, eight and fifteen for Mercury, Venus and Mars 'are to be classified among the *arcana*'. Robbins refers to Bouché-Leclercq with obvious agreement, but then quotes the Michigan papyrus P.Mich.149 (Loeb p. 445, footnote) 'which speaks of the "period of Mars, who returns to his original position in fifteen years" (ἐν τῷ Ἄρεως κύκλῳ, ὃς ἐν ἔτεσιν ιε' τὴν ἀποκατάστασιν ἔχει).' And the ἀποκατάστασις, apokatastasis, return to the original position, is the answer. 'Sepharial' explains it clearly:[26] 'They (sc. the Chaldaeans) found that Saturn came to the conjunction with the same asterism or group of stars after a period of 30 years, Jupiter after a period of 12 years, Mars after a period of 15 years, the Sun after a period of 19 years, Venus after a period of 8 years, and Mercury after a period of 10 years, *as seen from the earth.*' The italics are mine: the important point is that the *apokatastasis* is when Saturn is seen by us against the same star-group. A glance at any astrologer's ephemeris to check the positions of the planets in the zodiac over a long period will show that the periods quoted are roughly correct. Indeed, even Norton's Star Atlas,[27] having defined an opposition as 'favourable' when the Earth and the planet are near the point where their orbits most closely approach, and as this point is always about the same longitude, favourable oppositions *always take place about the same date in the year* (original italics), then says (pp. 33–34) that Venus' maximum magnitude occurs about every eight years, that favourable oppositions of Mars come every 15 or 17 years, Jupiter's every 12 years, and the most favourable conditions for Saturn every 29–30 years. So there was nothing arcane or magical about these planetary periods; they are soundly astronomically based. But it looks as though Ptolemy was as unaware of this as the modern commentators, for although he usually provides explanations, none is offered here.

Having done with the ages of life and their general characteristics, Ptolemy goes on to particulars, and this takes us back to ἀφέσεις, or prorogations. This time we have to base our deductions on 'all of them, not just on one, as in the matter of the length of life: the one from the ascendant applies to affairs of the body and to journeys abroad; that from the Lot of Fortune to matters of property; that from the moon to spiritual (mental) affairs and to marriage and personal associations; that from the sun to matters of honour and reputation; and that from the *Medium Caeli* to the other particular affairs of life, such as business affairs and friendships and the begetting of children.' We also have to take into account all the planets and all their aspects. This is so that everything shall not be governed solely by one beneficent or malevolent star, because as Ptolemy says, a man's fortune is always mixed: 'a man may lose a relative and gain an inheritance, or take to his bed ill and at the same time receive some honour or promotion.'

---

[26] *Transits and Planetary Periods* (London, 1920; reprinted 1970) 14.
[27] Arthur P. Norton, *A Star Atlas and Reference Handbook* (15th edn, Edinburgh and London, 1966).

We then have to identify the 'rulers of the times', the 'time-lords', the chronocrators. We find the chronocrator of the year for each aphetic house by setting out from there and counting round the zodiac, one sign for each year since birth, and taking the ruler of the last sign. The ruler of the month is found by counting twenty-eight days to a sign, and that for the day by counting two and a third days to a sign. These calculations have already been discussed in relation to chapter 11 of Book III. Lastly, we have to pay attention to what Ptolemy calls ἐπεμβάσεις, which seems to include 'ingresses' proper and 'transits': that is, the entry of a planet into a sign and its passage through it. Here the transits of Saturn refer to the general houses of the times, those of Jupiter to the houses of the year, those of the sun, Mars, Venus and Mercury to those of the month, and those of the moon to those of the day. The whole picture is then related to the original birth-chart, and assessed: it is, in fact, very similar to what is now called a progression.

A progression is what it says it is, a moving forward of the birth-chart into the future to see what effects the changed positions of the heavenly bodies will have. But the same procedures can be used to find out about an event or action now, by setting up the chart for this time, and then working, as it were, backwards to the birth-chart. This is what the ancients called a καταρχή, an 'inception', and the Middle Ages and later an *electio*, a choice. Ptolemy does not mention or deal with *katarchai*, but most other Greek astrologers do, some at very great length and in detail, and in later Greek astrology it was obviously one of the most important activities of the practising astrologer. There was, it seems, some disagreement about their propriety, since there is no mention of them either in Paulus Alexandrinus' *Introduction* or Heliodorus' commentary on it, nor are they dealt with as such by Firmicus Maternus, but others such as Dorotheus of Sidon in the first century A.D. and Antiochus of Athens, a younger contemporary of Ptolemy, wrote books on them or 'On Interrogations', which are the same.

While genethlialogy seems to have grown from a rational astronomical basis, under the influence especially of Stoic philosophy, the part of astrology that deals with *katarchai* has its origins in magic and superstition, and always preserves the 'family face', as it were. We shall stick for the present to the Greek word (the singular is *katarchē*), since it is a word of wide meaning in the texts, *katarchai* ranging from inceptions properly so called – beginning a journey, for example – to enquiries about lost property and the outcome of sacrifices; it became, in fact, as did so many words, a technical term of astrology.

Both the ancient Egyptians and the Babylonians used lists of lucky and unlucky days, like that of Hesiod, and linked them with the heavens, especially with the moon and its phases. It is after all the most rapidly and predictably changing body in the sky. We have also seen how days can be linked with star-groups, both through the mansions of the moon and the Egyptian decans. The planets are connected both by the hours of the day, and hence the days of the week, and by their paths in the zodiac. On the other hand, Manilius' chronocrators are based on the signs, not on the planets; possibly he was working from ultimately Babylonian sources. The earliest Greek astrologer known to have drawn all this together and written on *katarchai* is Dorotheus of Sidon, who wrote in verse in the middle of the first century A.D., and whose work is preserved in an eighth century Arabic version (made from a third century Persian translation) now published by David Pingree.[28] But the practice must be a lot older than Dorotheus, for Nigidius Figulus in 50 B.C. was doing something very like it in relating the positions of the planets to the houses, and a short time after Dorotheus Aquila was consulting his charts every day.[29]

Dorotheus' Book V, the last and by far the longest, is wholly concerned with 'interrogations', *katarchai*. It begins (Pingree, p. 262): 'This is the book of Dorotheus, King of Egypt. There are five books; he wrote four of them on nativites in which he mentioned every good and evil, and misery or happiness that men may attain from the beginning of their situation till its end, and he wrote one of them about the matter of commencements, and it is this book, which is called the fifth book, in which he mentioned the condition of every action which is begun, whether its limit is determined or it is not determined where the beginning of this action or its middle or its end will end up and what of good or evil will happen in it.' The book opens with the general rules. Dorotheus classifies the signs as 'straight' or 'crooked': a very simple division into those that rise in less than two equinoctial hours and those that rise in more. Then he tells us what the general effect is if the ascendant is in such and such a kind of sign – straight, tropical, twin and so on. *Katarchai* depend mainly on the ascendant and the moon, and how they are aspected; of the forty-three chapters, about thirty are mainly concerned with the moon's position and relationships. For example, in c.17 he says: 'Look every time concerning the matter of marriage at the sign in which the moon is'; all four of the chapters on slaves are mainly lunar, as are most of the seven medical chapters. For instance, c.29 says: 'But if the moon is flowing from Saturn, then it indicates a fever that shakes him and a hidden malaise in his diet, or some of this will reach him in his

---

[28] *Dorothei Sidonii Carmen Astrologicum*, ed. David Pingree (Leipzig, 1976); Arabic text, English translation and collected Greek and Latin fragments.
[29] For Nigidius and Aquila, see Chapter III, pp. 44 and 55.

belly or in his body, or his spleen will swell, and sometimes it will bring down a miserable disease on him, and a wound and difficult sore will reach him so that his limbs will be wounded or will be dislocated, and sometimes his black bile will be stirred up in him until his intestines are cramped and burn, and it is an indicator that every illness which reaches him will stay in him a long time.' We can notice here in passing the association of black bile, *melancholia*, with Saturn. The houses are also important, especially the four *cardines*, whose special place is probably a relict of the old four-fold division: 'There were some of the ancient scientists who looked concerning the matter of theft from the four cardines, and if one of them was asked about a theft or something lost he would look concerning what was stolen or lost from the ascendant, and at the midheaven for the owner of the goods, who is the one from whom these goods were stolen or who is seeking them, and for the matter of the thief from the sign opposite the ascendant, and the shelter of the thieves for what they stole and where they put the goods from the cardine under the earth' (Pingree p. 297). There is in Dorotheus the usual confusion of names, 'house', 'sign' and 'place' being interchangeable in the later versions and reflecting that confused use of the Greek terms we have already noticed.

Not only houses and signs are important. Dorotheus also employs the dodecatemoria, decans and terms; his list of the latter is exactly the same as Ptolemy's 'Egyptian terms'. Planetary ingresses and transits have their significance, as do their retrogradations and 'stations' – when the planet appears to stand still. But the moon remains the most important, and was clearly so for Hephaistion of Thebes, a compiler of the late fourth to early fifth century.[30] His third book, on *katarchai*, is based on Dorotheus' fifth, but he also links the moon (c.6) with what are called 'active' and 'inactive' days: 'Days are thought to be "active" (ἔμπρακτοι) whenever the moon is in the birth-sign or in trine with it along with beneficent planets, or in any sign with beneficent planets in the absence of malevolent ones, except at full and new moon; hours become "active" whenever the birth-sign is in the ascendant or in trine with it, or rises with the horoscope of the moon (that is, the Lot of Fortune) without being in aspect with any malevolent planet. Days are "inactive" (ἄπρακτοι) and bad whenever the moon is square with the birth-sign or the opposite sign, with malevolent planets, and at full and new moon, or when one of the malevolent planets is in the ascendant or in aspect with the full or new moon in the absence of beneficent planets.'

---

[30] *Hepaistio Thebanus: Apotelesmatica*, ed. David Pingree (2 vols, Leipzig, 1973–4).

For the Greeks this was a fairly advanced part of astrology, which is presumably why it did not get a mention in Paulus Alexandrinus' *Introduction*; but most later astrologers included in and wrote 'on *katarchai*' or 'on interrogations' (ρωτήσεις). Julian of Laodicea, at the end of the fifth century, says firmly that one must examine the sun and moon and their lordships, and the ascendant and the *Medium Caeli*, and 'the beginnings (*katarchai*) of every affair are understood from the moon and their ends from the lord of the moon's house' (CCAG, vol. I, p. 138). Rhetorius, of about the same period, has a chapter on 'the horoscope of the *katarche*' (CCAG, vol. V.4), and most of the later (and generally anonymous[31]) Greek sources provide many examples such as: 'Find the lord of the ascendant and the moon and the lord of the Lot of Fortune; the most powerful of these shows what the question is and who the questioner. Then find the lord of the house of the ruling planet, note its nature and what house it is in, and judge accordingly. If you wish to know the reason for the question, find the planet indicating the questioner, and see what planets it is moving away from, and judge according to their natures. And if you also want to know the result, look at the planet indicating the questioner and find what planet it is going to join with, and judge according to that planet's nature' (CCAG, vol. IX, p. 161).

This obviously requires a fair knowledge of astronomy; it required more before the age of accurate observation and cheap printed books. But it also required a good deal of astrology, to 'judge according to the natures' of the planets and so on. It was just this difficulty with the divinatory art which made room for magic, to assist. Vettius Valens among others introduces into this whole complicated picture an element of pure magic: number symbolism. Numbers are curiously fascinating, of course; and there are many people today who would maintain that the manipulation of the ancient rules of such symbolic use of numbers can yield surprising and plausible results.[32] But it

---

[31] The assigned authorship of most of the texts printed in the appendices of *CCAG*, especially the older volumes, should be treated with cautious scepticism, the editors being overgenerous in accepting manuscript attributions and allotting passages to named authors on the basis of similarity of text. There is far too much doubt as to dating, and far too much borrowing for such certainty – not to mention forgery; Pingree (*Dumbarton Oaks Papers*, 25 (1971) 203–4) has shown that 'Palchus', given not only a date and provenance but considerable authority in *CCAG*, is merely a corruption of *al-Balkhi*, the 'place-part' of an Arabic name (like the 'Cricklade' in Robert of Cricklade), and the work attributed to him a fourteenth century compilation of Eleutherius. This is easily confirmed by a look through the passages attributed to Palchus in *CCAG*: all are attributed to him because of similarities to MS Angelicus Gr.29, which is the only one in which the name of Palchus is given; but that manuscript was written in Mitylene in 1388 by Eleutherius.

[32] See, for example, 'Astro-Numerology ... Fact or Fiction'? by Philip A. Moritz, in *Astrology*, 46 (1972) no. 3.

originally had nothing to do with astrology, and astro-numerology is just one of the many areas where 'occult sciences' attached themselves to astrology. There is a great deal of this sort of mixture in later Greek (or Byzantine) astrology: magical stones and plants, alchemy and cheiromancy and geomancy, and other 'blacker' arts. Their history does not belong here, for none of these really influenced astrological principles or fundamental methods. They could be attached to and make use of any kind of astrology, and their development is matter for the historian of the occult. But the ramifications of the theory of *katarchai* illustrate the need to remember that astrology always exists on many levels; in antiquity it ran from Ptolemy's scientific-philosophical systematisation to this sort of method for finding your zodiacal sign: take the letters of your own name, and those of your mother (if you are male: of your father, if female), and taking letters as numbers, add them together (a-j = 1–10; k-s = 20–100; t-z = 200–800, for example). Divide the total by twelve, and using the remainder count round the zodiac, beginning with Aries and counting, as usual, anticlockwise (CCAG, vol. IX.1, p. 138). Performing this operation with my own and my mother's names gave Cancer as the result: my ascendant is actually in Virgo, and my sun-sign is Aries. Doing it again in Greek, using the Greek equivalents of the names and the actual Greek number-values of the letters was no better: it produced Pisces. Or to find out which sign governs the year (CCAG, vol. IX.1, p. 170) simply discover where the moon is on 13 March.

One famous book emerged from this period – or at least, later than Ptolemy and earlier than the eighth century: the *Centiloquium*, known in Greek as ὁ Καρπός, and attached under Ptolemy's name to the *Tetrabiblos*.[33] It consists of a hundred astrological aphorisms of from two to eight lines (hence its Latin name) derived from the *Tetrabiblos* and other sources: a little under a third of these sayings are non-Ptolemaic. A number are concerned with *katarchai*, as e.g. 42: 'When a sickness begins when the moon is in a sign in which at birth there was a malevolent planet, or in one in square with it or in opposition, it will be very hard to bear; if a malevolent planet is in a bad aspect, it will be dangerous; if the moon is in a house where at birth there was a beneficent planet, it will not be dangerous.' The links between the moon and medicine are there also in half a dozen others; which is not surprising since the moon is the chief influence on physical, bodily, matters, as 61 says: 'The moon shows that bodily matters change in the same way as she does in her movements.' There is indeed a good deal on the moon in these sayings, which is in accord with the general background of fifth and sixth century astrology, with

---

[33] Greek text edited by E. Boer, in *Claudii Ptolemaei Opera*, III.2 (2nd edn, Leipzig, 1961).

its greater magical content. Another un-Ptolemaic feature is the emphasis put on the houses, which play so small a part in Ptolemy's work: a third of the hundred are concerned with the moon or the houses or both, and the evil nature of the eleventh house is particularly stressed (39, 55 and 79), even though according to Ptolemy it is the house of the Good Daemon.

This suggests that the system of houses was still in a somewhat confused, or at least 'fluid', state in this period; which reminds us that we must not be misled by Ptolemy's *Tetrabiblos* into thinking that all was thereafter settled and clear. As well as the houses, the *Centiloquium* makes reference to the decans (95) and to the *paranatellonta*, the stars which rise at the same time as a sign or a decan (95, 96): 'It is the nearest "centres" which show the effects of the eclipse; examine the nature of the conjoined stars, wandering and fixed, and the *paranatellonta*, and judge accordingly.' There is more emphasis on the influence of the fixed stars than there is in Ptolemy: 'When you cannot make the moon conjoint with two planets, make it conjoin with a fixed star having the constitution of the two' (28). 'The fixed stars bring about good fortune which is without explanation and contrary to expectation, but for the most part they mark such good fortune with misfortunes' (29). 'Make use of the fixed stars in the building of cities, of the planets in the building of houses' (36). So, although this work was early fathered on Ptolemy, it in fact reflects the astrology of the fifth century and later. It was translated into Latin in 1136 by either Plato of Tivoli or John of Seville and became one of the basic textbooks of late medieval astrology; with Ptolemy's authority, and with its many commentaries (especially those of the Arabs), it made that astrology less Ptolemaic and more like the Byzantine.

It is really a matter of choice when we stop talking of 'late Greek' or 'late Classical' and begin using the term 'Byzantine'; there was, of course, no break, no 'Fall of the Roman Empire'in the east until the fifteenth century. Byzantium was a small Greek colony on the Bosphorus founded in the seventh century B.C., and it was there that Constantine decided to found his New Rome, inaugurating the city on 11 May, 330 A.D. It has ever since been known as Constantinople, the city of Constantine; but the culture and history associated with it is called Byzantine. If a date is required, one could reasonably take 476, when the last Roman emperor in the west was deposed and only the Greek half was left; or, more in line with common usage, the reign of Justinian, 527–565; or perhaps, as is often done, that of Diocletian, the emperor who in the late third century divided the empire formally into halves and ruled in a style that could properly be described as Byzantine. It matters very little; at any rate we shall from now on speak of Byzantine, not late Greek, astrology.

The city soon duplicated everything possessed by Old Rome on the Tiber: the imperial court and another Senate, one of the Consuls, Prefects and other magistrates, and all the apparatus of the civil service and the law. It had its university, state maintained, with professors of Greek and Latin rhetoric and language, and hosts of students. And it was the seat of a Patriarch who soon came to call himself 'ecumenical' and regarded himself as more or less the equal of the Bishop of Rome. Constantinople was the capital of administration, of learning and of the Church in the east. Though the official language of imperial law was Latin, the language of Constantinople and the east was and remained Greek, so that all the writings of the ancient Greeks, including the astrologers, were in theory at least available to later readers in their own language. In actual fact, of course, not everything was there to start with, and there was a long process of selection, learned and unlearned, conscious and unconscious, especially in a time like that of late antiquity, a time of epitomists and excerptors. But a great deal of astrology from the early centuries A.D. did survive, and the conservatism of astrologers, reinforced by that of the Byzantines, ensured that Greek astrology changed very little indeed in a thousand years.

Rhetorius, whose *floruit* is put at about 500 A.D., is fairly typical. His system, so far as one can judge from the many sections of his work printed in the appendices to CCAG, was basically the same as Ptolemy's, and derived from similar sources as well as Ptolemy himself; but the scope of his writings was wider than that of the *Tetrabiblos*, and there is considerably more interpretative detail. His account of the triplicities or *trigons* (*cf.* Ptolemy, *Tetr.*, I.19) includes, as most later astrologers do, the elements: the fiery triplicity is Aries, Leo and Sagittarius; the earthly one, Taurus, Virgo and Capricorn; the airy *trigon*, Gemini, Libra and Aquarius; and the watery, Cancer, Scorpio and Pisces: which is exactly what you will find in a modern textbook of astrology. Whereas Ptolemy has only one Lot, κλῆρος, of Fortune, Rhetorius lists eighteen daytime κλῆροι, and seventeen night-time ones, in addition to the Lots of Fortune, of the Good and of the Daimon. He suggests that some astrologers take as the beginning of the zodiac the sign Cancer, because Cancer was in the ascendant in the 'horoscope of the world', the *thema mundi*, which we shall consider later; and others begin with Leo, as the sun's sign; but it is better to begin with the spring equinox and Aries. The moon is more important to Rhetorius than to Ptolemy: its exaltation and depression is the most important of all, 'because it is the fortune of all: where fortune is exalted, none is depressed; where she is depressed, none can be exalted.' His list of houses is the same as Ptolemy's, but he makes them, as well as the signs and planets, male and female, and he goes into detail; for example, 'if Mercury is in a good house, especially the house of Saturn, and well aspected by Jupiter, Saturn and Mars, it will produce astrologers, prophets and priests; if Saturn is in the ascendant in Mercury's house, or Mercury is the ascendant, it will produce superb mathematicians.'

There is no need to go on at length with such detail; we shall see more like it when we come to Firmicus Maternus, who drew on the same sources as Rhetorius, especially Antiochus of Athens. But the great age of astrology was passing. By the time of Rhetorius astrology had long been frowned upon by both church and state. The Christian emperors proscribed it: in 357 Constantius counted the *mathematici* as undesirable along with magi and haruspices and dream-diviners and so on. In 409, Honorius and Theodosius required astrologers to burn their books in the presence of the bishops and return to the Catholic faith, under penalty of exile. And in 425 Theodosius and Valentinian banished various heretics, including the *mathematici*.[34] It did not, of course, disappear because prelates frowned and emperors issued edicts; but it must have declined and at least 'gone to ground', for in the eighth century a Persian called Stephanus Philosophus, 'Stephen the philosopher', could claim to be reintroducing astrology to 'Rome', that is, Constantinople. Among his self-justificatory arguments he insists that the stars are not gods, they only express the will of God; they act not through any power of their own, but by God's power; and consequently it is a sin for man not to use it. That there was a revival of interest in astrology in the ninth century is perhaps shown by the fact that the oldest manuscripts of the Greek astrologers we have been dealing with go back only to the tenth and eleventh centuries; but that it was not a massive revival is clear also, for of all the astrological manuscripts listed by the *Catalogus*, only twenty-four are earlier than the twelfth. But there was enough to stimulate argument about the propriety or otherwise of the art.

In the middle of the twelfth century one Peter the Deacon (also called 'the Philosopher') wrote a letter justifying some interest in astrology to the Patriarch Lucas of Constantinople;[35] it is an argument in favour of *iatromathematica*, of the use of astrology in medicine. He quotes Hippocrates (*Aphorisms* IV.502) to show the importance of Sirius, for the stars affect the heat and cold in our bodies. But he is scathing about the 'old astrology of the Greeks'. More interesting is an exchange of tracts between the Emperor Manuel Comnenus and a monk called Michael Glycas.[36] Manuel Comnenus was, according to

---

[34] Cod. Theod. (ed. Mommsen) VIIII.16.4; 16.12; Sirm. 6.
[35] D. Bassi and E. Martini, *CCAG*, IV.156ff. Lucas Chrysoberges was Patriarch of Constantinople from 1156 to 1169.
[36] Edited by F. Cumont, *CCAG*, I.106ff.

the Byzantine historian Nicetas, utterly ruled by his astrology: he even thought he had fourteen more years of conquest ahead of him not long before he died. But before he did die, he was convinced of the error of his ways by the Patriarch Theodosius Boradiotes, and repented and became a monk. A treatise against astrology had been written by a monk of the Pantocrator monastery in Constantinople, and Manuel wrote a refutation, reconciling astrology with his Christian beliefs and with the Scriptures. He describes the monk's work as 'worthy of the simplicity of a monk', but unlearned and ignorant. Michael Glycas' treatise was an answer to the Emperor's; it was written after 1147, but before 1156, when Glycas was imprisoned and died, for what crime is not known.

Manuel admits that astrologers have been accused of heresy, but argues first, that the influence of the sun and moon on the earth and all creatures on it is undeniable, and 'if these produce effects, so also must those', that is, the other stars and planets; and second, that medicine uses astrology, and medicine uses 'physics' which being natural cannot be against God's laws: the stars, he says, are signifiers, not causes – δηλωτικοί, not ποιητικοί – and to be given these signs by God and not use them is the real impiety. Superstition, on the other hand, such as the use of talismans, and deceiving the gullible, are sinful. He refers to the Star of Bethlehem and the Magi, taking them to be skilled astrologers; and even if it was a new star, and not one whose aspects could be calculated and so on, knowledge of *astrologia* (Manuel uses the two terms, *astrologia* and *astronomia* without distinction) was necessary to recognise it as a new star and therefore significant, and that the eclipse at the Crucifixion was 'unnatural'. To use signs is good: to treat the stars as living is wrong: the heresy is to think to them as living causes. Astrology is like medicine: sometimes it fails, and sometimes God intervenes, but we do not blame the doctor. The true astrologer recognises the power of God in the heavens, which are his throne; for 'the heavens declare the glory of God', for they are his works, and are therefore good. 'But you may say,' he ends, 'the devil is also one of the works of God: ought we then to listen to him? But the devil was given the free choice to oppose the good because of his pride, and he is and is known to be against God. But the stars are lifeless works of God and without perception or forethought, and therefore are not against God, but keep their natural places, and always, since they behave according to the natural laws of their creation, behave in the same way. Indeed, if they were conscious actors, the astrologer would not be able to understand what they signify, since their meanings would be hidden in the mystery of their volition.'

Glycas begins, and ends, with the Star of Bethlehem: if, he says, that justifies astrology, then the Dove at Jesus' baptism justifies augury, and the raising of the dead, necromancy. The Magi were inspired by God; and in any case, that was the end of the old order. (There follows a longish passage refuting the idea of a *thema mundi*, a birth-chart of creation, but there is nothing about this in the treatise of Manuel as Cumont found it.) All mystery is God's, and all revelation and prophecy is from him, not from the arts of men. Some arts are allowed, but the Scriptures and authority reject astrology, partly because for astrology the stars must be causes, not merely signs. If all is fated, where is freedom? And if there is no freedom, why the Judgment? It is no good quoting medicine; first, it works by physics, not by astrology (οὐκ ἀστρολογικῶς, φυσικῶς δὲ μᾶλλον), and second, its astrology is not consistent but involves self-contradiction. But he leaves a rather involved argument confessing the limits of his knowledge of the subject, and returns to the Star: it was inspiration from God and the instruction of an angel that directed the Magi, not astrology. Although in this treatise Michael Glycas uses *astrologia* and *astronomia* indiscriminately, he does in another work give the traditional distinction between the descriptive and interpretive arts, and says that Seth and Enoch were instructed in astronomy by the angel Uriel.

Vaguely interesting though this is as a twelfth century dialogue, there is absolutely nothing new here. The quotation of authority and counter-authority, including disagreement about what one of them actually said, is typical of the age, and all the arguments both deploy are to be found in the Fathers and the ancient writers. Nevertheless, it is obvious that astrology was sufficiently restored to public view to be worth arguing about, and indeed the next two hundred years saw a great multiplication of books on the subject, excerpted from older authorities and compiled by men with no critical sense and little logic, and often very little understanding of astrology itself. A fifteenth century *Prognostica* is typical of much of this stuff: a girl born under Gemini, it says, is hawk-eyed; inclined to illness until she is five; gregarious; has much trouble with her eyes ('Hawk-eyed' may refer to colour rather than excellence of vision); loves many men who are special to her; she will not eat hare; she will inherit an ancestral livelihood; she will marry twice and have twins; she will earn a living by her own toil, will be worn out by her own parents, will labour much and have no thanks from her own family; she will leave her father's house at fourteen to find a husband, giving grief to her parents; she will have a mark in a hidden place and one on her shoulder ... and so on and on; and after all that she will live to be eighty! Astrology has clearly become a sort of fossilized mumbo-jumbo, and its development does not lie here in the east.

V

The Latin Middle Ages

It is 'a fact the whole world knows': the Roman Empire fell in 410 A.D., when Alaric and his Goths sacked the city of Rome. The legions were withdrawn, and the Empire was submerged under a tide of barbarians, just as the Roman roads vanished under the grass, and an age of darkness followed – Fielding's 'centuries of monkish dulness, when the whole world seems to have been asleep'. It is probably less widely known that Gibbon's *Decline and Fall of the Roman Empire* ends only in the fifteenth century, with the fall of Constantinople. In truth, the first two sentences do contain some oversimplification. It was only the Latin West which ceased to be Roman, while the Empire in the East continued right through the Middle Ages, the capital still where Constantine had set it. But a problem remains, since the Western Empire did fall: why was it not in the Greek East, with its continuity of language and culture and tradition, but in the new barbarian kingdoms of the West, that not merely astrology, but Christian philosophy and the natural sciences and technology, developed and flourished?

Why were there two halves of the Empire, anyway? It was divided linguistically into Greek and Latin speaking areas, and Diocletian had towards the end of the third century divided it administratively, with two capital cities, Constantinople and Milan – a better base than the too southerly Rome from which to control the northern frontier. The two divisions very nearly coincided; for our purpose the West includes Italy, Gaul, Britain, Spain and North Africa as far east as Libya. In this mainly Latin area, the knowledge of Greek, once a normal part of the accomplishments of a Roman gentleman, declined steadily through the fourth and fifth centuries, and had all but disappeared, at least outside Italy, by the end of the latter. It was this Latin West which fell; but in a sense it did not fall, it crumbled, under the weight of the west- and southward movement of the barbarian tribes from beyond the Rhine-Danube frontier. A century or more of sometimes costly attempts to keep them out finally failed when the pressure of the Huns from further east increased the need to move into the richer and underpopulated lands of the Empire. The East was wealthier and stronger and less empty, so the tribes turned to the West. Once the frontier was breached the peoples moved in, and by the mid-fifth century it was really all over. Italy was an Ostrogothic kingdom, Gaul was taken by the Franks, Spain by the Visigoths and Africa by the Vandals. This was not the sort of 'invasion' which simply crushed and destroyed what was there before. It was, after the battles were done, a movement of whole peoples into lands in large measure uncultivated and underpopulated. There was living space there, so they occupied it, and were assimilated. Though the official imperial administration disappeared, the new rulers changed less than might be imagined, and many of them, like Theodoric in Italy, were even rebuilders of Roman cities after the ruins of the fifth century. While some of the great Roman landowners fled, many stayed and 'collaborated', or became important churchmen; and it probably did not make a great deal of difference to an oppressed and overtaxed peasantry that their masters had changed.

Through it all Latin and the Church survived, preserving for the West a unity which transcended the political divisions. Whatever the vernaculars of the regions, Latin was the language of religion and of learning, such as there was. When Roman rule vanished, so too did the imperial organisation of education, and most of the secular schools. But the Church needed literate men. It had already provided and had to continue to provide for the education of at least its clergy; and that education was basically the same as what had been given in the state schools. There had in earlier centuries been a conflict: should Christians be given a pagan education? Was it right for Christians to read pagan literature, with its tales of gods and heroes and immorality? The history of the affair is complex and stretches over four or five centuries, but the outcome is simply described. The Church in the end simply assimilated the late antique system of education, pagan authors and all. Among the most important reasons was that it was the only system available; and all the great churchmen, including those most hostile to pagan learning, were themselves products of it. And it is always difficult for anyone to believe that the system of education which produced himself was anything but good. The greatest and most influential of the western Fathers, St Augustine, had himself been a professor of rhetoric, and justified the use of all that was of value in paganism and putting it to the service of Christian understanding, by reference to the Israelite's 'spoiling the Egyptians' on their release by Pharaoh (Exodus XII.35–6). So the old curriculum with its pagan authors and textbooks was preserved in church schools, in theory always and for centuries in practice also only as a preparation for the study of the Scriptures and the understanding of the Faith.

It is a commonplace and there is much truth in it, that in northwest Europe education was until the later eleventh century largely confined to the monasteries. The combination of the increased independent power of the towns and the great monastic reforms of the tenth and eleventh centuries, which turned monks more away from the world, led to the growth in importance of the cathedral schools which by the beginning of the thirteenth century was to produce the universities. This is, however, largely untrue of Italy, where there was greater continuity of culture through from Roman antiquity to the Middle Ages. Despite the decline in the seventh century because of the ravages of the Lombard invasions, there is some evidence that many schools survived throughout the period, or were closed only for short times. It is almost certain that the schools of Rome, Ravenna and Milan, all administrative capitals, continued in however attenuated a state, and the same is probably true of Verona and Pavia, and possibly of Arezzo. All of these except Rome are north Italian cities, and of over twenty schools which existed in the eighth and ninth centuries and may have survived from much earlier, all but two, Naples and Benevento, were also in the north. South Italy and Sicily, along with Spain and North Africa, the rest of the old western Empire, are left out of this account because they really only become relevant when we deal with Arabic scholarship and influence. All these areas became parts of the Islamic empire in the late seventh and early eighth centuries. There was a brief period at the end of the sixth century and the beginning of the seventh when Seville under Bishop Leander and then his greater brother Isidore became an important centre of studies, and more will be said of Isidore later. At that time, too, the Anglo-Saxon schools of England, the product of the combination of Irish and Roman learning, were probably more important and better developed than those anywhere on the continent. But when continental Europe north of the Islamic lands of Harun al-Rashid was united under Charlemagne, who was crowned emperor by the Pope in Rome on Christmas Day, 800, all these streams were brought together, and Latin education and culture began to develop under royal and ecclesiastical patronage in a common and recognisably medieval way.

This Latin West – Western Christendom – was to some extent, though not entirely, cut off from contact with the east by the Muslim empire. It had inherited little Latin and less Greek. But paradoxically, this very poverty and isolation go some way to explain the development of thought in the West, rather than in the East. Western scholars did not labour under the weight of the whole ancient Greek learning. Despite medieval writers' constant and exaggerated respect for their predecessors, they could not find there all the answers to their questionings. Education, too, was freer. In the West it depended almost entirely on individual masters, and a succession of schools flourished and declined as scholars died or moved. The Roman Church, having a virtual monopoly, was both more tolerant, and, because it was never identified and frequently at odds with the state, more independent. The Caesaropapism of the Byzantine Empire made education the handmaid not of the Faith but of the Administration. The attitudes to secular learning were different. The East was largely dominated by a tradition holding the study of philosophy only to be of use for the understanding and refutation of pagans, and therefore useless if not actually dangerous in a wholly Christian society. But the West was Augustinian. For St Augustine there was not and could not be a division: philosophy and theology were one in their search for understanding of the Faith. Add to all this the differences in social and economic development, producing in the West an advancing, expanding world which looked to the future for improvement, where Byzantium dwelt overmuch upon the past; and there are reasons enough to go some way towards answering the question asked in the first paragraph of this chapter.

In all of this we have not yet seen what was the *content* of this education. Late antique and early medieval schooling consisted in theory in the 'Seven Liberal Arts'. They were invented by the Greeks. The Latin name, *artes liberales*, is a translation of the Greek ἐλεύθεραι τέχναι, and a better English version would be 'freeman's arts', that is, the arts or skills fit for a free man, as opposed to a slave. The word 'liberal' in 'liberal arts' has nothing to do with liberality or with liberalism: the phrase meant those skills suitable for free men. Now free men in antiquity did not work for their living, or at least not with their hands; the only ancient writer who confessed to such degradation was St Paul. What they used above all was words – in the law courts, in politics, in polemics, in arguments on anything and everything. It followed that their education, the liberal arts, should be practically useless except for making speeches or writing books. So Greek, and then Roman, education was fundamentally rhetorical. There were attempts to include in the arts the practical disciplines of architecture and medicine, both respectable occupations, but without any lasting success. It is from this ancient Greco-Roman tradition that stems that prejudice, longer and more strongly preserved in England than elsewhere, for the intellectual and largely verbal arts as against all those involving the use of the hands. It was, of course, a tradition suited to the Church. The clergy do not labour with their hands, and they are largely concerned with the understanding of what is written and the preaching of the message. It is not surprising that the Church adopted the seven liberal arts as the proper initial schooling for its ministers.

What were these seven? They were by the sixth century divided into two groups: the *Trivium*, Grammar, Rhetoric and Dialectic; and the *Quadrivium*, Arithmetic, Geometry, Music and Astronomy. The division represented the separation of grades of difficulty, and stages of instruction: a knowledge of Grammar, Rhetoric and Dialectic was necessary for the study of the other four. So the Trivium was the elementary stage: hence our 'trivial'. *Grammar* meant what it said, and meant Latin grammar. Medieval students laboured at it without the benefit of Kennedy's Primer, of course; for most, at least until the eleventh century, when Priscian's longer work became commoner, the textbooks were the two very short works of the fourth century Donatus. Once the rudiments of the parts of speech were learnt, Classical texts were read: first and most especially Virgil's *Aeneid*, and then extracts from such authors as Terence, Horace, Ovid and Statius, all contained in school anthologies. *Rhetoric* meant the study of figures of speech, forms of oratory, metrics and literary devices. Grammar and Rhetoric together provided a sufficient training in language, and most men, even in antiquity, were content with those, and went no further. For *Dialectic* meant Aristotelian logic, which was not easy and seemed less relevant. Dialectic, however, was to prove from the ninth century on the ground out of which Scholastic philosophy grew, for it raised many of the most important questions of philosophy while providing few suggestions for answers.

The Quadrivium was little studied either in antiquity or in the early Middle Ages, but it was held in theory to be necessary for the proper understanding of the Scriptures. *Arithmetic* did not mean what we mean by the name: that the Middle Ages called *algorism*, and it was only introduced in the twelfth century. Calculation was done on the abacus, and Arithmetic was not concerned with calculation but with numbers, including, among other things, their shapes – we still use the names 'squares' (e.g., 9: ⋮⋮) and 'cubes' (e.g., 8: ⋮⋮). *Geometry* included both elementary geometry as we know it, and 'geography', the description of the earth and its lands; both subjects could be called 'earth-measurement', the literal meaning of 'geometry'. *Music*, like Arithmetic, had little or nothing to do with the practice of the art, but was all to do with theories of harmony and modes and their effects on man's soul. Lastly, *Astronomy* meant *astrologia*, of which more in a moment.

However, not only was this neat scheme of seven liberal arts not a curriculum ever studied as a whole by anyone; it was not so rigid as to be incapable of evolution. Some idea of the expansion of the ancient scheme in the twelfth and thirteenth centuries is given by a comparison of three outline curricula. The first is that of Cassiodorus, who in the early sixth century succeeded Boethius as secretary to Theodoric, the Ostrogothic king of Italy, and in his retirement wrote two works for the instruction of his monks, known as his *Institutiones*.[1] For

---

[1] Edited by R. A. B. Mynors, *Cassiodori Senatoris Institutiones* (Oxford, 1937).

secular letters, he lists the seven arts and the textbooks to be used, with Boethius and Martianus Capella prominent among their authors – the only two given for Astronomy. In 1142 Thierry of Chartres drew up an encyclopaedic syllabus for his school.[2] It is still officially a list under the same seven heads, but now not only is the 'new logic' (the translations of Aristotle's major logical works, just arriving in the schools) included, but we find four authorities for geometry, including Gerbert d'Aurillac (the late tenth century Bishop of Rheims and Pope); and Gerland's book on the abacus; and Hyginus, Ptolemy and the Arabic writer al-Khwarizmi (of whose name *algorism* is a corruption) all mentioned under Astronomy. The third curriculum is one for a medieval Arts Faculty in a Ripoll manuscript of about 1230–1240.[3] The old *artes* have gone, and now *philosophia* is divided into three parts: 'Natural', which includes Metaphysics, Physics and Mathematics, which last is the old Quadrivium. Euclid is now there for Geometry and Ptolemy for Astronomy.[4] The authorities for the second division, *Moral* philosophy, include Aristotle's *Ethics*. *Rational* philosophy, which is the Trivium, now consists almost entirely of Dialectic, of logic, now obviously the only really important subject in the whole curriculum. The sciences developed, of course, out of the Natural Philosophy of such a curriculum.

Astronomy – *astronomia* or *astrologia* – was included among the advanced studies from the beginning. Both Latin names are used with varying or no distinctions, but before the twelfth century the content is almost entirely what we would call astronomical. There was probably little practical, professional astrology in the late Empire except perhaps at court, apart from popular horoscope-pedlars and a few learned men like Firmicus Maternus. Belief in astrology was widespread, no doubt, particularly among the uneducated, but it seems not to have been much to the fore in men's minds, where

[2] The work, known as the *Heptateuchon*, existed in two manuscript volumes (MSS 497 and 498) at Chartres, which were destroyed by fire in May 1944. Microfilms of the work exist at Toronto and Louvain, but it has not been published. The short prologue was edited by E. Jeauneau in *Medieval Studies*, XVI (1954) 171–5. A summary of the contents is given by A. Clerval in *Les écoles de Chartres au moyen âge, du Ve au XVIe siècle* (Paris, 1895) 220ff. Ptolemy and Al-Khwarizmi are only there for their Tables: the *Almagest* was still unknown in Latin.

[3] The MS is Ripoll 109, at Barcelona; see M. Grabmann, *Mittelalterliches Geistesleben* (Munich, 1936) II.193–199 and F. van Steenberghen, *Siger de Brabant, Les Philosophes belges* (Louvain, 1942) II.415–420.

[4] The Ptolemy is now the *Almagest*. The Ripoll MS is an account of works to be read, and specimen questions for discussion, under each heading. The interesting thing is that while seven 'pages' suffice for the whole of Natural and Moral philosophy, without any questions, the remaining forty-two 'pages' of the (incomplete) manuscript are concerned with the Trivium, the last two-thirds of these with Dialectic, with more than two hundred and sixty questions.

Chance was more likely to hold sway than Fate. There is no real astrology in late Roman art. There are zodiacs, it is true: but throughout the centuries, from Roman times to the Renaissance, the representation of the zodiac, or its description in books, cannot be taken as evidence for the presence of astrology. The 'Monnus-mosaic' in Trier, for example, as well as those from Münster-Sarmsheim, Selinum, Avenches and the Yonne, with zodiacs round the sun in his chariot, or with Atlas the heaven-bearer, or with the seasons and the months, are all time-pictures, the sun portrayed as *Sol invictus*, the time-lord, *chronocrator*.[5] The same is true of those in synagogues, as at Beth-Alpha or Doura-Europos: 'the picturing of the zodiac in the pavements of synagogues is less a representation of the heaven with its stars than a schematic image of Time'.[6] Zodiacs on coins and gems are associated with the sun, with the sun and moon, with the planets and their gods – especially with *Zeus* (Jupiter) *chronocrator* – and all seem to be connected with religion and the calendar.[7] It is very important to remember that zodiacs are not necessarily astrological; indeed the chances are that they are not.

This is particularly relevant to the consideration of the worship of Mithras. It was in his function as time-lord that he collected zodiacs and zodiacal figures round him, as on a stone of the second or third century from Housesteads, on Hadrian's Wall (Plate I). Other such representations of Mithras with zodiacs are found, for example, at the Wallbrook Mithraeum in London and at Modena. He is often associated with figures of the moon and planets, and of winds, and others possibly but not wholly convincingly representing elements – air, fire, water and so on. Despite J. Vermaseren's frequent insistence[8] there is in fact no evidence to establish any strictly astrological connection between Mithraism and the heavens. Mithras was certainly a sun-god, and also Saturn (the 'sun of the night'), who was also identified 'with the god of Eternal Time, the Persian Zervan, and the Greek Aion'.[9] The importance of the sun's position in the zodiac and the association with the planets and moon are most probably linked with this time-god aspect of Mithras, and with the sort of religion and mythology which

---

[5] See K. Parlasca, *Die römischen Mosaiken in Deutschland* (Berlin, 1959) 41, 87; V. von Gonzenbach, *Die römischen mosaiken der Schweiz* (Basel, 1961) 43; J. P. Darmon, 'Sur deux mosaiques de l'Yonne', in *La Mosaique Gréco-romaine* (Paris, 1975) II.313.

[6] A. Grabar, *L'Art de la Fin de l'Antiquité et du Moyen-Age* (Paris, 1968) II.781.

[7] See W. Gundel, 'Zodiac', in *Enciclopedía dell' Arte Antica*, VII (Rome, 1966).

[8] In his *Mithras, the Secret God* (London, 1963).

[9] Vermaseren, *op. cit.*, 78. For the lack of real connection between Mithraism and astrology see also R. L. Gordon, 'Franz Cumont and the doctrines of Mithraism', in *Mithraic Studies*, ed. J. R. Hinnells (Manchester, 1975) I.215ff. Nothing in the two volumes of papers from that international conference supports the idea of anything more than the most tenuous association of Mithraism with astrology.

I 'Birth-stone' showing Mithras and a 'reverse' zodiac, 2nd or 3rd
century A.D., from Housesteads on the Roman Wall
(Museum of Antiquities of the University, Newcastle-upon-Tyne)

included catasterisms and associated the Bull and Venus with creation, and Taurus with spring. The time-god relationship is clear in the Modena relief[10] 'depicting the egg-birth of the snake-entwined Orphic-Mithraic god Phanes-Aion, within a zodiac frame, but not with a cut-out background.' The time element is also seen in the frequent arrangement of the planets in the order of the days of the week, as at Bologna, for example. (The order when they are associated with the seven grades of the cult – Saturn, Sun, Moon, Jupiter, Mars, Venus, Mercury – is neither calendrial nor astrological, but seems to be hierarchic.)

An odd thing about the Housesteads stone is that it shows the signs in the 'reverse' order: if we assume we are facing south, with east on our left, we see Gemini rising before Taurus, which is followed by Aries, and that by Pisces and Aquarius. This is also true of the zodiac with the 'bull-slayer' Mithras on a relief from Osterburken now in the Badisches Landsmuseum, Karlsrühe.[11] There are two possible explanations. It could be that we are actually facing north, so that east is on the right. This is unlikely, not only because the left-hand east is more natural to northern countries (if one faces the sun, one is looking south), but all ancient horoscopes are drawn with the ascendant on the left. The probable explanation is that the artist was working from a celestial globe. Books of the constellations were often illustrated in the way the tenth century al-Sufi's was.[12] Although it is late, it was derived from Classical sources, with two drawings of each constellation, 'giving its image in symmetrically opposed figures, the one as it appears in the sky, the other as it would be presented on a celestial globe, where the beholder sees it as it were from the outside, so that left becomes right and vice versa.' (See Plate II) 'Classical constellation images are best known from the "Farnese Globe", a huge celestial marble globe in the Museo Nazionale at Naples, which is generally considered to be a Roman copy of a Greek original, and from a number of medieval copies of classical texts.' So the zodiac on the Housesteads stone is shown as it would be on a globe, seen 'from the outside'; which is another reason for thinking that the artist was not interested in astrology (which would naturally have had a 'normal' zodiac with the ascendant on the left) but in the heavenly bodies as time-reckoners. It might be added as further confirmation[13] that on the

---

[10] J. M. C. Toynbee, *Art in Roman Britian* (London, 1962) 154, note 4.

[11] F. Saxl, *Lectures I & II*, Warburg Institute (London, 1957) Plate 20b.

[12] Bodleian MS Marsh 144; see Emmy Wellesz, *An Islamic Book of Constellations* (Bodleian Picture Book No. 13) (Oxford, 1965) from which the quotations are taken (p. 4).

[13] I owe this information to the kindness of Dr D. J. Smith, FSA, Keeper of the Museum of Antiquities, Newcastle-upon-Tyne, who provided the photograph of the stone.

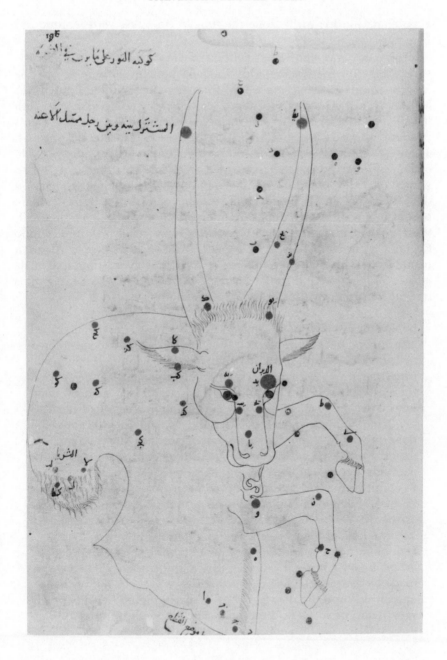

II Taurus, from a manuscript of al-Sufi's book of constellations
(Oxford, Bodleian Library MS Marsh 144, p. 96)

altars flanking this birth-stone the time-epithet *saecularis* is, uniquely here perhaps, applied to Mithras.

Mithraism was the only serious ancient rival to Christianity, spreading with the Roman army the length of the Empire. When the Empire and its armies vanished, Mithraism faded, and the Church was left alone in the field. The Church was opposed to astrology as both pagan and magic, and as appearing to diminish or to deny man's freedom, and possibly also God's omnipotence. Into the scale against astrology went the weight of Augustine's unparalleled authority. No other author is so much represented in medieval libraries, none so widely read: not only his two most famous works, the *Confessions* and the *City of God*, but his letters and sermons and commentaries and the host of less well-known books. In many of these works, particularly in those written in the first few years after he became bishop of Hippo Regius (the modern Bône – or Annaba, to give it its proper Algerian name) in 395, after about ten years of consciously Christian living, he attacks astrology;[14] and in the *Confessions*, written in 397, he describes how he was himself attracted to it in his younger days:

So I did not cease to consult openly those impostors called astrologers, because it seemed they had no sacrifices and offered no prayers to any spirit for their fortune-telling; though true Christian piety always rejects and condemns it. I knew at that time a wise, very skilled and very well-esteemed medical man, who when he learned from my conversation that I had devoted my time to astrological books, advised me in a kindly and fatherly way to throw them away, and not to waste my time and energy, which would be better spent on useful pursuits, on such vain falsehoods. He had himself, he said, so far studied the art as to want, in his early years, to become a professional: after all, if he had understood Hippocrates he would be able to understand astrology. Yet he had left it aside and followed medicine, simply because he had found it to be entirely false, and he could not as a serious-minded man seek his livelihood by cheating people. When I asked him why it was that many true predictions were made by astrologers, he replied that this was the result of chance, operating throughout nature. Yet at that time neither he nor my very dear friend Nebridius, who mocked every kind of divina-

---

[14] See for example, *De Doctrina Christiana*, II, c.21; *Enarrationes in Psalmos*, Ps.58 and 140; *De diversis 83 quaestiones*, q.45; *De Actibus cum Felice Manichaeo*, I.10. All these were written in the later 390s. In *De Doct. Christ.* II, c.29, Augustine points out that a knowledge of astronomy is necessary for the understanding of the calendar and of the Scriptures.

tion, could persuade me to throw it aside, because I was more influenced by the authority of the astrological writers, and I had not yet found any certain and unambiguous proof, such as I looked for, to show me that those things truly said by astrologers who were consulted were right by chance not because of the skill of those who inspected the stars.[15]

It is an instructive passage. Augustine was an intelligent and educated young near-pagan, who had learned enough of astronomy to be impressed (he refers elsewhere in the *Confessions* to the accuracy of the astronomers' predictions of eclipses and so on), and who had sufficient Christian background from his mother Monica to reject magic and superstitious divination through prayers and sacrifices to 'the gods'. He had not found any good reason to reject the authority of the astrologers; though who these authors were is a bit of a mystery, since he knew very little Greek. Perhaps Augustine was referring to popular prediction-books, 'almanacks', the fourth-century equivalent of 'Old Moore'. At any rate, he had no proof that the true revelations of astrology were due to chance not skill. Two of his friends tried to persuade him to leave astrology alone: Nebridius, his contemporary, who also later became a bishop, and the old ex-Proconsul, Vindicianus, a doctor. As might have been expected, given the close association between medicine and astrology, he had at first studied astrology and intended to make it his career, but rejected it as swindling.[16] Ten years after his conversion Augustine, now a bishop, frequently found occasion to condemn what he had earlier accepted; which shows not only that it was something to be reckoned with at that time, but also that it was still on the bishop's tender conscience.

The obvious place for an extended attack was in *The City of God*. It was begun as a proof that the pagan gods had not taken care of Rome, as a refutation of the accusation that it was because the City had forsaken her ancient guardian deities that she had fallen to the Goths. It developed, of course, over fifteen years, into something much wider in scope and of much greater and lasting importance. In Book V, cc.1–7, written nearly twenty years later than the *Confessions*, Augustine set out his criticism of astrology. The opening of the Book shows that whatever the status of astrology among the educated and however much it was disapproved of by the Church, nevertheless at the popular level there was sufficient belief to make most people equate

---

[15] Book IV, c.3 (abridged).
[16] Cf. *Conf.* VII.6, where Augustine again refers to these dissuaders and explains that he was finally convinced of his error by the different fates of two children born with precisely the same natal chart.

'fate' with the influence of the stars. If, he says, anyone means by 'fate' the will of God, 'let him hold to his opinion but correct his language. For when men hear that word, "fate", by the ordinary usage of current speech they simply understand by it the power of the stars' arrangement, as it is when a man is born, or conceived.' There is a further hint of the common popularity of the astrologer-soothsayer in the number of references (as in *De Doctrina Christiana*, II.21 for example) to their hawking their predictions around.

Now some men hold the 'power of the stars' to be independent of God, while others believe it to be dependent upon his will. The first opinion is to be rejected as really a form of atheism, whether it is held by pagans or professed Christians. In the second case, either the stars act of their own volition, the power being given them by God, or they merely carry out, by necessity, the will of God himself. If the first, how is it that these heavenly bodies, in all their beauty and grandeur – *clarissimus senatus et splendidissima curia*, says Augustine – can cause evil? It is unthinkable. Then surely it is even less thinkable that God causes evil through them? But if it is said, as it has been by men of great learning, that the stars *signify* events but do not cause them, that is not in fact how the *mathematici*, the professional astrologers, put it: they do not say, 'Mars in such and such a position signifies that a man will be a murderer'; they say, 'makes him a murderer'. And even allowing that they are wrong in using such phrases, and following the learned, what about twins? If, as is usual, the fates of twins are different, the astrologer says that they were not, of course, born at the *same* time. Nigidius Figulus illustrated the difference a small interval can make by striking a spinning wheel twice in quick succession, and then stopping the wheel and pointing to the distance between the marks. Against this Augustine argues that the time of birth, or *a fortiori* of conception, and even the times of the ascending of signs, cannot be measured accurately enough; which was indeed a permanent difficulty in the centuries before the invention of reliable mechanical clocks. And anyway, as he points out in Chapter 5, exactly the opposite is said by the astrologer in the cases of twins falling ill at the same time, namely that they were born or conceived under the same heavens, at the same time. The classic case of twins with different fates is, of course, that of Jacob and Esau, with whose story Chapter 4 is taken up. There is much more argument about twins, particularly about the relative importance of the times and dates of conception and birth, concluding with the difficult question, 'Is it not true that the will of those who are now living changes the fates decreed at their nativity, when the order in which they are born changes the fates decreed at their conception?' It is interesting that Augustine betrays his former involvement in astrology in his use of the technical language of the subject: 'Then I ask, if there is so much difference in the times of the births of twins that they are born under different constellations, because their ascendants are different and therefore all their *cardines* are different (that is, the MC etc.; his words are: *propter diversum horoscopum et ob hoc diversos omnes cardines*), in which that power is located which causes them to have different fates, I ask, how can this happen, when their conceptions cannot have occurred at different times?'

The final passages, in Chapter 7, concern 'elections' – *katarchai* – and the consequent opportunities for interfering with what is supposed to be the 'course of fate'. 'Suppose a man to be born,' he argues, 'under stars promising not an admirable but a contemptible son; and that, since he is learned, he chooses the particular hour to have intercourse with his wife, so that he has made for himself a fate he did not have, and by that chosen act of his, that has begun to be fated which was not there in his nativity.' That is, although the 'house of children' in his birth chart made it clear that he would have wretched children, he can by a judicious use of *katarchai* so plan their conceptions that they are destined to be the opposite. Nevertheless, the plausibility of astrology is admitted; astrologers are very often surprisingly correct. But this, says Augustine, is because of the hidden influence of evil spirits, whose concern it is to encourage the growth of this superstition in men's minds, not because of any skill in determining and interpreting horoscopes – 'there is no such art'. The most difficult case for the Christian to deal with was, of course, that of the Magi and the Star of Bethlehem, which could hardly be put down to demonic causes. Augustine's answer is set out most clearly in a treatise he wrote about 397–8 against Faustus the Manichee:[17]

Now we (as opposed to the Manichees) set the birth of no man under the fatal rule of the stars, so that we can loose from any bond of necessity the free choice of his will, by which he lives well or ill, for the sake of the just judgment of God. How much less then do we think that temporal begetting of the eternal Creator and Lord of all to be under the influence of the stars! So that star which the Magi saw when Christ was born according to the flesh was not a lord governing his nativity but a servant bearing witness to it, it did not subject him to its power but in its service pointed the way to him. What is more, that star was not one of those which from the beginning of creation keep their regular courses under the Creator's law, but at the new birth

---

17 *Contra Faustum Manichaeum*, II.5 (*PL* 42: cols 212–3); and *cf.* Sermon 201.

from the Virgin a new star appeared, which performed its office by going before the faces of the Magi in their search for Christ until it led them to the place where lay the infant Word of God ... So Christ was not born because it shone forth, but it shone forth because Christ was born; so if we must speak of it, we should say not that the star was fate for Christ, but that Christ was fate for the star.

In all this, Augustine is in line with the attitude of earlier Latin Christian writers. Another great African writer, Tertullian, had written[18] two centuries earlier a passage much quoted later by Bede, Alcuin, Ivo of Chartres and many others: astrology 'was allowed only until the time of the Gospel, so that no one from then on, after Christ's appearance, should interpret anyone's nativity from the heavens. For the Magi offered incense and myrrh and gold to the infant Lord as it were to mark the passing of this world's glories and rites, which Christ was to remove'; and since magic was condemned, so too was astrology, a kind of magic. In his *Apologeticum*[19] he says that Christians do not consult 'astrologers or haruspices or augurers or magicians, even about their own affairs (since these arts came from demons and were forbidden by God), much less about Caesar's life' – of which no doubt they had been accused. The same linking of astrology with other forms of pagan magic and divination is found in the very early fourth century in Lactantius;[20] and in the Lives of the Fathers[21] the demonic origin of even true astrological forecasting is an example of the way God uses even his adversaries as agents of his truth, so that no excuse for ignorance might be left for the wicked.

Not only was astrology thus associated with pagan magic and superstition, but it was tainted with heresy. It was among the beliefs of the Priscillianist heretics in Spain. Orosius, Augustine's disciple, says[22] they believed in the soul's journey through the spheres, when it was influenced by the planets in turn, and in the allocation of the parts of the body to the signs of the zodiac – the *melothesia*. The same associations were made by Gregory the Great, and so passed into medieval literature.

And to all this as an at least equally potent force working against astrology's survival must be added the decline of learning in the centuries immediately following the break-up of the Western Empire.

---

[18] Tertullian, *De Idololatria*, c.9 (*PL* I: col. 747).

[19] Ch. 35 (*PL* I: col. 521).

[20] *Divin. Inst.*, II.17 (*PL* VI: cols 336–7).

[21] *Vitae Patrum* (*PL* LXXIII: col. 452).

[22] See *Priscilliani quae supersunt*, ed. G. Schepps, *CSEL* 18, 1889, 153–4.

As M. L. W. Laistner has written:[23] 'Not persecution or prosecution, but the lack of proper manuals caused the disappearance of "scientific" astrology in the West for four or five centuries after Firmicus composed his astrologers' handbook.' There was virtually no knowledge of Greek, and the study of the Liberal Arts dwindled to the acquisition of a very rudimentary smattering of grammar and rhetoric, from very elementary textbooks. Now the preservation of any art or skill from generation to generation, even at the most rude and popular level, depends upon the continuity of a high professionalism; without understanding and development at the highest level, the bottom is starved and dies. There is no 'pop' without the philharmonic. There could be no hack horoscope-mongers or star-gazing soothsayers without skilled astrologers, no production of popular almanacs or prediction sheets without the expert provision of the material on which they must all be based. In the late fourth and early fifth centuries there were few good textbooks of astrology in the West, and probably fewer learned masters of the subject. Considering that it was a time of transition, of great insecurity and therefore of great anxiety, and that in such times men turn to religion and to magic and astrology for help and comfort, we can reasonably ask why astrology virtually disappeared from western Europe at this time. The hostility of the Church and the decay of learning are probably enough to account for it. Only the very few scholars who progressed beyond the Trivium (and did not go on to law and civil administration) – and before the ninth century few enough even got as far as dialectic – only those few would reach 'astronomy'; and all of that had to be in Latin. Now it is fair to say that there could be no accurate making of birth-charts, no real genethlialogy, without Ptolemy's *Almagest*; neither that nor his *Tetrabiblos* existed in Latin. The Latin 'textbooks', including those of Manilius and Firmicus Maternus, were useless without the mathematical apparatus; and if there were books such as those Augustine consulted, derived perhaps from Nigidius Figulus or even Posidonius, whom Augustine described in *The City of God* (Book V.5) as 'a great astrologer and philosopher', they were probably very much like the sort of stuff found in the late Greek works represented in the appendices of the CCAG, or possibly like the 'Elements of Astronomy' of Geminus, a sort of *sphaera*, or description of the heavens, with some account of astrological terms such as trigons, tetragons (squares) and so on.[24] At any rate such books must have disappeared very early, for

---

23 In *The Intellectual Heritage of the Middle Ages*, ed. C. G. Starr (New York, 1957) 82 (= 'The Western Church and Astrology during the Early Middle Ages', *Harvard Theological Review*, 34 (1941).)

24 *Gemini Elementa Astronomica*, ed. K. Manitius (Leipzig, 1898). If Manitius was right, the Greek text is a fourth/fifth century epitome of a Stoic Geminus' first century B.C. commentary on Posidonius' *Meteorologica*.

only a few relics remain. So, what *astrologia* did the men of the Latin West inherit, and how much of it was astrological?

Two of the chief Classical sources of later 'scientific' knowledge were the *Quaestiones naturales* of Seneca and the *Natural History* of Pliny the Elder. Both contained much astronomy. But whereas Seneca's work was unknown and unused until the twelfth century, Pliny's was used, at first or second hand, by very many medieval scholars. There is no astrology in either author, but neither makes any clear distinction between astrology and astronomy. In Pliny's second book, concerned with the *mundus*, the world, the universe, and largely astronomical, Saturn, for example, is described as 'of a cold and frozen nature', and the sun is the ruler of the stars and the heavens, 'the soul, or more precisely, the mind of the whole world'. The authorities Pliny claims to have used include, apart from his Latin sources, Hipparchus, Petosiris and Nechepso, Posidonius, Eudoxus, Thrasyllus, Archimedes, Eratosthenes and Aristotle: but despite the inclusion of Nechepso-Petosiris, Posidonius and Thrasyllus, there is no astrology here. He has indeed the Roman Stoic's contempt for popular superstition:

> Everywhere in the whole world at every hour by all men's voices Fortune alone is invoked and named, alone accused, alone impeached, alone pondered, alone applauded, alone rebuked, and visited with reproaches; deemed volatile and indeed by most men blind as well, wayward, inconstant, uncertain, fickle in her favours and favouring the unworthy. To her is debited all that is spent and credited all that is received, she alone fills both pages in the whole of mortals' account; and we are so much at the mercy of chance that Chance herself, by whom God is proved uncertain, takes the place of God. Another set of people banishes fortune also, and attributes events to its star and to the laws of birth, holding that for all men that ever are to be God's decree has been enacted once for all, while for the rest of time leisure has been vouchsafed to Him.[25]

Along with Pliny the three chief authorities for the early Middle Ages on matters astronomical were the later writers Calcidius, Martianus Capella and Macrobius, of whom the last was by far the most influential. The earliest, Calcidius, translated the first, cosmological part of Plato's *Timaeus* and wrote a long Neo-Platonist commentary on it, at about the end of the fourth century.[26] He accepted from his late

---

[25] Pliny, *Natural History*, Loeb Classical Library, vol. I, tr. H. Rackham, 1944, pp. 183–5.
[26] *Timaeus a Calcidio translatus commentarioque instructus*, ed. J. H. Waszink, Plato Latinus (Leiden, 1962) vol. IV.

Greek sources the Aristotelian (*Meteor.* I.2) principle that processes of generation and decay in the sublunary world are caused by changes in the heavens. This clearly makes possible divination by astrology, as he says (c.157); but he is clear (c.125), following Plotinus, that 'the stars do not cause what happens, they merely foretell future events.' A fatalistic astrology would raise the problem, how could the stars, which all have the same higher nature, possibly cause evil? It would also destroy God's providence and man's freedom (cc.174–5). Consequently, although astrology is possible, it is (c.186) 'only conjecture about things pertaining to the body, or affairs belonging to the body, or that part of mind subservient to the body.' Calcidius is interesting as giving us the opinions of an intelligent late fourth century astronomer, but his influence was small. His work was virtually unknown until the twelfth century, and not much read then; it is significant that whereas Macrobius was first printed in 1472, Calcidius had to wait nearly half a century for the first edition of 1520. Perhaps he was just too long and difficult.

The same cannot be said of the early fifth century encyclopaedia of Martianus Capella, 'The Marriage of Mercury and Philology'.[27] This curious work is the account of the wedding, before all the assembled gods, of the lady *Philologia* to the god Mercury (of course: language and learning were properly his). Philology has been given seven sisters as bridesmaids. As each in turn introduces herself, she explains what she does: the first is Grammatica, the second Dialectica, the third Rhetorica, and so on – so Books III to IX are in fact a summary encylopaedia of the seven liberal arts. Book VIII is concerned with *Astrologia*,[28] and it is wholly astronomical. The only hint of astrology is a reference (885) to Jupiter as health-giving; but the author does not even bother to give the names of the signs of the zodiac, because 'everybody knows them'. He does pass on Heraclides' notion that Venus and Mercury move, not in eccentric circles round the earth like

---

[27] *Martianus Capella,* ed. James Willis (Leipzig, 1983). It is written partly in prose and partly in verse; the form is known as 'Menippean satire' and was used with a much more regular structure by Boethius in his *Consolation of Philosophy*.

[28] Willis in fact (following Dick's 1925 Teubner edition) prints the title of Book VIII as *De Astronomia,* on the grounds that the sister in question is called Astronomia in Book VI (581) and that the word *astrologia* does not occur in Martianus; but without MS authority – those MSS which do have a title call it *de astrologia,* as do also those which have a sub-scription at the end of the book, save one. Martianus has *astrologus* meaning 'astronomer' in Book VIII (858), and *astronomus* with the same meaning in Book III (230). Neither Martianus nor his later copyists would have made any distinction. It is true that among the divinatory arts not actually admitted to the wedding is *Genethliace* (Book IX, 894), 'who knowing the heavenly reason discloses the thread of fate spun by Lachesis and declares the things to happen in the close-pressing centuries', but this does not mean that Martianus was making any modern distinctions; after all, the *ratio aetheria* was exactly what was studied by the *astrologus/astronomus*.

the rest of the planets, but round the sun (854, 857), which itself goes round the earth. The only point of real astrological interest in the work occurs not in Book VIII but in Book II, 200, where Philology on her arrival at the sphere of the fixed stars, 'jumping out of her litter, saw the immense plains of light and the springlike calm of the ether, and now she saw the differences and the shapes of the decans, now wondered at the eighty-four ministers (liturgi) of the heavens standing near, and saw besides the shining globes of the many stars . . .' etc.[29]

We know about decans, of course, though we are not used to finding them personified, as they are here, and as they are occasionally elsewhere in pagan religious and occult writers. But what are these 'ministers', the liturgi, of which there are, apparently, eighty-four? The footnote in the Teubner edition sends us to Firmicus Maternus (a century earlier than Martianus Capella), who deepens the mystery: 'Some authorities, wishing to go into more complications in this matter (sc. of the decans), attribute three divinities to each decan; these they wish to be known as ministers (munifices), that is, liturgi; so that nine ministers can be found in each sign, and each decan is equipped with three ministers. Then again, they divide the nine ministers which they say are established in each sign among countless powers of divinities; by these, they say, sudden chance events, pains, sicknesses, colds and fevers are caused, and all else that comes upon us unexpectedly without our knowledge; and monstrous births are also caused by them'.[30] Three liturgi in each decan, nine in each sign, and therefore 108 in all, according to Firmicus. Neither he nor Martianus explains any further.

Modern scholars do not help. Franz Boll (Sphaera, 1903, pp. 392ff) merely follows Bouché-Leclercq, and he Saumaise before him, and says that the liturgi belong to the sphaera barbarica, the Egyptian description of the heavens, and are paranatellonta, the stars which rise with the decans. This is also the view, unsupported by evidence, of a modern editor and translator (into Italian) of Book II of Martianus Capella, Luciano Lenaz.[31] However, they clearly are not paranatellonta. Not only is there no list of 84, nor of 108, such stars, but in Martianus

---

[29] *Ipsa quippe Philologia lectica desiliens, cum immensos luminis campos aetheriaeque tranquillitatis verna conspiceret ac nunc tot diversitates cerneret formasque decanorum, tunc octoginta quattuor liturgos caelo moraretur adstare, videretque praeterea fulgentes crebrorum siderum glogos*, etc. The Latin is worth quoting, since there are ambiguities in it concealed in translation. For instance, does the *decanorum* go with *diversitates* as well as *formas*, or are the *diversitates* separate, as early commentators seem to have thought?

[30] II.4, 4. *Iulii Firmici Materni Matheseos libri VII*, ed. W. Kroll and F. Skutsch (Leipzig, 1897) vol. I; ed. W. Kroll, F. Skutsch and K. Ziegler (Leipzig, 1913) vol. II.

[31] (Padua, 1975) 34, note 86. He suggests that the 84 is simply produced from the seven of the planets multiplied by the twelve of the signs.

they are obviously like the decans and similarly personified, and separated from the stars; and Firmicus does not even hint at such a solution, but treats them as divisions of the decans (though of course it is possible that *paranatellonta* could be so used). The early medieval commentators, such as John Scottus Erigena and Remi of Auxerre in the ninth century, both drawing on older glosses, are at a loss. Erigena says:[32] '*Liturgi* means ministers. The space between the earth and the firmament is divided into eighty-four "varieties" (*varietates*).' And Remy says the same[33] and adds: '*liturgi* according to some authorities are divinities which inflict sicknesses on mortals.' It looks as though their 84 varieties are derived from a possible but unlikely interpretation of *diversitates* in Martianus, and the sicknesses come ultimately from Firmicus or at least the same tradition.

So what are *liturgi*? And why are there 84 or 108 of them? There is no certain answer. They are not mentioned by any other ancient astrological writer, and there is no reference to them in Bede's astronomical works or in those of later commentators. It is fairly safe to assume that Martianus had little or no idea what they were, but merely listed them with the decans in the same way as an anonymous Gnostic quoted by Boll puts them in a list which includes angels and archangels! Firmicus Maternus may possibly have known more, but it looks unlikely. His three *liturgi* per decan is too tidy and too complicated at the same time. It looks like a guess, making *liturgi* thirds of thirds, and it gives an odd unit of $3\frac{1}{3}°$, a third of the 10° decan; which looks like the 'ninths', the *novenarii*, of later astrology.[34] These were probably of Babylonian origin. So also were the lunar mansions, of which there were 27 or 28. If a 28-mansion sign were divided between the seven planets, there would be 84 such divisions in a twelve-month (lunar month) circle. All of which makes sense in a lunar calendar based astrology, but is not easily fitted into a solar zodiac. Firmicus may be forgiven for simplifying, if that is what he was doing. If something like this is the explanation, Martianus' encyclopaedia of the liberal arts, not widely but continuously known through the early Middle Ages, gives us a glimpse of yet another complication of late antique astrology.

Nothing about astrology, and little of any value of astronomy is to be learned from the muddled commentary Macrobius wrote, about 430 A.D., on Cicero's 'Dream of Scipio', the *Somnium Scipionis*. It was a popular work not only throughout the Middle Ages but through the Renaissance also and down into the eighteenth century. Cicero,

---

[32] *Ioannis Scotti Annotationes in Marcinum*, ed. Cora E. Lutz (New York, 1939) 73.
[33] *Remigii Autissiodorensis Commentum in Martianum Capellam I & II*, ed. Cora E. Lutz (Leiden, 1962) 302.
[34] But see pp. 164f below on *navamshas*, 'ninths', for further remarks on *liturgi*.

following Plato, had written a *Republic*, which, like Plato's, closed with a myth. In Cicero's book this took the form of a dream experienced by Scipio Aemilianus, in which he is shown the mysteries of the universe by his adoptive grandfather, the great Scipio Africanus. Macrobius, of whom practically nothing is known save that he was a pagan,[35] wrote a Neo-Platonist commentary on that *Dream* (commonly referred to simply as the *Somnium*)[36] which is one of the chief sources for the Middle Ages of late antique doctrines of the soul and immortality.

The cosmology and the astronomy are muddled, as is the mathematics. A passage of some obscurity (I.19) preserves ancient doubts about the relation between the inferior planets, Venus and Mecury, and the sun, the obscurity being due not to difficulties in the Latin but to the fog in Macrobius' mind. He gives the usual lists of characteristics of the planets, from the *genethlialogi*, and then advances fantastic numerical 'explanations' derived from Ptolemy 'On Harmony'; and quotes Plotinus as saying that the stars do not cause but only signify events on earth. But if Macrobius offers us nothing new, he does serve to illustrate two interesting and important aspects of astrology, which he helped to preserve into the Middle Ages: the idea of the soul's journey down through the spheres on its way to join the body, acquiring various characteristics from the seven planets as it descended; and the *thema mundi*, the horoscope of the world, the 'birth-chart' of the creation.

The Platonic separable soul imprisoned in the body became in the Neo-Platonic amalgam of Plato, Aristotle and Stoicism (which introduced the idea of the soul having the same fiery nature as the outermost heaven) a soul which had to descend from the etherial regions where it was at home to the earth, to enter a body. On the way it passed, necessarily, through the spheres of the planets, and Macrobius tells us (I.12, 14) that 'in Saturn's sphere' the soul receives 'reasoning and intelligence, which the Greeks call λογιστικόν and θεωρητικόν; in Jupiter's sphere, the power of acting, which is called πρακτικόν; in Mars', the fiery ardour of spirit called θυμικόν; in the Sun's, a nature for feeling and opinion, which they call αἰσθητικόν

---

[35] His other, larger, work, the *Saturnalia*, is a conversation on literary, mythological and religious themes – mostly on Virgil – between pagan Roman senators of the preceding generation. It shows Macrobius to be a supporter of the 'pagan party' in the state, and his somewhat idealised portraits of Symmachus, Praetextatus and th others were probably intended to counter the hostile propaganda of the historian Ammianus Marcellinus. See Alan Cameron, 'The Date and Identity of Macrobius', in *Journal of Roman Studies*, LVI (1966) 25–38.

[36] *Ambrosii Theodosii Macrobii Commentarii in Somnium Scipionis*, ed. James Willis (Leipzig, 1963).

and φανταστικόν; and the soul then receives the motion of desire, called ἐπιθυμητικόν, in Venus' sphere, of speaking out and interpreting what it feels, called ἑρμηνευτικόν, in Mercury's; and the φυτικόν, that is, corporeal begetting and growing, it obtains on entering the globe of the Moon.' The idea that the soul was affected by this journey was probably an astrological one,[37] since Servius (the grammarian and commentator on Virgil who is one of the characters in Macrobius' *Saturnalia*) says, on *Aeneid* VI, 714, that 'the astrologers claim that when the souls descend, they draw with them the sluggishness of Saturn, the anger of Mars, the lust of Venus, the desire for wealth of Mercury, the desire for power of Jupiter.' The Sun and Moon are left out of his list. It is a list of five of 'the seven deadly sins': sloth, anger, luxury (or lust), avarice and pride – the two missing ones are gluttony and envy. As Zielinski says: 'Of course, anyone could see how well gluttony could be attributed to the all-consuming Sun, and envy to the pale Moon.' The Classical poet Horace already had the same seven vices listed in Ep.I.1, 33ff; and their origin, together with their link with astrology, is probably in Posidonian Stoicism. Victorinus, Bishop of Pettau, who died in the Diocletianic persecution of 304, put together Psalm 32.6 and Isaiah 11.2–3, and had seven heavens with seven spirits: 'the highest heaven of wisdom, the second of understanding, the third of counsel, the fourth of virtue, the fifth of knowledge, the sixth of piety and the seventh of the fear of God'.[38] St Ambrose made the same connexion and called them 'the seven principal virtues of the Holy Spirit' (Ep.XXXI.3), and so the association of astrology, the seven deadly sins and the seven gifts of the Holy Spirit all passed into medieval thought.

The *thema mundi*, the horoscope of the world, was very much more ancient than any of this. As it is presented in our late sources, it is strikingly consistent, which suggests that it was long established and accepted.[39] It is normally introduced to explain why Aries is regarded as the 'beginning' of the zodiac, although a circle has of course no beginning. So Macrobius (I.21, 23ff): 'They say that when that day

---

[37] For what follows, see Th. Zielinski in *Philologus*, LXIV (1905) 21f; and *Saturn and Melancholy*, by R. Klibansky, E. Panofsky and F. Saxl (London, 1964) 159ff.

[38] *Tractatus de fabrica mundi*, 7; in *Victorini Episcopi Petavionensis Opera*, ed. J. Haussleiter, *CSEL* 49 (1916).

[39] Cf. Macrobius, *Somn.*, I.21; 23; Firm.Mat., III.1; Paul.Alexandr., c.37; *CCAG*, IX, ii, ed. S. Weinstock, pp. 176ff; and S. Weinstock, 'A New Greek Calendar and Festivals of the Sun', *Journal of Roman Studies*, XXXVIII (1948), pp. 37ff. It is interesting that Firmicus puts all the planets at 15° of their signs, which is a relic of Eudoxus' astronomy, a much older tradition. Bede in his *De temporum ratione*, c.VI (ed. Ch. W. Jones, *CC(SL)*, CXXIII B) explains how the day of the Creation, the 'beginning of the zodiac', was worked out not by the Greeks but by the Chaldaeans, and concludes: 'And so according to the division of the zodiac the sun enters Aries on the 15th of the kalends of April, the day light was

began which was the first of all and is therefore rightly called the world's birthday, Aries was in the Midheaven; and because the Midheaven is as it were the vertex of the world, Aries was therefore held to be the first among them all, the one which appeared like the head of the world at the beginning of light. And they add the reason why these twelve signs are assigned to the powers of different gods. For they say that in that same birth-chart of the world, Aries being as we have said in the Midheaven, the *horoscopus* of the world coming to birth was Cancer, bringing forth at that moment the Moon. The Sun was rising next with Leo, Virgo with Mercury, Libra with Venus, Mars was in Scorpio, Sagittarius had Jupiter and Saturn was wandering in Capricorn. So it came about that each was said to be the lord of that sign in which it was believed to be when the world was being born. To the two luminaries antiquity allotted only the signs, one to each, in which they had been then, Cancer to the Moon and Leo to the Sun. To the other five stars, however, besides those signs in which they then had been, ancient times so added the other five as to begin the new series at the end of the first. We said earlier that Saturn, last of all, was in Capricorn; so the second set of attributions made the previous last one first, and Aquarius, which follows Capricorn, was given to Saturn. To Jupiter, who preceded Saturn, Pisces was allocated', and so on, thus explaining the 'planetary houses'. All of which is found in other authorities; and indeed Firmicus says that the explanation is the reason for the construction of the *thema mundi* by wise men in the first place. The more probable ancient order of logic is restored by later authors – it clearly fits better with the Christian doctrine of Creation, as John of Salisbury says in the twelfth century:[40] 'Each planet has its natural house, in which each was created, provided the astrologers agree that they were created by God.' He then lists the houses of the *thema mundi* in the traditional order.

The origins of all this may go back to Babylon. We can get some idea of its mythological beginnings from the Epic of Creation.[41] According to this myth, Marduk (who like his Sumerian predecessor Ninurta was a solar god, so that later Marduk was equated with Jupiter, and Ninurta with Jupiter's predecessor Saturn, the 'sun of the night') slew Tiamat, the dragon, who represented the salt waters of the oceans. He

---

made.' So the day of the Creation was 18 March, three days before the equinox (since the sun and moon were not created till the third day) as he earlier suggests; though in c.XXX he gives the date of the equinox as 25 March, the Feast of the Annunciation, Lady Day.

[40] *Ioannis Saresberiensis Episcopi Carnotensis Policratici ... libri*, VIII, ed. C. C. J. Webb (Oxford, 1909) II.441d.

[41] S. Langdon, *The Babylonian Epic of Creation* (Oxford, 1923). The epic was first composed about the twenty-second century B.C.

divided her into two 'like an oyster', that is, lengthways, and set up half arched over the world, with the heavens as a covering. Then he made the 'stations of the great gods': *manzazu* – the word is used also of the stations of the moon, and later for exaltations; and sometimes *bîtu*, house, is used instead. Marduk fixed the year and designed the signs, and defined the days of the year by signs,[42] and then (if the interpretation is correct) set Nibiru, Marduk's planet, at the equinox, Aries or Libra, 'to fix all of them', and set the ecliptic between the northern and southern stars, and 'caused the new moon to shine forth', that is, in the west. Of course, there is not much here of the *thema mundi*; but there is the notion of the stars and planets being set in place at the creation, and the confusion is itself instructive. If Nibiru is a planet and not simply a 'crossing' – that is, one of the equinoxes; if it is, as Langdon thought, a 'crossing planet', a planet at the equinox; and if the planet was originally not Marduk's (Jupiter) but Ninurta's (Saturn), then Saturn was in the house of his exaltation, Libra. If Saturn was above the horizon in Libra, then the Sun was set in Aries and the new Moon was in Taurus – all three in the signs of their later exaltations; and there is some evidence that the other planets were in their corresponding places. The confusion over the words *manzazu* and *bîtu*, stations and houses, we have seen persists in late antique astrology, and one cannot press distinctions as far back as the Epic.

More interesting is Tiamat, the dragon stretched across the heavens, her head and her tail on the equator at opposite ends of a diameter. Now 'the head and tail of the dragon', *caput* and *cauda draconis*, are of great importance in later astrology, taking their places with the planets, and given symbols of their own, ☊ and ☋ . Astronomers will recognise these as representing the south to north, or ascending, node of the moon, and the north to south, or descending node. What are and were they? The lunar nodes are the points on the ecliptic where the moon crosses from south to north and back again, its slightly wobbly orbit being inclined to the ecliptic. The ascending node, ☊ , is the point where the moon (or, in modern astronomy, any planet) passes from south to north of the ecliptic, so it was frequently referred to as the northern node, and this was the *caput draconis*, the head of the dragon. The descending node, where the moon crossed the ecliptic

---

[42] Langdon is perhaps anachronistic in inserting '(of the zodiac)' after 'signs' (p. 153); 'constellations' is probably all that is meant. The Assyrian word used is not known elsewhere. The text at this point also says that Marduk 'placed three stars each' for the twelve months. The literature on these 'decans' is immense and unrewarding: it is safe to say that what it meant is now unthinkable, and that much that has been suggested is too anachronistic to be possible.

on its way south, was the *cauda*, the tail of the dragon. These nodes move round the ecliptic, precess, in the same way as the equinoctial points precess round the equator. They take about eighteen and a half years to go right round the ecliptic from east to west. The time taken for the moon to get from *caput* to *cauda* and back again is between 27 and 27½ days, a period (the mean is 27.212220 days) still known to astronomers as the Draconitic period. In late medieval and Renaissance astrology the head and tail of the dragon became 'things', with aspects and so on and almost the powers of planets, but they have virtually dropped out of modern astrology. Their connection with the modern constellation Draco, which snakes round the Little Bear, is probably that the modern line of stars is all that is left of the ancient Dragon. From the number of different myths Greeks and Romans attached to this constellation we might guess that they inherited it, its name, and its associations from a time before memory. It looks most likely that it is to be traced back over the millenia to the dragon of Babylonian mythology, especially since the *caput* and *cauda draconis* turn up in some strength in Hindu astrology later, and so come, through the Arabs, into the late Middle Ages and the Renaissance.

There is no mention of any of this in Macrobius, although an attentive reader could gather a great deal of astrological jargon from his book, and much that looks like astrological reference in later writers is really only from Macrobius' *Commentary*. For all early medieval learning is book learning, and almost all that is concerned with *astrologia* is from Macrobius, Isidore and above all Bede. So much were books considered the source of all knowledge that Cassiodorus derived the name 'liberal arts' from *liber*, a book.[43] Cassiodorus (490–583) was Master of the Offices, or secretary, to the Ostrogothic king of Italy, Theodoric; he retired from his duties to his estate at Vivarium to found a monastery and live his old age out in peace. There he wrote for his monks, as the darkness of paganism and ignorance deepened over western Europe, 'an Introduction to their studies', and 'divided his work into two books: one dealt with Christian learning and in general with their monastic life, and the second contained a compendium of such secular knowledge as was indispensable to the study of Holy Writ' (Mynors, p. ix). 'In which books,' says Cassiodorus himself in his Preface, 'I am not putting forward my own teaching, but the sayings of the ancients, *priscorum dicta*, which for us coming later it is right to praise and glorious to set forth.' The motive, that it is all for the better understanding of Scripture, and the attitude, that not original ideas but *priscorum dicta*

---

[43] *Cassiodori Senatoris Institutiones*, ed. R. A. B. Mynors (Oxford, 1937) II, 4.

matter, are both utterly typical and persistent throughout the story of medieval scholarship.

There is in Book II of the *Institutes*, which is really a sketch of the liberal arts and a list of their textbooks, a section *de astronomia*; Cassiodorus himself always uses the forms *astronomia, astronomus*, but he is quite happy to refer to Varro's *De astrologia*: there is no distinction. He gives, three times with nearly identical wording a definition of *astronomia* which he probably got from Varro (Inst.II.iii.6 and 21, vii.2): '*Astronomia* is that discipline which examines all the movements and shapes of the heavenly constellations and rationally enquires into the relations of the stars to one another and to the earth'. The same words are used by Isidore and later authors. Cassiodorus says there are many books in both Greek and Latin on astronomy (of which Ptolemy's are the most important) including handy tables of positions and so forth, but apart from Ptolemy he names no authorities, nor does he suggest that there are any translations into Latin of Greek books.[44] He admits the usefulness of *astronomia* to navigators and farmers, but then warns (vii.4): 'But the other things which go

[44] That he does not mention Latin books (other than Varro) is one piece of negative evidence against the view that there was a textbook of astronomy by Boethius. Boethius, who had preceded Cassiosorus as Theodoric's *magister officiorum*, was executed in 525 on suspicion of having plotted with Byzantium. He had set out to translate into Latin and comment on the works of Plato and Aristotle, but got no further before his death than the *Organon*, the logical works of the latter. In prison he wrote one of the most famous and widely read of all medieval books, the *Consolation of Philosophy*. Before that he had written textbooks on some of the liberal arts, using Greek sources, in the knowledge that the West would need Latin books when there was no longer any Greek. He certainly wrote a Geometry, an Arithmetic and a Music. Did he also write an Astronomy? For an affirmative answer there are four arguments. Cassiodorus in one of his letters written in 507 (*Variae* I.45, 3f) actually says: 'In your translations Pythagoras' Music and Ptolemy's Astronomy are read by the Italians, Nichomachus' Arithmetic and Euclid's Geometry are heard by western men.' Against this is the undoubted hyperbole of the letter's conclusion: 'and whatever arts and disciplines eloquent Greece produced in the works of individual men, Rome has received in clear Latin at your hand, yours only.' Secondly, there are occasional references in medieval library catalogues to works on astronomy along with or among Boethius' works – two at least seem clearly to refer to a work by Boethius (Becker, *Catalogi*, 1885, Nos 32 and 77), and one of them may be the book at Bobbio referred to in Gerbert's eighth letter. (I fear I cannot share the certainty of George Goold on p. cviii of his Loeb edition of Manilius that the reference is to Manilius.) But the attributions are neither absolutely certain nor textually always reliable, and there are many occasions and places where one might have expected to find Boethius' Astronomy if it had existed but where it is not. Thirdly there are the two very doubtful references in Gerbert's letters (Epp. 8 and 130). Lastly there is the stated intention of Boethius himself in his *Arithmetica*; but he died with so many unfulfilled intentions! The main argument against there having been a Boethian version of Ptolemy, besides the lack of reference in Cassiodorus' *Institutes*, is the total absence of any text or any clear citation of it. On the whole it must remain an unanswerable question, with the balance in favour of the Noes rather than the Ayes. It can safely be said that if it did ever exist it was never read or used by anyone in the early Middle Ages.

along with the knowledge of the constellations, that is, things pertaining to knowing men's fates, which are without any doubt contrary to our faith, ought to be so far unknown to us that they seem not even to have been written.' He goes on to refer to St Basil and St Augustine to support his condemnation of such astrology. He returns to the same theme in the immediately following Conclusion to the book, a very revealing passage: 'But some, charmed by the beauty of the constellations and their bright splendour, seeking out most zealously the very causes of their own perdition, rushed blindly into the study of the stars' motions so that they might believe themselves able to foreknow events by unlawful calculations.' He maintains that Plato and Aristotle as well as Scripture are against this, and that if anyone wants to know about 'the powers above' and the future he should read the Apocalypse of St John! But clearly in the second half of the sixth century there were still some who were tempted by the 'books of the astrologers' just as Augustine had been a century and a half before.

There may have been practising astrologers and real believers in the art in Spain among surviving Priscillianist heretics, though the evidence for actual astrological practices, apart from various magical activities, soothsaying and such-like, is very slender indeed.[45] At any rate by the time of Isidore astrology was really a matter of history. Isidore was Bishop of Seville after his brother Leander, in the Visigothic kingdom of Spain, from 602 until his death in 636. He is remembered especially for his *Origines* or *Etymologiae*, a vast twenty-book encyclopaedia of learning culled from other men's books which fills two volumes of the Oxford Classical Texts.[46] Its title is accurate: the names of all the topics, and hosts of words not forming separate topics, are furnished with 'etymologies' only very rarely and quite accidentally correct. We have already noted (Chapter II, p. 19) how Isidore needed, because there were two words, *astronomia* and *astrologia*, to make some distinction. Many later medieval authors felt the same compulsion – if there are two terms, they must denote two things – and either followed Isidore or produced different, sometimes quite contrary, definitions. The natural tendency, given their respect for words and 'etymology', was to take the *nomos* bit of *astronomia* to refer to law or custom (the meaning of the Greek), and the *logos* part of *astrologia* to mean reason, account, and thus make almost precisely the opposite distinction to that we now make. The essential point is that no one in the Middle Ages or for centuries after made *any* real

[45] See the somewhat unconvincing case in J. Fontaine's 'Isidore de Séville et l'Astrologie', *Revue des Etudes Latines*, XXXI (1953) 271ff.
[46] Ed. W. M. Lindsay (1911).

distinction between what we call astronomy and what we call astrology: they were simply complementary aspects, theoretical and practical, of the same art, as they had been for Ptolemy. The distinction drawn by Christians was not made on theoretical, scientific grounds, but simply against superstition, against anything which derogated from the omnipotence of God or the freedom of man. Astrology is simply part of *astrologia* (or *astronomia*); but there is some *astrologia* which is not lawful for Christians.

The result of this is that although one could learn very little astrology from Isidore's encyclopaedia, in an important way it contributed to astrology's future. Isidore was bound to treat *astrologia* in his work, which began, naturally enough, with the liberal arts. Much of what he says is taken literally from Cassiodorus, and the rest is equally third hand, so that much ancient lore is preserved, without any great understanding. In the course of his *sphaera*, his description of the heavens (in Book III), Isidore produces the standard account of comets as signifying 'pestilence or famine or war' and adds the interesting detail that it was 'the Stoics' who classified them under more than thirty different types 'the names and effects of which certain *astrologi* have written about'. On the names of the signs of the zodiac Isidore indulges in some very fanciful 'explanations'; it might not be unfair to quote his ideas on Cancer (III.71, 26 – entire): 'Cancer they call so because when the sun comes into that sign in June, it turns back after the manner of a crab and makes the days shorter. For that animal has an indistinguishable front end, and in fact moves in both directions, so that the front becomes the back and the back the front.' Isidore is brief and definite on a question on which ancient and medieval astronomers were divided, that of the stars' and planets' light (III.61: *De lumine stellarum*, on the light of the stars – entire): 'The stars are said not to have their own light but to be illuminated by the sun, like the moon.'

Book VIII is 'On the Church and the Synagogue, on Religion and Faith, on Heresies, on Philosophers, Poets, Sybils, Magi and Pagans and their gods.' In Chapter 9 of that book, 'On Magi', is a section on *astrologi* (22–27): '*Astrologi* are so called because they make predictions from the stars (*astri*). *Genethliaci* are named thus because they consider the dates of birth, for they draw up the births (*geneses*) of men round the twelve signs of the heavens and attempt to predict the characters of those born and what they will do and suffer from the courses of the stars. These are commonly called *Mathematici* ... but these same interpreters of the stars were at first called *Magi*, like those in the Gospel who announced the birth of Christ; after that they were known only by the other name, *mathematici*. The knowledge of that art was allowed down to the Incarnation (*usque ad evangelium fuit concessa*), on condition that once Christ had come into the world no one from then on should interpret anyone else's birth by consideration of the heavens. Horoscopes are so called because they look at the hours of the births of men in the light of the different fates involved.' There is here no suggestion that astrology is mistaken, that it does not work, that it is empty superstition: only that it is no longer allowed. The conscientious early medieval, Christian, student – monk or priest or layman – who might otherwise never have known about astrology, apart from the quacks at fairs along with all the other magicians and conjurors, was bound, if he was interested enough to read Isidore, or indeed most of the commentators on St Luke's account of the Star of Bethlehem, not to be left with a simple and acceptable miracle, but to be introduced to the fascinating but illicit subject of astrology. The idea, at least, of a potentially valid science of astrology was kept alive by the very authorities who condemned it.

But not by the most popular and the greatest of the scientific authorities of the Middle Ages, Bede (673–735). Known to most of us as the author of the superb *Ecclesiastical History of the English Nation*, Bede also wrote a large number of commentaries on Scripture, and textbooks, including the most important Latin works on the reckoning of time and on the *computus*. Nowhere in any of his work is there any astrology; even the Star of the Magi only calls for a brief comment as symbolising that art of prophecy in which the Magi, as successors of Balaam, were skilled enough to know that a great prophecy had been fulfilled. Just as his *Ecclesiastical History* made acceptable and normal the Dionysian reckoning of years from the supposed date of the Incarnation, which Bede explained and argued for in the *De Temporum Ratione* and used in the annals in that book; so his methods for working out dates, and in particular for finding the date of Easter, on which the other movable feasts in the Church's calendar depend, became standard, until the Reformation, at least. Bede was, for the Middle Ages, *the* authority on the calendar and the *computus*.

What was this *computus*? The Latin word means reckoning, or computation; but in the special sense in which medievalists use it, it has no translation, and is best left as it is in Latin. In the words of a modern editor of Bede's works on time and the calendar, C. W. Jones:[47] '*Computus* ... denoted a body of knowledge and its art, a department in the curriculum, and all or part of the text-book codex which

---

[47] In his *Baedae Opera de Temporibus* (Cambridge, Mass., 1943) which gives an account of the development of the *computus* to the eighth century, and of the complicated details of dating equinoxes and new moons. See also W. E. van Wijk, *Le Nombre d'Or: Etude de chronologie technique, suivi du texte de la Massa Compoti d'Alexandre de Villedieu avec traduction et commentaire* (The Hague, 1936).

contained it.' The art was that of computing the calendar, and especially the date of Easter. Why should anyone want to calculate the calendar, or such a well-known date? Because there were no almanacs, no calendars on the walls, no clocks. Time-reckoners there were: hour-glasses and marked candles and even perhaps *clepsydrae*, water-clocks. But these measured *how long*; they did not tell you *when*. You cannot tell the time from an egg-timer, unless you know precisely *when* you turned it over; and when, in the ages before clocks and watches, was different. It is very difficult, but absolutely essential, for the modern student of the ancient and the medieval world to make the mental effort needed to understand how men thought and lived and organised their lives when there were no clocks and no calendars; when the time and the date meant something very far from what they mean to us. Time – hours, days, months, years – was not figures or names, but natural, visible even: the positions of the sun and of the moon.

> Whan that Aprille with his shoures sote
> The droghte of Marche hath perced to the rote ...

So Chaucer begins the Prologue to the *Canterbury Tales*; and when was this? When ... 'the yonge Sonne/ hath in the Ram his halfe cours y-ronne.' And how would you know when that was? You might have on the church or town hall a zodiac sun-dial, such as can be seen on the wall of the Royal Observatory at Greenwich. Then the shadow of the sun at midday would tell you where the sun was in the zodiac – when he had run half his course through the Ram, Aries, at the beginning of April, for example.[48] Such dials go back at least to the second century B.C. and were still being erected in the eighteenth century.[49] And what of the time? We can again get a good idea from Chaucer:

> Our Hoste sey wel that the brighte sonne
> Th' arc of his artificial day had ronne
> The fourthe part, and half an houre, and more;
> And though he were not depe expert in lore,
> He wist it was the eightetethe day
> Of April, that is messager to May;
> And sel wel that the shadwe of every tree

---

[48] There is a difficulty here, in that it is elsewhere implied that the Pilgrimage started in mid-April, not at the beginning of the month. See Chauncey Wood, quoted in note 50, pp. 161ff.
[49] See Sharon L. Gibbs, *Greek and Roman Sundials* (Yale, 1976) 94.

Was as in length the same quantitee
That was the body erect that caused it.
And therefor by the shadwe he took his wit
That Phebus, which that shoon so clere and brighte,
Degrees was five and fourty clombe on highte;
And for that day, as in that latitude,
It was ten of the clokke, he gan conclude,
And sodenly he plighte his hors aboute.

(Beginning of the Man of Law's Tale)

Length of shadows and the height of the sun in the daytime, then; and the positions of the stars at night; these told you the time. Night-time too, for the monks needed to know when to say the night office, and lists of stars were set out to help them.[50]

Time was natural, months and seasons fitted into agricultural life; the calendar superimposed on this pattern was that of the Church, the succession of feasts and fasts that made the liturgical and working year. Many of these feasts were fixed – Christmas, the Annunciation, saints' days, and so on – but the greatest feast, Easter, and all that depended on it – Ash Wednesday and Lent, for example, or Pentecost – were, and are, movable. That is, they occur on different dates from year to year. The fixing of the date of Easter was a complicated problem. Usually in the early Middle Ages the date was promulgated from Rome, taken in the letters and safe-conducts carried by priests returning from the City, but it was often necessary for local bishops to do the job for themselves, and the clergy needed to understand the business, so the *computus* became part of the curriculum. Along with the *computus* went the necessity for astronomy as a liberal art. And although Bede himself avoided nearly all astrology – even he says that the study of the stars can help with weather forecasting – his successors could not always resist the temptation to warn the student off 'the folly of the wise men of old' who thought that 'man got his spirit from the Sun, his body from the Moon, his intelligence from Mercury' and so on.[51]

---

[50] See for example a sixth century work in *MGH Scriptorum Rerum Merovingiarum*, I, 2: *De cursu stellarum*, ed. B. Krusch (1885) 854ff. For some interesting observations on Chaucer and astronomy see 'Kalenderes Enlumyned Ben They: some astronomical themes in Chaucer', by J. D. North, *Review of English Studies*, NS XX (1969) 129ff and 418ff; and also Chauncey Wood, *Chaucer and the Country of the Stars* (Princeton, N.J., 1970); and the note by Frank D. Gilliard, 'Chaucer's Attitude to Astrology', in *Journal of the Warburg and Courtauld Institutes*, XXXVI (1973) 365–6.
[51] *Byrhtferth's Manual (A.D. 1011)*, ed. S. J. Crawford, EETS 177 (1929) p. 130. It is just possible that some 'scratch dials' on church walls which face east or west were calendar, not time, dials.

The full calendar with all the feasts and their proper prayers was set out in the breviary, the priest's prayer book for his private devotion, the Office (his duty, *officium*). In the later Middle Ages, developing from the ninth to the fifteenth century, similar books were compiled for devout lay men and women. They began in the ninth century as the 'Little Office of the Blessed Virgin Mary', a collection of private devotions to Our Lady set out in eight parts corresponding to the canonical 'hours', *horae*, of services: Matins, Lauds, Prime, Terce, Sext, None, Vespers and Compline. Such books were consequently called 'Books of Hours', and from the twelfth century on they gathered not only more psalms and prayers but also a calendar, and became what has been called 'the breviary of the laity'. The first half of the fifteenth century was the great age for the illustrations of these books of hours, the best known being those of the Duke of Berry. The calendar illustrations from his *Très Riches Heures* are often used to illustrate books on astrology: but despite the signs of the zodiac, they are purely calendrial. They contain all that is needed to tell the date from the state of the heavens, and have nothing directly to do with astrology at all. The same is true of zodiac pictures in the stained glass of churches and cathedrals, and of signs carved in stone or wood on arches or tympana or misericords. They are to do with time, with the year, and when, as at Vézélay, for example, they surround Christ in the tympanum of the central doors, their function is exactly what it had been round Mithras. They signify that Christ is Lord of time, of the year; they do not indicate an invasion of the Church by astrology.[52]

There was indeed before the twelfth century nothing more than a faint memory of a lost, and illicit, art flickering in the minds of those with a genuine interest in astronomy awakened partly by the *computus* and largely by the simple fascination of the night sky and the seasons, so much more regularly and consciously observed in those clockless centuries. They were, broadly, the centuries of monastic culture. Bede was a monk in the Benedictine house founded by Benedict Biscop at Jarrow. In Northumbria, converted from Ireland, the learning preserved in the Irish schools and that brought from Rome by Benedict Biscop fused into a tradition which, established at the cathedral school

---

[52] There is, of course, some astrology in the *Très Riches Heures*, which was written in the fifteenth century, after the revival of the art. It is not however in the calendar but in the 'zodiacal man' which is so often reproduced. It is actually derived from medical astrology, and for it and its like see Harry Bober, 'The Zodiacal Miniature of the Très Riches Heures of the Duke of Berry – its Sources and Meaning', *Journal of the Warburg and Courtauld Institutes*, XI (1948) 1–34. On the matter of zodiacs in medieval sculpture etc., see James Fowler, 'On Medieval Representation of the Months and Seasons', in *Archaeologia*, XLIV (1873), 137ff, and A. Katzenellenbogen, *The Sculptural Programs of Chartres Cathedral* (Baltimore, 1959) (s.v. 'Zodiac' in Index).

of York by Bede's pupil Egbert, passed at the end of the eighth century with Alcuin of York to the continent, to inform Charlemagne's movement of educational reform and encouragement, the Carolingian Renaissance.

Charlemagne established his rule over most of continental western Europe south of Scandinavia except southern, Islamic, Spain. He desired, partly for genuinely pious reasons and partly from the need for a literate 'civil service' of clergy, that education (which was almost entirely in the hands of the clergy) should be revived after the ravages of centuries of invasion and war had reduced it to a perilously low condition.[53] He called to his itinerant court a number of scholars from Italy, Spain and England – Alcuin from York in about 781, who became not only his 'minister of education', as it were, but also his private tutor. Charlemagne was eager to learn, though he began too late to achieve real literacy. He did, says his biographer Einhard, learn grammar from Peter of Pisa, and the other arts from Alcuin: and he 'gave much time and labour to learning rhetoric and dialectic, and especially astronomy (astronomia); and he tried to learn the art of computus and with great curiosity and concentration sought to understand the course of the stars.' His interest in astronomy was obviously genuine: he caused to be made for himself a 'celestial table', a map of the heavens, in silver, which was, alas, too valuable to survive him long.[54] The result of his and his successors' exhortation and encouragement was less impressive than much written on the 'Carolingian Renaissance' suggests, but certainly there were more schools and scholars because of it. A line of 'academic descent', as it were, can be traced through such ninth century pupils of Alcuin and his generation as Rhabanus Maurus and Walafrid Strabo and Lupus of Ferrières, to Eric and Remi of Auxerre and Hincmar of Rheims, and on into the tenth century to Gerbert of Aurillac, also Archbishop of Rheims, who died in 1003 after nearly four years as Pope Sylvester II. The tenth

---

[53] In about 595 the Bishop of Cartagena wrote to Pope Gregory the Great (MGH Epistolarum, I, pt. 1, ed. Ewald (1887) 60): 'We are compelled by necessity to do what you say should not be done: you order that no uneducated man may be ordained. But pray consider whether perhaps it is not sufficient for a man to be called educated if he knows Christ Jesus and him crucified; if it is not enough, there will be none in this place who can be called educated: there will indeed be no priest, if none but the educated may be a priest.' Things certainly cannot have improved on the continent of Europe in the even darker years of the seventh century, not until the spread first of Irish and then Anglo-Saxon missionaries and the foundation of such houses of monks as Bobbio and St Gall, and the others which followed in the eighth century such as Reichenau and Fulda.

[54] F. N. Estey, 'Charlemagne's Silver Celestial Table', in Speculum, XVIII (1943) 112–117. It was probably modelled ultimately on late antique maps, like Muslim ones such as that on the vault of the eighth century castle of Qusayr 'Arma in the Transjordanian desert. Like the latter it would have been a planispheric projection, from the south, since Capricorn was the outside, largest, circle.

century also saw those movements of monastic reform, notably that of Odo of Cluny, which turned the monks back inward to their vocation and left the new learning to the cathedral schools such as Rheims and Chartres and Paris.

New learning? New indeed, from the Arabs. We must begin with that same Gerbert.[55] Not that he was ever a pupil of the Arabs, nor is there evidence of any Arabic influence in his work. It should not be said of him as it still is by some that he went to the Arabs for astrology. That tale begins in the early twelfth century with William of Malmesbury, who says:[56] 'There followed (sc. as Pope) Gerbert, of whom, I think, it will not be a waste of time to set down in writing what is heard on the lips of all.' Among the gossip is the 'fact' that Gerbert, after growing up as a monk of Fleury (which he did not), 'fled by night into Spain, longing especially to learn from the Saracens astrology and the rest of such arts'; and there he 'surpassed Ptolemy' in the astrolabe, Alchandreus (? Al-Kindi) on the distance of the stars, and Julius Firmicus on fate. A little later, William says Gerbert 'was first to bring the abacus from the Saracens, and gave rules for its use that are scarcely understood by abacists who sweat over them'.

The truth is less dramatic, but not less significant. In 967 the Count Borel of Barcelona, duke of the Christian Spanish march established by Charlemagne and his successor Louis, returned home from a journey to Rome (to get his bishop of Vich raised in dignity to archbishop) and Gerbert went with him. He went for the quadrivium, the 'mathematical sciences'. The Spanish march was Visigothic, and had re-established, after the expulsion of the Arabs, the old culture of Isidore, of Boethius and of Cassiodorus. Not only is there only the slenderest of evidence for Arabic culture there; the Arabic culture in the west itself, even in Andalusia, was poor enough for the Emir Al-Mansur of Cordova (from 976 to 1002) to send to the east for a tutor for his second son. The flowering of Islamic culture in Spain was not until the next century. It was really for 'mathematics', including and perhaps especially astronomy, that Gerbert went to Vich. And it was very elementary stuff. There are references in Letters 17 and 25 to a book 'On the multiplication and division of numbers' by a Joseph of Spain (neither book nor man is otherwise known), and we have seen how

---

55 On Gerbert d'Aurillac (or of Rheims) see F. Picavet, *Gerbert: un Pape Philosophe* (Paris, 1897); and his letters, edited by Fritz Weigle, in *MGH, Die Briefe der deutschen Kaiserzeit*, II (1966), or by J. Havet, *Lettres de Gerbert 983–997* (Paris, 1889). It is true that John of Gorze, a generation earlier, had gone to Arab Spain, to Cordova, but there is no evidence that he brought much back from his two years there; which is perhaps not surprising, as his pious biographer tells us he forsook the liberal arts for Holy Scripture in his youth on his Prior's instructions. See also J. W. Thompson, 'The Introduction of Arabic Science into Lorraine in the Tenth Century', in *Isis*, XII (1929) 184–193.

56 *De Gestis Regum Anglorum*, ed. William Stubbs (Rolls Series 90, 1887) I.194.

complicated William of Malmesbury much later thought Gerbert's instructions on abacus-reckoning were. There are two references to astronomy in the Letters. The short Letter 24 is to Lupitus of Barcelona asking for 'a book on *astrologia* translated by you'. If the book was actually an Arabic one on astronomy (*astrologia* and *astronomia* are completely synonymous for Gerbert as Letter 153 shows, where *astrologia* is used of Martianus Capella's book, two lines after a mention of *astronomiae subtilitates*), it seems certain that Gerbert never received it, for there is no trace of Arabic astronomy in his works. It was more likely a book on either the astrolabe or the armillary sphere. Gerbert certainly knew how to make, and made, a sphere with rings to represent the circles of the horizon etc.; Letter 134 to Remi, a monk of Trier, promises such a sphere in exchange for a copy of Statius' epic, the *Achilleis*. Gerbert mentions the difficulty involved in making it, and his biographer Richer refers (III.50) to the amazing way in which Gerbert and his sphere made this 'almost incomprehensible science' clear to his students. Letter 153 is on the varying length of the day and night and the *climata*, simply and without explanation, and is all from Martianus Capella. So Gerbert's astronomy and mathematics probably went no further than a grasp of the *sphaera* and of the armillary sphere (and *possibly* of the astrolabe), and of the abacus and its workings. This, which would have seemed elementary even to Isidore or Bede, seemed so startlingly advanced to Gerbert's contemporaries that the legends of his magical powers were invented and grew! Nevertheless he is symptomatic of, and probably through his teaching also partly the cause of, a revival of interest in *astrologia* in the late tenth and the eleventh centuries.

William of Malmesbury says (wholly wrongly) that Gerbert surpassed Julius Firmicus in matters concerned with fate. In another of his works he tells the story of Gerard, Archbishop of York, who died in May, 1108. Gerard, described as well-lettered and eloquent, was guilty 'whether truly indeed or merely according to unfettered rumour I cannot tell,' of many crimes of lust, and said to be in league with demons, 'for he used to read Julius Firmicus secretly in place of his afternoon devotions.' As a result of which and because they found a book of the evil art under his cushion when he died sitting in his garden, the canons refused to let him be buried within the minster church (whither he was transferred later by his successor Thomas, who was presumably either more enlightened or more charitable).[57]

---

[57] *Gesta Pontificum Anglorum*, ed. N. E. S. A. Hamilton (Rolls Series 52, 1870) 259. William's first edition was written in 1125; and a second, revised edition was issued in 1140, in which William removed what Hamilton calls 'offensive personalities', including this tale of Gerard. It looks a reliable story, however, even if 'hearsay', since William was writing only seventeen years after Gerard's death and leaves the account of the

Who was Julius Firmicus (to whom we have referred more than once already), that he should have been regarded as an authority in matters of fate, and be so disapproved of by the pious canons? A number of other pieces of evidence show that he was known of and being read in the late eleventh and early twelfth century. His name is mentioned as an astrological authority in the early twelfth century *Philosophia mundi* of Honorius (II.v; PL 172, 59B) – a work itself containing no astrology. The earliest extant manuscripts of Firmicus are of the eleventh century.[58] There is imitation of Firmicus in an anonymous English legal author of the early twelfth century, probably a servant of that same Archbishop Gerard.[59] Later in the century but before 1175 the Englishman Daniel of Morley disputed in Toledo with the translator Gerard of Cremona on the propriety of astrology; 'and to me Gerard said, "Have you read Julius Firmicus?" And I said I had'.[60] So Firmicus' *Mathesis* was certainly around in the late eleventh century.

It was written in the fourth century, possibly in 337 A.D. It has been left for consideration until now because there is no evidence of its being known before the eleventh century.[61] It is the last ancient Latin source, and its rediscovery, or the revival of interest in it, coincides with the arrival in the West of the first Greek learning from the Arabs. Julius Firmicus Maternus may have been a Sicilian, and some time after writing the *Mathesis*, his astrological textbook which now concerns us, he wrote in the late 340s *On the Error of Profane Religion*, against the mystery cults, to which he was probably opposed both as a Stoic-Neo-Platonist and as a Christian.[62] The title *Mathesis* is the Greek

---

extra-ecclesial burying in 1140. The tale is repeated by Higden in the fourteenth century in his *Polychronicon*; he identifies the book found under the cushion as Firmicus Maternus.

58 All references are to the Teubner text (see note 30) and for MSS see Vol. II Praef., p. v. See also Jean Rhys Bram, *Ancient Astrology: Theory and Practice* (Park Ridge, N.J., 1975), which is an English translation of Firmicus with an Introduction and some notes. Unfortunately the translation is frequently wrong and the notes avoid all the real difficulties.

59 See Firmicus, II, Praef., p. iv.

60 See Valentin Rose, 'Ptolemaeus und die Schule von Toledo', in *Hermes*, VIII (1874) 348–9. Firmicus was also named and quoted by Marbod of Rennes in the late eleventh century (*PL*, col. 1705), which suggests that his work was introduced into England from Normandy. (See 147 below).

61 W. H. Stahl says in the *Dictionary of Scientific Biography* (1971), 622, that it is mentioned by Sidonius Apollinaris in the late fifth century – and indeed in the Budé text of his Carmen XXII, Firmicus Maternus is named in the prefatory epistle. But the name only occurs in a single MS and is almost certainly an eleventh century addition to the two names already there. It is not included in either the Teubner or *MGH* texts, though Mohr, the 1895 Teubner editor, had doubts.

62 Th. Mommsen, 'Firmicus Maternus', in *Hermes*, XXIX (1894) 468–472; O. Neugebauer, 'The Horoscope of Ceionius Rufus Albinus', in the *American Journal of Philology*, LXXIV (1953) 418–420. The *De Errore Profanarum Religionum* was edited by A. Pastorino (2nd edn, Florence, 1969) and the identity of the authors of the two works, the *Mathesis* and

word μάθησις, meaning 'learning', in both the usual English senses; the Latin for it was *doctrina*. It meant at first learning in the Liberal Arts, especially in the quadrivium, the 'mathematical sciences'. Later its scope was restricted to *astrologia*. By the twelfth century a distinction had been established between *mathēsis* with a long ē in the middle, and *mathĕsis* with the accent on the first syllable and a short ĕ (the doubt over the quantity of the e is as old as Prudentius, and indeed the distinction of meanings may also go back to the fourth century). In Chapter 18 of Book II of his *Policraticus* John of Salisbury refers to the 'good *mathesis* which is pronounced with a short middle syllable, which nature induces, reason proves and practical utility approves', and the 'bad *mathesis*, pronounced with a long middle syllable': the first is true learning, the second vain superstition. Firmicus' work is, of course, on *mathēsis*. It has eight books, and is an ill-sorted compendium of interpretative detail which, as Stahl says, 'best represents popular traditions of the previous four centuries and bears little resemblance to Ptolemy's quasi-scientific manual of astrology, the *Quadripartitum*'.

Astrology consists of three parts: the mathematical-astronomical basis from which the chart is derived and which has to be understood to be able, for example, to dispute over the division into mundane houses; the astrological 'machinery' – aspects, decans, houses and so on, and all the agreed 'characteristics' of signs and planets; and interpretation – when the chart is made and the planets inserted and the aspects and so on listed, what does it all mean? For the first, astrologers used 'handy tables', with or without Arabic additions and refinements, and the sole mathematical basis lay in Ptolemy's *Almagest*. Firmicus' work, like that of almost all the Arabic and Latin astrologers of the Middle Ages, takes all that for granted and proceeds straight to the second and third, with, more often than not, a preface like Ptolemy's in defence of astrology. Book I of the *Mathesis* is such a preface. The second book runs through the preliminary classifications of signs, planets, houses and so forth; Book III deals with the relations between the macro- and the micro-cosm, the *thema mundi* and the effects of each planet on its own and in conjunction with Mercury. Book IV treats of the moon, the Lot of Fortune and various refinements

---

the *De Errore*, was established by Clifford H. Morre in a dissertation published at Munich in 1896, *Julius Firmicus Maternus, der Heide und der Christ*, to which very little has since been added. It is usually said (without evidence) that Firmicus was converted to Christianity in the interval between the 'pagan' *Mathesis* and the later Christian work. It may indeed be so, but it is by no means impossible that he was always a Christian. There is plenty of evidence for the mixture of paganism and Christianity in the minds of men of the fourth (or twentieth) century, and perhaps Firmicus needed to assert his Christianity after the kind of reception his *Mathesis* most likely received.

such as 'empty' and 'full' places and masculine and feminine degrees! The next book returns to the effects of the Horoscope (the ascendant), and of the planets in individual signs, and Book VI deals with aspects and interpretation concerning such particular topics as marriage, slaves and so on. Book VII continues in the same vein, being, says Stahl, 'marked by undue attention to sexual and moral deviates' (but so perhaps is the last book of the *Quadripartitum*). Book VIII purports to be a *sphaera barbarica*, the Egyptian description of the heavens. In all this, the mechanics are mostly the same as in other astrologers, Greek or Arabic, and the interpretation has certain consistencies running through the idiosyncracies of the author's personal choices. The whole is jumbled and without any very clear organisation, and Firmicus Maternus succeeds in being even more complicated, ambiguous and muddled than Manilius – of whom he was certainly not ignorant even if he does not mention the name but actually says (*Praef.* Book II) that no one had written on astrology in Latin except for some bits of translation by Julius Caesar (?) and by Cicero (presumably his Aratus), thus claiming to be the first in the field.

There is no need to go to any length to illustrate Firmicus Maternus' complications and muddle. Anyone feeling the need for examples might look at what he says about *chronocratores*, 'lords of times', in Books II and VI, or rising times, or *dodecatemoria*, or the *dator vitae* in the same Book II.[63] He preserves some of the older confusions, with relics of the *octatopos* and the muddle over *locus* and *signum* (II.14 and 16), and by insisting frequently and finally that *every* scrap of 'information' must be used in the interpretation, multiplies confusion, and of course ambiguities! For example, if one adds up all the various references, there are 114 degrees of the zodiac in which Mars is 'at home'. His understanding of the mathematics is fairly rudimentary. He often seems to be assuming that the quadrants – ascendant to *medium caeli* and so on – are all equally ninety degrees. It is indeed typical late antique astrology compiled by a man who was not being entirely conventional, merely using a familiar literary *topos*, when he wrote (*Proemium* 8): 'I have but a modest intellect and poor power of expression, and, I must truly confess, little astrological knowledge.' However, there are two or three peculiarities of Firmicus' worth dwelling on.

---

[63] Book II, c.25 should be read with Book IV, cc.18 and 19; Firmicus is thoroughly confused about the *dator vitae*, the 'giver of life', and the *dominus geniturae*, the 'lord of the nativity' – sometimes they are synonymous, sometimes not, and there is more than one meaning for each. There is a quite spurious clarity about his setting out of alternative views in IV.19.

Chapter 29 of Book II is headed 'On *antiscia*' (*sc. signa*). By this Firmicus seems to mean 'reflections', since he says that Antiochus explained them by saying that since Libra cannot 'see' Aries because of the earth in between, 'as it were by a mirror it is related by reflections', each sign or degree both reflecting the other of its pair and being reflected by it. Our author may have invented the term or at least first deliberately used it in this sense.[64] But he did not invent the notion, the relationship. As he says, Ptolemy has it; though he seems to have been wrong about Dorotheus. Firmicus' *antiscia* are Ptolemy's βλέποντα, 'regarding' or 'looking at' one another (*Tetr.*, I.15). Ptolemy explains that degrees equidistant from the tropical signs, Cancer and Capricorn, are equal in power, and as usual gives reasons why. Firmicus merely pairs off the signs and the degrees without explanation but the result, though long-winded, is the same. Virgo 17, for example, is given by Firmicus' calculus as reflecting Aries 13; and both are 76° from 1 Cancer, and so fit into Ptolemy's scheme. The use and importance of these reflections for Julius Firmicus are illustrated by a birth-chart and its interpretation. It is the nativity of Ceionius Rufius Albinus and can be dated to 14 March, 303 A.D. The analysis keeps Firmicus busy for four pages of the Teubner text. It emerges from this that *antiscia*, degrees and signs, can substitute for one another, so that a planet at Virgo 17 not only has all the effects and aspects and so on it has because it is there, but also all the effects, aspects etc., which it would have at Aries 13, its 'reflection' behaving exactly as it does itself.[65]

---

[64] Jean Rhys Bram in the Glossary to her translation (pp. 333ff) has: '*Antiscia*: Sometimes known today as Mundane Parallax. Relation between degrees or signs equidistant from the MC or the IMC. A rare kind of aspect especially favoured by F., who seems to have invented the term for it.' By 'Mundane Parallax', Mundane Parallel is presumably meant, but that, being generally concerned with planetary positions, has nothing to do with *antiscia*; which are not equidistant from the MC or the IMC but from the tropical signs; nor is 'it' a rare aspect, but they are in a permanent relationship. But the rest of the note is fair. The Greek word meant 'casting shadows in the opposite direction' – or at least it could mean that – and the word was used at the end of the fourth century by the Latin historian Ammianus in just this sense, of antipodeans. Only in Firmicus has it this meaning, 'reflection', which is a reasonable derived meaning from the Greek: things in mirrors do cast shadows in the opposite direction.

[65] See O. Neugebauer, *op. cit.* note 62 above. The details given by F.M. are: Sun in Pisces, Moon in Cancer, Saturn in Virgo, Jupiter in Pisces ('at the same degree as the Sun'), Mars in Aquarius, Venus in Taurus and Mercury in Aquarius ('in the same degree as Mars'). He begins the analysis as follows: 'The father of the subject of this birthchart ... was exiled, and he himself was exiled for adultery ... Now anyone knowing nothing of the calculation of reflections, noticing that the Sun and Jupiter are in the same position in the fifth house from the Ascendant, that is, the House of Good Fortune, would declare that the father was rich and fortunate and powerful, and other such about the subject himself; and would be unable to declare anything of his exile and troubles, unless he transferred his attention to calculating the reflections. You remember we said that Pisces cast reflections in Libra in Pisces. So the Sun and Jupiter together in

The student astrologer reading Firmicus' Latin will stumble, in-evitably, on the strange word he finds at the end of the first chapter of Book V: *myriogenesis*. 'Now, Lollianus, my honoured friend, I do not want you to expect to see *myriogenesis* in these books ... For now everything must be learned step by step, for we cannot reach *myriogenesis* by any other way except that our minds have first grasped the secrets of the beginnings of the art.' Now should the student be a modern one, he may look the word up. If he thinks, rightly, that it is a Greek word, and consults Liddell and Scott, he will be told, with reference to two passages of Firmicus, that it means 'the signs that rise with Pisces' (*sic!*). If he then, rightly again, feels that this is nonsense, and turns to Lewis and Short's Latin Dictionary, he will read, with a reference only to Firmicus 8.18, that it means 'multiple generation'; which indeed from its roots it might, but which makes little sense of our text.[66] So what is *myriogenesis*? From all the passages in Firmicus it emerges that it was the title of a work (in thirteen books?) by 'Aesculapius', who was instructed by Mercury (that is, Thoth, the Egyptian god); that the work was concerned with 'expounding all birth-charts by the single minutes (of the zodiac) without adding any planet' (V.1, 36); and that Firmicus in Book VIII is presenting a sort of elementary *myriogenesis*, with single degrees instead of minutes (VIII.18ff). So what we have is an account of the meaning and influence of each degree (or even each minute in 'Aesculapius') of the zodiac, irrespective of signs and planets; and this is derived from Egypt, as the mention of Mercury (and in one or two places, Anubis) and the context of the *sphaera barbarica* indicate. It looks as though the origin is the list (non-astrological) of 360 lucky and unlucky days of ancient Egypt; when these become degrees of the zodiac, one degree equals one day, and one minute of arc equals twenty-four minutes of time, so that a man's fate could be determined to some extent by the exact minute of his birth, 10.20 and 10.50, for example, being more than 1' apart. All this may sound a little fantastic, but Chapter XXIII of Alan Leo's popular *Astrology for All* (1910) is headed: 'The Character and Destiny of each Degree of the Zodiac' and has lists beginning: 'Aries: 1° – Positive, forceful, uncontrollable; creates own destiny. 2° – Enterprising ...' and so on right through the 360°, sign by sign. So in a sense *myriogenesis* does mean 'countless births' – 21,600 if each minute

---

Pisces cast reflections in Libra, in the sign in which it (the Sun) is humbled and depressed, and in the twelfth house of the chart, that is, of Evil Daemon; which shows the father to be of base family and decrees a notorious exile for him.' And so on, finding evil predicted by the *antiscia* of the signs of the other planets also.
66 The Thesaurus says the same: *generatio innumerabilis*; but the Latin could bear a meaning closer to the correct one than the English 'multiple generation'.

of arc is counted! – but in the sense of 'countless birth-times'; it is probably better left in the 'Greek'.[67]

Lastly, there is the astrologically most interesting part of the *Mathesis*, Book VIII, the *Sphaera barbarica*. Firmicus himself gave the book that title, at the end of Book VII: 'Now that we have explained all these things, let all our efforts be turned to expounding the *sphaera barbarica*.' The phrase referred in antiquity to any non-Greek description of the heavens, and usually to the Egyptian pattern of constellations. There is, however, more to Mathesis VIII than that.[68] At the end of the first chapter the author lists the intended contents of the book: that is, all that has been left out of earlier books, except *myriogenesis*, which he again says he is postponing. In the order in which he gives the contents they run as follows; the actual order of treatment is given by the chapter references in brackets. First, signs 'seeing' and 'hearing' each other (c.3); the 'measures of degrees' – that is, the size of the zodiac (end of c.4); where in the heavens to find each degree of the signs (c.4); and what the effect is of the ninetieth degree, 'called by the Greeks *enenecontameris*' (c.2). 'And so when all this is set out we may the more easily approach the *sphaera barbarica* and learn the effective power of the brighter stars.' Chapters 5–17 in fact are concerned with the *paranatellonta*, the stars rising with the signs of the zodiac, in order, beginning with the assertion that this kind of astrology was unknown to 'many Greeks and all Romans', and undiscovered by Petosiris and Nechepso: a piece of flagrant dishonesty since these chapters are based on Manilius V.[69] The uncritical copying of 'authorities' is demonstrated by the different rising times of some of these fixed stars given in later chapters of this same book, derived from another source. And whether any of this really belonged to a *sphaera barbarica* is now beyond establishing: the Greeks themselves were not clear what was Greek and what was Egyptian or from some other tradition.[70]

---

[67] The footnote in the Teubner text to III.1, 2: 'μοιρογένεσις Salmas.535' etc., refers to Claude de Saumaise's *De annis climactericis* of 1648, where he says that the word was corrupted to μυριογένεσις by Firmicus; but it is possible that *myriogenesis* referred to calculations involving minutes, *moirogenesis* to those involving degrees.

[68] On Firmicus' misuse of this title for all that he crams into his last book, see Houseman, *Manilius*, V.xlff.

[69] On which it may be worth quoting Houseman's remark that 'some of his statements are statements made by competent astronomers in other climes and times, but no competent astronomer ever or anywhere made them all'. Firmicus like Manilius before him has no idea of astronomy, but follows his source books blindly.

[70] Firmicus' own confusion is shown plainly in Book II, c.2, where he writes: 'The Egyptians call these planets by different names from those used by us and the Greeks: what we call Saturn, the Egyptians call Faenon, our Jupiter is the Egyptians' Faethon', and so on, giving the ancient Greek names, with 'f' for 'ph', which are later replaced by

Chapter 18, entire, runs: 'Now I shall concentrate on the subsequent parts of the *sphaera barbarica*, which to some extent are similar to the *myriogenesis*: for what *myriogenesis* says about single minutes of arc, we shall set out about single degrees. So the exact reading of the ascendant is to be set down, so that the true degree ascertained by skilled calculation may cause the *apotelesma* (the interpretation of the influences) to be set out properly. If it is done in any other way, the whole of what may be forecast is clouded with faults and falsehoods. So now, beginning with Aries, let us set out the powers of the single degrees and their astrological meanings according to the *Sphaera barbarica*.' Chapters 19–30 then tell us the astrological significance of each degree of each sign, beginning with Aries: 'Those who have their ascendant in the first degree of Aries, if they are favoured by the rays of benevolent planets, will be born kings and leaders, always leading their armies successfully. Those who have their ascendant in the second degree of Aries will be persistent thieves who always use unnecessary and extraordinary violence in their attacks; such as keep shifting their residence to places where they are not known. Now if Mars affects this degree, their ascendant, and the Moon aspects it in square or opposition, these crimes will be detected and they will be publicly punished.' Which shows how important it could be to be very accurate about the degree of the ascendant! The mind boggles at the idea of this sort of thing being set out for every *minute* of the zodiac. At any rate, we have had, despite the expressed intention to keep it for another time, a sort of poor man's *myriogenesis*, though Firmicus includes consideration of planetary influence which should really not be there.

Only two other things in Book VIII call for remark, the 'nonagesimal' and the 'seeing' and 'hearing' signs (Chapters 2 and 3). Firmicus says that the *enenecontameris*, 'that is, the ninetieth degree', was unknown to most astrologers, only briefly dealt with by a few, and deliberately kept secret by Petosiris. It is, however, of great importance since 'from these (ninetieth) degrees the end of life, death, misfortune, dangers and happiness and the whole substance of the nativity is gathered.' The two nonagesimals, 90° angles, are the one from the ascendant and the one from the Moon's position. One should consider whether they are in good or bad places and aspects, under good or bad rulers, and so on. So, he repeats at the end of the chapter, 'you will find the kind of death, the order of life, and the whole nativity.' Only the first of these, the nonagesimal from the ascendant, is now used at all in

'the star of Saturn' etc., and finally just by the gods' names, as Firmìcus found them in his late sources. But it really has nothing to do with 'Egypt', except perhaps Greek Alexandria.

birth-charts: it is still so called, and is the cusp of the tenth house in the Equal House system, being 'at any time of the day the highest degree of the ecliptic in the heavens' (M. E. Hone). Firmicus may have derived the idea of the importance of the nonagesimal partly from the notion that the quadrants were all of ninety degrees. That he dealt with the nonagesimal separately from the ascendant at all suggests that he was aware that that point was not always the *medium caeli*; but not necessarily, for he was quite capable of both repetition and inconsistency. There is however the idea of unequal quadrants also in c.15 of Book II, where he writes: 'The *medium caeli* is the tenth sign from the ascendant, but sometimes, in terms of degrees, the *medium caeli* is found in the eleventh sign.' So, if one is working only with whole signs – and not only are many late Greek horoscopes simply expressed in terms of signs, with no degrees given, but most of Firmicus' own interpretations are the same: 'if the Moon is in the tenth place from the ascendant, that is, in the *medium caeli* ...' (III.13, 9), and so on – if the chart is simply plotted in signs, the tenth from the ascendant sign is the *medium caeli*: if the ascendant is Libra, the *medium caeli* is Cancer. But, says Firmicus, if you are working in degrees, the *medium caeli* may be a degree in the eleventh sign from the ascendant. By 'sign' here he must mean 'house', for he goes on: 'So that you may get this clear, count from the degree of the ascendant through the following signs 270 degrees, and the 271st, wherever it is, is the *medium caeli*.' Now if *signum* meant 'sign' – and all signs are thirty degrees – this would still be in the tenth sign; but if it means 'house', and the quadrants are unequal, then the 271st degree from the ascendant could be in the eleventh 'sign', i.e. house. Four chapters later in the book, however, he describes the twelve houses as exactly equivalent to signs, each of thirty degrees.

Chapter 3, which follows that on the nonagesimals, is one of the most curious and most muddled in the whole of the *Mathesis*. It is about 'seeing' and 'hearing' signs. 'Seeing' originally meant 'casting rays upon', and was derived from the very common theory of vision according to which the eye sends out rays to 'grasp' the object. 'Hear' meant 'obey, listen to'; the two Greek words used and the Latin *audire* have both meanings. The basic idea, then, is the emission and reception of influence. Precisely the same is behind 'aspect', the Latin *aspectus* meaning 'seeing'. On signs which 'see' and 'hear' one another, most ancient authorities are in agreement.[71] But Firmicus'

[71] Signs equidistant from the tropical signs Cancer and Capricorn 'see' one another, those equidistant from the equinoctial signs Aries and Libra 'hear' each other; seeing and hearing having become mutual influences, it seems, though there is confusion over 'commanding' signs – a notion surviving long enough to be discounted as 'fanciful' rather than logical by a modern astrologer (Sepharial's *New Dictionary of Astrology* (1921)

chapter is quite different, and incredibly muddled. Some of this must have been due to the scribes who copied an incomprehensible chapter, but not all. For example: 'Aries sees and hears Cancer equally. Cancer does not see Aries but hears him. Taurus both sees Leo and hears him equally, and similarly Leo Taurus. Gemini see Virgo and hear her a little, Virgo sees Gemini a little and very fully hears them. Cancer sees and hears Libra equally, but Libra does not see but hears Cancer. Leo neither hears nor sees Scorpio, but Scorpio sees and hears Leo equally.' And so on and on in the same disordered and contradictory fashion. However, if one tabulates the various *videt*s and *audit*s, it becomes apparent that Firmicus is drawing on two different systems, one of trigons and one of squares, as the Teubner editors note (p. 285); so that, moving in an anticlockwise direction in both cases, in the first case, according to trigons, Taurus sees Leo which hears him; Gemini see Virgo, who hears them, and so on; and in the second, according to squares, Taurus sees Virgo, and Gemini see Libra. The two systems are inextricably jumbled and modified, with some mistakes, and absolutely no account is offered as to what it might all mean. It is peculiar to Firmicus Maternus, and he says it is all excerpted 'from the books of Abraham', though there was almost certainly no astrological author of that name (but Vettius Valens did refer to 'books of Abraham' at CCAG, V.2, p. 71). Some astrological writings may have been attributed to the patriarch, who was generally credited with an important role in the transmission of astrology from Seth.[72] The relationships of trigons and squares are of course aspects,

---

93). Manilius, Ptolemy, Dorotheus and the later Rhetorius (*CCAG* I.155) all agree, as does Porphyry in his commentary on Ptolemy's *Tetrabiblos* (*CCAG* V.4.208), though he has a complication in that signs of equal rising times are equipollent, an idea possibly derived from one understanding of the (now slightly dubious) Greek of Ptolemy, *Tetr.*, I.15. At any rate, whatever the meanings of 'seeing' and 'hearing' the diagrammatic relationships are simple: the lines of seeing and hearing are parallels at right angles to each other:

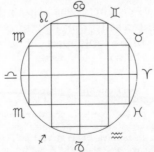

[72] 'Abraham' in later authors of the Middle Ages, when the Arabic sources have been used, often refers to Hipparchus, by a misunderstanding of the Arabic form of his name.

which are described and explained as normally elsewhere by Firmicus, and it looks as though he is here in Book VIII preserving a relic of an older day before the aspects and the 'seeing and hearing' signs separated.

It must be stressed that although Firmicus' work is long and very detailed, if confusing, nobody could actually have practised astrology with only the *Mathesis* to hand. To use the book at all one would have needed to be expert, to sort out his muddles; or unprincipled or stupid enough to ignore them. And one would have needed to possess and to understand a set of Tables and the rules for setting out a chart. There may have been some who could make a considerable impression on their more ignorant contemporaries with a bit of jargon culled from Augustine and Macrobius and a good dosing of Firmicus; but is there any evidence for such men before the late twelfth century? It is clear that the medical tradition, and perhaps herbals, preserved some *iatromathematica*, some of the astrology bound up with medicine; but although confusion of *astrologia* with astrology and the inference to the presence of astrology from descriptions or representations of the zodiac have led some to see astrologers where there were none, there is really no evidence for active practitioners of the art before the mid-twelfth century when Firmicus Maternus' *Mathesis* emerged from its obscurity.[73]

It was that half-understood farrago which poor Archbishop Gerard browsed through in his garden and which so horrified his clergy. The same book lay behind some of the anti-astrological chapter 6 of the 'Book of Ten Chapters' (in verse) of Marbod, Bishop of Rennes, about the end of the eleventh century.[74] He set out some 'doctrines', such as: 'Mars, in square aspect with Saturn, and with none of the good planets in aspect, makes men bold – gladiators, murderers, demoniacs, thieves, full of all kinds of lust,' which, he says, 'I remember I once read in the astrologers: Firmicus tries to prove all this with weak arguments but I think his *themata* are false.' As so often, however, the fascination of the erroneous doctrines was stronger than the force of their rejection or refutation. There was also undoubtedly a cumulative effect: the revival of interest in *astrologia* produced more interest in astrology (a perfectly respectable part of *astrologia* for all ancient

---

[73] Erwin Panofsky and Fritz Saxl, from an art history background, were long ago aware of the absence of astrology in the West in the earlier Middle Ages: 'The assimilation of Arabic knowledge brought to the Western countries not only a new conception of astronomy, medicine and other natural sciences, but also knowledge of astrology, which until the twelfth and thirteenth centuries was almost unknown, or at least not practised, in the West.' *Classical Mythology and Medieval Art*, Metropolitan Museum Studies IV.2 (1938) 241.

[74] *PL*, clxxi, cols 1704–1707.

authors), which provoked more caveats and repudiations, which awakened and stimulated interest; and so on.

Certainly there was increasing curiosity concerning the quadrivium in general and *astrologia* in particular in the eleventh and early twelfth centuries, following the work and teaching of Gerbert and others. This curiosity had to work with the old Latin sources, and views of the universe were mainly derived from Macrobius and Boethius, with a strong vein of Platonic cosmology from the *Timaeus* running through the whole. Alongside this purely Latin revival there grew the awareness that there was more to be had from the Muslim world to the south, particularly in the Mathematical arts. At the beginning of the twelfth century, Guibert of Nogent in his history of the First Crusade could write, of the prognostications of the fall of Jerusalem: 'The knowledge of the stars is as poor and rare in the west as it is flourishing through constant practice in the east, where indeed it originated.'[75]

But the revival was slow in its effects. Despite the occasional mention of Firmicus and Ptolemy (a bit of twelfth century 'name-dropping' very often) there is really no astrology in such well-known and widely read encyclopaedic writers as William of Conches, Hugh of St Victor or Honorius. What they have to say about the stars and about cosmology is derived from the same old Latin sources. For example, Hugh's *De eruditione docta*, Bk II, c.xi, deals with astronomy, *de astronomia*:[76]

The difference between astronomy and astrology is that astronomy is so called from the laws of the stars, and astrology is as it were discourse about the stars: *nomos* means law and *logos* means discourse. So it seems that astronomy deals with the laws of the stars and the turning of the heavens, the positions and circles, the courses and risings and settings of the constellations, and why each is called what it is. Astrology considers the stars with relation to the observation of birth and death and all sorts of other events, and is partly natural and partly superstitious. The natural part deals with corporeal things and their make-up, things which vary with the constitution of the heavens, such as health and sickness, storms and calm weather, fertility and

---

[75] *Gesta Dei per Francos*, VIII.8 (PL clvi, col. 816).
[76] PL clxxvi, col. 756. Hugh's dates are 1097–1141. Incidentally, on the word *mathesis* Hugh makes a different distinction from that which we saw made by John of Salisbury (p. 134 above), one also made by other writers: in the *De eruditione docta*, III, c. 4 (col. 753) he says that *matesis* with a *t* means *vanitas*, emptiness, and *mathesis* with *th* means *doctrina*, learning.

barrenness. The superstitious part is concerned with contingent events, and those falling under the free will, and this part the *mathematici* deal with.

Which is the whole of that chapter, and it obviously owes as much to Isidore as to any other source. In Book VI superstitious astrology, there called *horoscopia*, is linked with haruspicy and augury among the magic arts.

There was much magic about at this time, as there had no doubt been throughout the centuries before.[77] There was little distinction between magic and superstition and belief even in scholars' minds; or between paganism in its literary and mythological guises and aspects of Christianity such as the lives of saints, real and legendary, and the books of miracles and the tales used as *exempla* in sermons, many of ancient origin.[78] For the Middle Ages generally the Book of Nature *was* another book, a revealed 'scripture' of God's making, to be interpreted in a similar way to the Bible, having many layers of meaning, the 'literal', face value being far less important than the symbolic truths to be discovered in it. (A not too different remark might be made about Kepler, as we shall see.) 'Natural science' was 'natural philosophy', and it was all 'book' learning, from simple description through fantasy to alchemy and astrology and magic. Many old forms of divination were revived, or at least were more openly discussed and written about than in earlier times, the general aim being the discovery of the future. Among the products were the 'Books of Fate', giving sets of answers to certain questions, the 'correct' answer being selected in some random manner,[79] and such mixtures of geomancy and other

[77] See for example, P. Riché, 'La magie à l'époque carolingienne', in *Comptes Rendus de l'Académie des Instriptions et Belles Lettres*, Paris, 1973, pp. 127–138. Six royal ·decrees against magic in the sixty years from 789 to 850, with the condemnations of Rhabanus Maurus and Hincmar (though they are really only quoting Isidore), with positive evidence from Ps-Bede and Paschasius Radbert, show that magical practices were known to be going on, even at court. Though when Riché writes (p. 133): 'Enfin, la divination astrologique est très souvent utilisée. Mais, bien que magie et astrologie soient très liées, nous n'avons pas à aborder ici les croyances dans la toute-puissance des astres,' which is all he does say about astrology, it is only a truism plus an unsupported assertion, unjustifiably extending to earlier ages what is true of the twelfth and later centuries.
[78] On this see J. Seznec, *The Survival of the Pagan Gods*, trans. Barbara F. Sessions (New York, 1961) and *cf*. Chapter 2, 'The Magic of the Mediaeval Church', of Keith Thomas' splendid *Religion and the Decline of Magic* (London, 1971) – towards the end of the chapter he writes: 'The difference between churchmen and magicians lay less in the effects they claimed to achieve than in their social position, and in the authority on which their respective claims rested.'
[79] See T. C. Skeat, 'An early mediaeval *Book of Fate*: the *Sortes XII Patriarcharum*', in *Medieval and Renaissance Studies*, III (1954) 41ff: 'The structure of a "Book of Fate" remains unaltered whether the enquirer uses dice, a volvelle, geomancy or other methods for this purpose', (*sc*. selecting the 'number' of the answer).

'magics' as the *Experimentarius,* some of which may be attributable to Bernard Silvestris.[80] The geomancy of that little anthology is typically twelfth century and pre-Arab – the Arabic 'mansions' were surely much later additions.

Astrology hovered on the fringes of all this, becoming involved in ways very similar to those which drew it into herbalism and alchemy and numerology. Geomancy provided patterns of numbers for the planets and these patterns found themselves still attached to illustrations in astronomical textbooks, even if the artist or copyist had little understanding of them and sometimes got them wrong (see Plate III).[81] A book which is a mixture of many curiosities, and certainly was by Bernard Silvestris, is the *Cosmographia,*[82] a largely Platonic work including some astrology, written in the 1140s. There is much less astrology in this strange work than might at first appear, and the signs of the zodiac and so on are treated much more mythically and allegorically than *astrologice,* even in the *sphaera* in the first of the two books. How distant it all is from astrology proper, so to speak, is best seen in Bernard's characterisation of the planets in Book II, c.5 – mixtures of myth and *astrologia* in every sense.[83] But the new astrology

---

[80] M. B. Savorelli, 'Un manuale di geomanzia presentato da Bernardo Silvestre da Tours (xii secolo): L'Experimentarius', in *Rivista critica di storia della filosofía,* 14 (1959) 283ff (incl. text); and Ch. S. F. Burnett, 'What is the *Experimentarius* of Bernardus Silvestris? A preliminary survey of the material', in *Archives d'Histoire Doctrinale et Littéraire du Moyen Age,* XLIV (1977) 79–125. See also note 82: Dronke has something on the *Experimentarius* (pp. 5–6).

[81] See Panofsky and Saxl, *op. cit.* note 73 above, 228ff. The illustrations to Michael Scot in Bodley 266 are copied from the Munich MS Cod. Monac. lat. 10268, of the mid-fourteenth century. The Arabs apparently took over from the Greek illustrations, kept the scientific aspects and ignored the foreign, Greek, mythological aspects, and so produced more accurate figures of the constellations with the stars marked correctly and marked according to magnitudes. Since the Arabic images were neither Classical nor contemporary European, the Latin illustrators left them alone and followed the text-descriptions to make contemporary images. The curious patterns of dots are the geomantic ones referred to in the text; in *Techniques of High Magic,* by Francis King and Stephen Skinner (London, n.d.), those here attached to Jupiter mean *acquisitio* and *laetitia,* 'gain' and 'happiness'. See also Fritz Saxl, 'Beiträge zu einer Geschichte der Planetendarstellungen im Orient und im Okzident', in *Der Islam,* III (1912), 151–177, esp. 165ff, 'Die okzidentalen Planetendarstellungen des spätern Mittelalters'.

[82] Ed. Peter Dronke, in Brill's *Textus Minores,* LIII (Leiden, 1978). See also Brian Stock, *Myth and Science in the Twelfth Century: A Study of Bernard Silvestris* (Princeton, N.J., 1972); though there is less astrology in the work than Stock sees there, and pp. 188–196 in particular should be read with a close eye to what Bernard actually says in his Latin text.

[83] For example, Urania and Natura on their way down through the spheres, come 'to the circle of Mars lying next beneath, and hear the murmuer of water as it were falling in a steep valley. When they were close enough to look properly, Natura recognised the river, from its dark, sulphurous banks, as Pirflegeton (fiery Phlegethon), a river flowing down from Mars' circle. But it happened that then the fiery one (Pirois) the star of Mars, was in his own proper sign, Scorpio, and being strong in his native powers was sending his threatening rays on to the fourth sign (*signum*) and the seventh and seeking the right

III Geomantic image of Jupiter copied from a fourteenth-century
illustrated text of Michael Scot
(Oxford, Bodleian Library MS Bodley 266 f. 197v)

was known, and by the 1140s translations from the Arabic were being circulated. John of Salisbury, who died as Bishop of Chartres in 1180, was aware of it, though there is no evidence he had read any of the new translations. His knowledge and his attitudes were typical of the mid-twelfth century, the end of the first 'renaissance', based only on the Latin sources, of which Abelard was the greatest representative in logic and theology. John's attitude to astrology in his *Policraticus* (especially Book II, c.19) is very much that of later churchmen: that the stars are signs, and signs not only of times but of physical processes and events, such as the weather and sicknesses; anything attributed to the stars which derogated from the omnipotence of God or the freedom of man was superstitious and dangerous. It was especially dangerous because it was based on natural, true foundations in *mathēsis*; but alas it led too frequently to *mathēsis*. Equally typically, in the passage where John is in fact taking such a line against 'judicial astrology', he presents the reader with a good deal of astrological detail, including the *thema mundi*, for example. The chief sources for it all are Macrobius and Augustine, with some Martianus Capella: John had done his homework. What his writing displays so clearly is that fundamental lack of distinction between astrology and astronomy (in the modern meanings), the acceptance of astrology, in fact, in all but those senses in which it seemed to introduce fate or other impersonal, non- divine causation. It is anachronistic to treat John of Salisbury, or any other medieval or Renaissance opponent of judicial astrology, as a modern sceptical philosopher or scientist before his time. He was no more a sceptic than the buyer of saints' relics in the market place, who also no doubt bought prognostications of all kinds. John was merely more aware of the theological implications of Isidore's distinctions.

Neither Adelard of Bath nor the Spaniard Gundissalinus (Domingo Gondisalvi), both John's contemporaries, was really concerned with astrology, though both were interested in science and belonged to the first generation of the translators who transmitted the ancient Greek learning from the Muslim cultures of Spain and Sicily to the schools of North-West Europe. Adelard indeed travelled in Muslim countries and himself translated in the 1120s the *Tables* and *Introduction to Astronomy* of Al Khwarizmi, the 'Smaller Introduction' (*Isagoge Minor*) of Abu Ma'shar, and in the 1130s a short astrological work of Thabit ibn

---

moment for a comet, a terrible, bloody long-tailed star, to appear from his circle. They were fearful of a region full of fury and seething with poisonous airs and hastened to fly over and out of it to reach the dwellings of the life-giving Sun' (Dronke, p. 130, §11). Notice that Bernard has the same confusion of signs an houses: the fourth house is the IMC and the seventh the setting point, both houses of death, disease and so on: only if Scorpio were the ASC could the fourth and seventh *signs* from Scorpio be intended here.

Qurra. But almost all of this, even the Abu Ma'shar, is really astronomical not astrological and Adelard is, like most similar twelfth century scholars, interested in all the sciences, which then included astrology.[84] Gundissalinus also translated works from the Arabic, including the *Metaphysics* of Avicenna and the *Fons Vitae* of Ibn Gebirol, and his *astrologia* is derived from Arabic sources.[85] But apart from the fact that he reverses the Isidorean distinction between *astronomia* and *astrologia* there is little of relevance to the history of astrology. In his work as in Adelard's astrology in our sense is included as part of the whole science without question. Almost the same might be said of the writings of another Englishman of the second half of the twelfth century, Daniel of Morley,[86] though there is more astrology there. His work was based on both the older Latin sources, including Firmicus, and Arabic writers like Abu Ma'shar and Al Fargani, whose works he studied at Toledo. He is among the first to introduce into Latin the lunar mansions, no doubt as a fascinating new piece of 'machinery'.

That astrology was accepted and practised in the late twelfth century is clear from the controversy which surround the various prophecies produced in anticipation of two eclipses and the conjunction of all the planets in Libra in 1186.[87] The chronicler Roger of Hoveden says: 'In that year, 1184, the astrologers, both Spanish and Sicilian – and indeed

---

[84] Adelard's early work, the *De eodem et diverso*, written before 1116, was edited by Hans Willner in Baeumker's *Beiträge*, IV.1 (Münster, 1903). The whole of what Adelard says there about astronomy (pp. 31–2) runs to only a dozen lines, but includes: 'If anyone possess this science he will know not only the present state of things below the heavens but also their past and future condition. For those higher and divine creatures (*animalia*: "ensouled", living beings) are the principle and the causes of lower natures. And concerning *astrologia* I should set forth many things no less to be desired than what has been said above, were it not that they could not be covered in few words, nor understood by anyone ignorant of that art.' The belief in and interest in astrology was evident; that the heavens were causes of sublunary effects was almost an Aristotelian commonplace; and the chief reason for the stars being *animalia* was that they moved, without apparently being *moved by* anything. But it is all part of the general interest in the new science. The *De eodem et diverso* was written before any influence from the Arabs was felt. Even the much later *Quaestiones Naturales* (ed. M. Müller in *Beiträge*, XXXI.2, Münster, 1934) is mainly derived from older, Latin sources and there is little Arabic learning there.

[85] See L. Bauer's edition of the *De divisione philosophiae* in *Beiträge*, IV.2 & 3 (1903) and G. Bülow's of *De processione mundi* in *Beiträge*, XXIV.3 (1925). The Neo-platonism of his sources comes through but very little more than generalities about astrology.

[86] Th. Silverstein, 'Daniel of Morley: English Cosmogonist and Student of Arabic Science', in *Medieval Studies*, X (1948) 179ff. See also the same author's '*Liber Hermetis Mercurii Triplicis de VI rerum principiis*', in *Archives d'Histoire Doctrinale et Littéraire du Moyen Age*, XXII (1955) 217–302, for an anonymous twelfth century work based on both Latin and Arabic sources.

[87] What follows is taken from the Chronicle of Roger of Hoveden: *Chronica Magistri Rogeri de Hovedene*, ed. W. Stubbs (Rolls Series 51, 1869), II, 290–298.

almost all the world's prognosticators, Greek and Latin – wrote much the same prediction about the conjunction of the planets.' Notice that the astrologers are still firmly anchored in their Islamic bases in Spain and Sicily. According to one Chorumphiza there were going to be great natural and political disasters, to the benefit of the Franks and the discomfiture of the Saracens, with the generations after the calamity living a much fuller life; 'whatever others may say, that is my opinion.' Then there was a William, a clerk to the Constable of Chester, who reckoned that a great Christian prince was to rise, who should also be 'numbered among the prophets', because Jupiter signified prophecy; but since England too would suffer from this conjunction, 'since as every astrologer knows, this region is under Saturn, and the Moon is with him ... there is but one remedy, that the king and the nobles should take counsel, serve God and flee from the devil, so that the Lord may turn aside these threatened punishments.' Roger of Hoveden also tells the wonderful story of the lay brother at Worcester Priory who went into a trance, recited thirty-three terrible Latin couplets[88] on the wrath of God to come, and promptly died. Comfort was only to be drawn, apparently, from the more sober predictions of an Arab of Cordova, Pharamella the son of Abdelabi, whose arguments against all the terrible prognostications were entirely astrological: the good and evil influences cancelled out, he said, and anyway the days were all wrong, and so on. But, as Stubbs' footnote says, 'considering the positive way in which the prophecy of the storm is contradicted (we shall conclude) that this explanation was written after the dangerous day had passed.' Pass it did, without major calamity, but the episode illustrates the emergence of astrology from its centuries of quietude.

It emerged from the Muslim lands, Spain and Sicily especially. And it emerged because there had been a revival and a growth of interest in the quadrivium, in the 'mathematical sciences', and in medicine, over the preceding two centuries. That interest drew first on the old Latin sources, and only gradually began to include, during the late eleventh century and the twelfth, the Islamic material, itself mainly derived from the Greek. The Latin scholars of North-west Europe went to the Arabs first for the quadrivium and for medicine; and medicine and *astronomia* naturally and unavoidably brought astrology with them. As Tullio Gregory says,[89] 'In the twelfth century astrology was

---

[88] Perhaps the worst (just) is:

> hic sonat assidue carmen lacrymabile, Vae, vae,
>
> quantae sunt tenebrae! vae mihi, vae mihi, vae!

[89] *The Cultural Context of Medieval Learning*, ed. J. E. Murdoch and E. D. Sylla, Boston Studies in the Philosophy of Science, XXVI (Dordrecht and Boston, 1975). Tullio Gregory's article, 'La nouvelle idée de nature et de savoir scientifique au XIIe siècle', is on pp. 193ff; the quotation is from p. 214.

one of the physical sciences men had to study – as a physical science, not as something based on imaginary data – because it really was a positive science for medieval men.' The point is that the 'astrological' description of the zodiac and the signs and the planets and their exaltations and so on was all part of the *sphaera*, the 'scientific' description of the universe in the earlier years before the revival of practising judicial astrology. It was not indeed until such astrology was established and flourishing as an art that John of Sacrobosco could in the mid-thirteenth century write a wholly astronomical *sphaera*.

What kind of astrology, then, was brought into the Latin culture of western Christendom? Who introduced it, where and when? And how did astrology find itself in Arabic in the Islamic empire? It is best to take these questions in the reverse order.

Whether directly because of the closing of the pagan philosophical schools of Athens in 529 by Justinian, or because the teachers of Greece had for perhaps a century or more been leaving the intellectually and spiritually hostile environment of the Christian Empire for the more liberal court of Persia, by the middle of the sixth century there had been transferred thither from Greece the scientific and medical works of Hellenistic scholars and most of the Aristotelian corpus – mainly, perhaps, for his biological writings, but including also the logic, the *Physics* and the *Metaphysics*, the book 'On the Heavens' and the one 'On Generation and Corruption' which contains the most explicit statement of the heavenly causation of earthly events. Two centuries later the Middle East and much of the Mediterranean world were under Muslim domination. In 622 the Prophet Muhammad fled from Mecca, where his teaching had upset the merchant obigarchy, to Yathrib, later called Medina (the City, *sc.* of the Prophet). The date marks the beginning of the Islamic era, dates in which are usually written A.H., *annus Hegirae*, the *Hegira* being the Flight (of Muhammad). In the following hundred years the Arab armies with their expansionist faith had conquered all the Near East except a remnant of the Byzantine Empire, Egypt and North Africa, Sicily and Spain; and had crossed the Pyrenees, when their raiders were stopped and sent back by Charles Martel after the Battle of Poitiers in 722.

Under Islamic rule a new civilisation arose which drew on the older Persian, Indian and Greek sources; all three affected astrology, but of the three the Greek were by far the most important – particularly since they lay behind much of the astrology of Persia and India. There were two great periods of translation into Arabic of works of Greek science and philosophy. In the ninth century men like Hunayn ibn Ishaq and Thabit ibn Qurra translated many medical and scientific books directly from the Greek into Arabic; and in the following century many more translations were made, largely from the Syriac or Pahlavi versions, of the works of Plato and Aristotle, the Commentators on these, the Neo-Platonists and the great medical authority Galen. To these two periods belong the two most important founders of Islamic philosophy and science: to the first Al Kindi, and to the second Al Farabi. The former was sympathetic to astrology, the latter opposed to it. The Arabs were bound, in taking over Greek *astrologia* and Greek medicine, to find astrology also. What was to be their attitude to it? It may be very briefly said that the medieval Muslim had a very similar world-view to that of the medieval Christians, and a very similar revealed, 'book', religion; and that consequently, and because their philosophical background also was Greek, their attitudes to astrology were very much the same as those of Christian scholars and church-men. Al Farabi, Avicenna, Al Ghazzali, Averroes – all these for various reasons rejected astrology, or at least judicial astrology; yet it became part of the Islamic tradition. The reason was that for many Muslim the wholeness of the universe and the one-ness of wisdom (ḥikmah) meant that the sage (ḥakim) gathered all knowledge into one penetrative understanding or gnosis of a world which was all symbol, all allegory. 'Despite the opposition of religious authorities to the predicative aspect of astrology, its practice has continued far and wide in Islamic civilisation over the centuries. Many notable astronomical treatises have astrological sections attached to them and numerous pages of Arabic, Persian, Turkish and other literatures of the Islamic peoples are concerned with the interrelation between man's terrestrial life and celestial influences. But on the highest level, namely in metaphysical and gnostic works, the powerful symbolism of astrology has been integrated perfectly into Islamic esotericism. In these works astrology is revealed to be in its symbolic aspect a means whereby man rediscovers his own cosmic dimension and becomes aware of his own angelic and archetypal reality and the influence of this reality upon his terrestrial existence. This was achieved without in any way destroying or weakening the direct relation which man possesses *vis-à-vis* the metacosmic Reality, which lies at once beyond the Universe and at the centre of his own being.'[90]

---

[90] Seyyed Hossein Nasr, *Islamic Science: an Illustrated Study* (London, 1976) p. 131; *Science and Civilisation in Islam* (Cambridge, Mass., 1968). The author presents Islamic science in a way which, as Giorgio de Santillana says in his Preface to the latter book (p. vii), 'may surprise some readers both West and East'. Islamic culture is too often presented as the indispensable link between Antiquity and our Middle Ages, but the achievement of its historic mission is implied when it has handed on the texts and techniques of the Greeks. This is a way of turning a great civilisation into a service department of Western history. It is the merit of Dr Nasr to have shown convincingly that the mind and culture of Islam embrace a far wider arc, and that the cultivation of the Greek heritage is only a phase in the development of an essentially independent thought'. Both books should be read with as unprejudiced a mind as can be managed,

The process of translation from Arabic into Latin began in the second half of the eleventh century with the medical writings of Constantine the African, and effectively gave way to translations made directly from the Greek in the middle of the thirteenth century. During these two centuries a whole body of astronomical/astrological works, both Greek and Arabic, were turned into Latin by various scholars.[91]

---

and with humility: they help one to see important differences more clearly as differences, not simply errors.

[91] What follows is derived mainly from the following works, and a perusal of many of the MSS referred to by Haskins, Thorndike and others:

M. Steinschneider, *Die europäischen Übersetzungen aus dem Arabischen bis Mitte des 17 Jahrhunderts*, Sitz. d. Klass. Akad. d. Wiss. (Wien, 1904/5; repr. Graz, 1956).

Lynn Thorndike, *History of Magic and Experimental Science* (London, 1923) II.

C. H. Haskins, *Studies in the History of Medieval Science* (Cambridge, Mass., 1924).

A. van de Vyver, 'Les plus anciennes traductions latines médiévales (Xe–XIe siècles) de traités d'astronomie et d'astrologie', in *Osiris*, I (1936) 658ff.

Francis J. Carmody, *Arabic Astronomical and Astrological Sciences in Latin Translation: A Critical Bibliography* (Cambridge & Los Angeles, 1956).

Lynn Thorndike, 'The Three Latin Translations of the Pseudo-Hippocratic Tract on Astrological Medicine', in *Janus*, XLIX (1961) 104–129.

Lynn Thorndike and Pearl Kibre, *A Catalogue of Incipits of Medical and Scientific Writings in Latin*, revised and augmented edition (London, 1963).

M-T. d'Alverney, 'Translations and Translators', in *Renaissance and Renewal in the Twelfth Century*, ed. Robert L. Benson and Giles Constable (Cambridge, Mass., 1982).

From these writers a list of translations of astrological and related works made in or before the twelfth century may be made up. They form, or course, only part of any complete list, which would have to include not only more medicine and mathematics, but logic, philosophy and theology.

Late 10th century at Fleury (? Abbo) 'Alchandreus' – traditional astrology.
Late 11th century Constantine the African: medical works.

1120–30	Adelard of Bath: Al-Khwarizmi's Tables; Euclid.
1127	Stephen of Antioch: medical encyclopaedia.
1134	Plato of Tivoli: Albuhali, *de electione horarum*
1136	Plato of Tivoli: Al-Battani
1138	Plato of Tivoli: Ptolemy, *Quadripartitum*
1136	Hugh of Santalla: *Centiloquium*
1138	Hermann of Carinthia: Saul b. Bishr, *de revolutionibus*
1140	Hermann of Carinthia: Abu Ma'shar, *Maius Introductorium*
1143	Hermann of Carinthia: Ptolemy, *Planispherium*
1142 on	John of Spain: a large number of astrological works
1144	Rudolf of Bruges: Ptolemy, *Planispherium*
	Rudolf of Bruges: ? *de astrolabio*
1140–50	Dominicus Gundisalvi: Avicebron, Al-Farabi, Al Ghazzali
1140	Raymond of Marseilles: planetary tables; astrolabe
1150–60	Henry Aristippus: Plato's *Phaedo* and *Meno*; Aristotle's *Meteorologica*; Ptolemy, *Almagest* (1160)
1169	Pascalis Romanus, at Constantinople: *Kyranides* (magic) and a dream-book, *Thesaurus occulti*
1160s	Eugene of Palermo: Ptolemy, *Optica*
Late 12th century	in Sicily, Euclid: *Data, Optica, Catoptica*
1176	Gerard of Cremona: Ptolemy, *Almagest*, and many other works. (He is the most prolific of the translators, but only six out of ninety works listed by Steinschneider are actually astrological.)

The *Tetrabiblos* and the *Centiloquium* were translated in the late 1130s, and Abu Ma'shar, the most widely used Arabic source, in the 1140s. Although the *Almagest* was put into Latin from the Greek in Sicily about 1160, it was unknown in the west until Gerard of Cremona produced a version from the Arabic in Toledo in 1175. Gerard was one of the most prolific of all the translators, producing more than ninety works, of which some half dozen were purely astrological. Of the translators, Haskins says (*Studies*, p. 10): 'Besides a large amount of astrology, inevitable in an age which regarded astrology as merely applied astronomy and a study of great practical utility, their attention was given mainly to astronomy and mathematics.' The part of astrology in the whole picture should not be exaggerated, but certainly John of Spain, for instance, seems to have specialised in it. He translated the *Centiloquium*, two works of Masha'allah, three of Abu Ma'shar including the *Greater Introduction*, two of Alcabitius, three other minor astrological works and the astronomy of al Farghani, as well as himself composing an *Epitome totius astrologie*. By 1180 the *Almagest*, the *Tetrabiblos* (in more than one version), the *Centiloquium*, sets of Tables (from those of Adelard in 1120 to Roger of Hereford's in 1178), together with Arabic commentaries and a number of other astrological works, major and minor, were all circulating in Latin. Some of the copyists may have had qualms of conscience over all this use of Saracen sources: one wrote after a Latin version of a text of Abu Ma'shar, 'finished, with praise to God for his help and a curse on Mahomet and his followers.' But the translations came and multiplied none the less.

So the Latin scholars and translators went to the Arabs for medicine and for science, the mathematical arts, which included *astrologia*, theoretical (astronomy) and practical (astrology). The mixture of these last and the balance of interest, to begin with at least, are shown in the mid-twelfth century concoction by 'an unknown Western writer with a bias in favour of astrology, who read no Arabic but consulted some of the Arabic texts in the current Latin translations'.[92] The author was acquainted with the old Latin sources, Bede and Macrobius, and probably Boethius, and with contemporaries such as Adelard and William of Conches; he refers to a *liber almanach*, some Arabic planetary names, and the Arabs' Greenwich, so to speak, Arin (their prime meridian city). His main sources, according to Silverstein, were Firmicus Maternus, Zahel ben Bishr, Alcabitius and 'others of this stamp'. Much of it is written in 'a language conventional to the subject since the tenth century' and despite its editor's opinion of its 'bias in

---

[92] Th. Silverstein, *Liber Hermetis Mercurii Triplicis de VI rerum principiis*, in *Arch. d'hist. doct. et litt. du moyen âge*, XXII (1955) 217–301; p. 217.

favour of astrology' most of the content is astronomical and such astrological matter as the rules for finding the horoscope, for example, is introduced naturally as part of the use of the astrolabe. There is of course no hesitation in including astrology or in showing an interest in it.

Among the early translations one of the works which appeared – or reappeared – in the West was the *Centiloquium*, falsely attributed to Ptolemy, which we have already noticed among the late Greek works.[93] It is a collection of a hundred astrological aphorisms. There were a number of such collections circulating in the later medieval centuries, three of which had this same title: apart from the Pseudo-Ptolemy there were the *Centiloquium Hermetis*, which only survives in the Latin version of Stephen of Messina, and the *Centiloquium Bethem* (i.e. al Battani), which also only exists now in Latin. We are now only concerned with the Pseudo-Ptolemaic version, to which *Centiloquium* will henceforth refer. The origins of this work are obscure and at present probably undecidable. The earliest text is Arabic, and its title is *Thamara*. This is a translation of the Greek title, καρπός, which gives its alternative Latin name, *Fructus* – 'fruit'. Or, of course, the Greek title is a translation of the Arabic. Richard Lemay seems to believe that it was compiled at the beginning of the tenth century by Ahmet abu Ja'far.[94] This Arabic text was translated into Latin in 1136 by Plato of Tivoli, with a commentary attributed in manuscripts to 'Haly' but probably by abu Ja'far. The work was known and quoted in Syriac in the thirteenth century, and in Hebrew in the fourteenth; a Greek text is known in manuscripts from the fourteenth century, which has been edited by Aemilie Baer.[95] There are a number of variants in both the Greek and the Latin texts – at least one other Latin translation, this time from the Greek, was made in the fifteenth century. There is no doubt that the general impression given by the aphorisms is of late Greek, Hellenistic, astrology. The great majority of them either can be parallelled in Hellenistic sources or are such commonplaces as might have been produced by almost any astrologer in the Greek tradition at any time; none, in fact, can really be traced directly to Ptolemy.

Two only appear to be foreign to Greek, numbers 56 and 60. Number 56 says: 'In the first *tetragon* of the moon the moistures of bodies flow out, until the second, and in the rest they diminish.' What are these tetragons of the moon? The Teubner note refers to Ptolemy and to Porphyry, but the passages are not really parallel; they refer to

---

93 P. 92 above.
94 See Helen Lemay, 'The Stars and Human Sexuality: Some Medieval Scientific Views', in *Isis*, 71 (1980) 127ff.
95 Bibl. Teubneriana, in *Opera Ptolemaei*, 2nd edn, 1961.

the quarters of the moon, and they cannot be called tetragons, and the reference to moisture is too commonplace in connection with the moon to be useful. Now number 60 says: 'With regard to the sick, look at the critical days and the position of the moon in the angles of the *hexkaidekahedron*; for when you find such angles not afflicted, it will be well for the sick man, if afflicted, the opposite.' So now we have a sixteen-sided figure for the moon as well. It can be seen at once that if the circle (of the zodiac) is divided into sixteen parts there are four and only four squares that can be drawn in the circle to touch the sixteen points: it is an isometry – if a square is rotated through 22½° four times it comes back to the same space, and 22½° is the full 360° of the circle divided by 16. Now Ptolemy at *Tetr.* III, 12 mentions 'bendings' (κάμπιοι) of the moon; and these, according to the Loeb editor, Robbins (p. 325), who follows 'the anonymous commentator', are 'the points quartile to the nodes', that is, to *caput* and *cauda draconis*. So this would give one a tetragon; a first tetragon, if it were of the new moon, with three more for the first quarter, the full moon, and the last quarter. This is, of course, pure guesswork. Any real answer will have to wait until there have been enough scholarly publications of all the texts – Greek, Persian, Indian and Arabic – to enable comparisons to be made. But at least it is possible that even these two aphorisms are ultimately derivable from Hellenistic sources. At present it seems reasonable to suggest that there was a collection of aphorisms like this one made in late Hellenistic times; such collections, *florilegia* (the Latin equivalent of the Greek *anthologia*, 'a collection of flowers'), were very common in all subjects, very often for teaching purposes. That collection, perhaps with the title *Karpos*, and fathered on Ptolemy, then passed down through the centuries through the hands of a number of compiler-revisers of whom abu Ja'far was one, and perhaps the most important and influential.

The *Centiloquium* has introduced into the background of these translations Persian and Indian as well as Arabic astrology. Indeed Arabic astrology, rather like the *Arabian Nights*, was a mixture of Indian and Persian ideas as well as Greek; much that was Greek came to the Arabs through Persia and perhaps through India too. Indian astronomy/astrology – they were inseparable on arrival in India before the sixth century, and remained so – were mainly derived from the Greeks.[96] Most, probably, of Persian astrology was also from Greek

---

[96] *Cf.* Gauranga Nath Banerjee, *Hellenism in Ancient India* (New Delhi, 1981), 130: 'From all these extraneous indications, coupled with the internal reasons of probability mentioned above, we conclude that the Scientific Astronomy of the Indians should be regarded as an offshoot of Greek Science.' See also D. Pingree, 'The Indian Iconography of the Decans and Horâs', in *Journal of the Warburg and Courtauld Institute*, 26 (1963) 232–254; and the same author's *The Yavanajataka of Sphujidhvaja*, Harvard Oriental

sources. It may be, however, that elements of older Babylonian traditions survived in or influenced Persian and Indian writers; as, for example, the lunar signs or houses, and perhaps the periods called *ferdariae*, which we shall come back to. It is safe to say that Syriac, Hebrew and Arabic scientists in the Middle Ages were the direct or indirect heirs of Alexandrian Greek science.[97] According to Pingree, his published Arabic text of Dorotheus' *Carmen Astrologicum*,[98] made about 800 by al-Tabari, is a version of a third century Pahlavi (Persian) translation of the first century Greek, the Persian having been revised, with additions from India, in the late fourth or early fifth century.

The second important thing about Arabic astrology is that the period of its development and its influence on the West was short. Before the eighth century the Arabs had virtually no astronomy, only 'a very crude method of telling the time by night by means of the twenty-eight lunar mansions, and a rough estimation of the seasons by means of their heliacal risings and cosmic settings'.[99] The high period of scientific development in Baghdad was the late eighth century and the ninth, and the sciences flourished in Islamic Spain especially in the tenth century under Abd er-Rahman III and his successor al-Hakam II. In the next century the translations were becoming commonly available in the Latin West. The chronological gap between the science of the Arabs and that of Western scholars is thus really quite short. This is especially true, perhaps, of acquaintance with and knowledge of the astrolabe and of astrological Tables, which began to be translated, as we have seen, as early as Adelard of Bath. So far as the astrolabe is concerned, one has to be very wary of scholars' generalisations. The word itself is Greek, and merely means an instrument for 'taking the stars'. Consequently any instrument used in observing stellar positions or altitudes could be so called. By the tenth century in Western Europe the word was also used of armillary spheres, systems of rings to represent planetary and stellar movements, such as were known to Gerbert d'Aurillac. The astrolabe proper, so to speak, is a projection of the sphere of the universe on a plane: it should properly be called a planispheric astrolabe, but the epithet is usually dropped in contexts where the meaning is plainly understood. It was the most important observational instrument before the invention of the telescope, and could be used not only for such observation of heavenly bodies, but for finding the time, or

Series 48, 2 vols (Cambridge, Mass., 1978), and 'The Indian and Pseudo-Indian passages in Greek and Latin astronomical and astrological texts', in *Viator*, 7 (1976) 141ff.

[97] *Cf.* J. Millás Vallicrosa, *Nuevos estudios sobre historia de la ciencia española*, (Barcelona, 1960), esp. c.vii.

[98] *Dorothei Sidonii Carmen Astrologicum* (Leipzig, 1976).

[99] D. Pingree, 'ILM at Hay'a', in *Encyclopaedia of Islam*, 2nd edn, III.1135ff.

latitudes, or heights and distances, and for constructing horoscopes and calculating the mundane houses. It was certainly known to the Greeks, probably being invented by Ptolemy (or possibly by Hipparchus), and as certainly not known to the Latin Middle Ages until its reintroduction from Arabic sources in the twelfth century.[100] The astrolabe is important to astrologers not so much (as a number of late medieval drawings might suggest) for taking accurate observations of the heavens at a given moment – of a birth, say – which were of less use than they might have been had there been good chronometers available, but for calculating from the Tables, which were essential, what was the horoscope (the ascendant) and how to divide the chart into its twelve houses.

So the Arabs of the eighth and nineth centuries adopted the Greek astrology they received from the Persians, the Syrians, and perhaps the Indians; but not without opposition. Islam might be expected to be more receptive to astrology than Christianity, with its determinist view of the Will of Allah – Islam means 'submission', and a Muslim is one who submits to Allah's will. But their very determinism and their absolute monotheism left little or no room for any sort of stellar fatalism, and in fact Arab arguments about the validity or admissibility of astrology are very similar to the Christian ones of earlier centuries. The great philosopher-theologians al-Farabi, Avicenna, Averroes and ibn Khaldun were against astrology; but the encyclopaedic al-Kindi and his pupil Abu Ma'shar were astrologers, as was their predecessor, the first voluminous Arab writer on the subject, Masha'allah (or Messahalla, in his Latin form). These last two, with al-Battani, are the most often cited Arabic sources of Latin astrologers,[101] with Abu Ma'shar far and away the most influential. Abu

---

[100] Anyone wanting to see what an astrolabe looked like should visit the Museum of the History of Science in the Old Ashmolean in Oxford, which has one of the finest collections in the world. There are good illustrations in *Time and Space: Measuring Instruments from the Fifteenth to the Nineteenth Century*, Samuel Guye and Henri Michel, trans. Diana Dolan (London, 1971), the text of which should be treated with great caution. The literature on the astrolabe is immense. J. D. North gives a clear account of its construction, with good illustrations, in 'The Astrolabe', in *Scientific American*, 230 (1974) 96–106. Two good articles on its history are O. Neugebauer, 'The Early History of the Astrolabe', in *Isis*, 40 (1949) and Emmanuel Poulle, 'Les instruments astronomiques de l'Occident latin au XIe et XIIe siècles', in *Cahiers*, 15 (1972). The best account of its principles and uses is Willy Hartner's (trans. Phyllis Ackerman) in *A Survey of Persian Art*, ed. A. Upham Pope, III.2530–2564 (London and New York, 1939). See also the same author's *asturlab* in *Encycl. of Islam*, 2nd edn, 1 (1960). For Chaucer's instructions to his 'litel sone Lewis' at Oxford, see R. T. Gunter, *Early Science at Oxford*, V (Oxford, 1929). From Hartner and Chaucer-Gunter anyone can make his own astrolabe.
[101] The eleventh century astronomer al-Biruni was best known for his tables, though he wrote astrological works also. His division of astrology, and his attitude, are interesting. In his *Elements of Astrology* (Arabic text and translation by R. Ramsay Wright, London, 1934), §515 he divides the art into meteorology, including earthquakes, floods and so on;

Ma'shar was born at Balkh, a city in what is now northern Afghan-
istan, in 787. The last element of his name, al-Balkhi, is behind the
non-existent Greek 'Palchus' of the appendices to CCAG. The authorities used by these Arab writers are difficult to sort out, since they
themselves were so eclectic, as were no doubt many of the books they
used, and they fathered anything and everything on the Greeks: 'For
them, everything was Greek which carried a Greek name,' says
Ullmann.

The beginnings of a philosophical basis not only for astrology but
also for magic and divination of other kinds, usually practised as
occult sciences, were laid down by al-Kindi.[102] He was born about the
end of the eighth century into an aristocratic family (his father was
governor of al-Kurfan under Harun al-Rashid) and was tutor and
physician to that great patron of arts and sciences, the Khalif
al-Ma'mun. He died about 866. His major task and achievement was,
with the translators, the creation of a new Arabic philosophical
language. His own thought depended largely on the Neo-Platonists,
and through them, Plato and Aristotle. He wrote copiously on all
subjects, including astronomy, astrology and the astrolabe. Some of
his works are now lost, and others only survive in Hebrew or Latin
translations. One of the most important of the latter, from our point of
view, is the *De radiis*, 'On (stellar) rays'.[103] In that book al-Kindi seems
concerned to establish a metaphysical basis for magic – that is,
rational, 'good' magic – on a sort of Stoic philosophy of cosmic
sympathy, physically expressed in 'rays' between objects, and
especially between and from heavenly bodies. As he says in Chapter 2
(Alverney and Hudry, p. 221): 'So the diversity of things in the world
of the elements apparent at any time proceeds from two causes,
namely the diversity of their matter (elements) and the changing

---

plants, and animals and humanity; the individual – life and posterity; the individual –
actions and occupations; and lastly, 'beyond these there is a fifth division where such
origins (as the other sections have) are entirely unknown. Here astrology reaches a point
which threatens to transgress its proper limits, where problems are submitted which it
is impossible to solve for the most part, and where the matter leaves the solid basis of
universals for one of particulars. When this boundary is passed, where the astrologer is on
one side and the sorcerer on the other, you enter a field of omens and divinations which
has nothing to do with astrology although the stars may be referred to in connection
with them.' For a chronological summary see M. Ullman, *Die Natur- und Geheimswissen-
schaft im Islam*, Handbuch der Orientalistik, Erste Abteilung, Ergänzungsband VI, 2
Abschnitt (Leiden, 1972), Chapter V.
102 For a summary of his life and work see G. N. Atiyeh, *Al-Kindi: the Philosopher of the
Arabs* (Rawalpindi, 1966).
103 Ed. M.-Th. d'Alverney and F. Hudry, 'Al-Kindi *De Radiis*', in *Arch. d'Hist. Doct. et
Litt. du Moyen Age*, XLI (1974), pp. 139–260.

operation of the stellar rays.' This leads him to a firm stellar determinism (of exactly the sort condemned as heretical in a Christian context by Bishop Tempier of Paris in the list of errors proscribed in 1277) and also to an extraordinarily Keplerian statement (ibid. p. 223): 'If it were given to anyone to comprehend the whole condition of the celestial harmony, he would know fully the world of the elements with all contained therein at any place and any time, as knowing the caused from its cause', and vice versa, knowing the cause from what what is caused. 'So that whoever has acquired the knowledge of the whole condition of the celestial harmony will know the past and the present and the future.' This was the teacher who interested the then 47-year old Abu Ma'shar in astrology. The commonplace as to causation is clearly repeated in the latter's *Introductorium* (and elsewhere in his works): in comparing medicine and astrology in his preliminary generalities, Abu Ma'shar writes, 'The doctor studies the changes in the elements; the *astrologus* (by which, as is evident from the context of 'the whole, *astrologia*', he understands the astronomer and the astrologer together as one person) follows the movements of the stars to arrive at the causes of elementary changes.'

Of Abu Ma'shar Duhem says (Système, II.369) that his '*Introductorium* is the work from which, for many centuries, astrologers most readily borrowed philosophical arguments to justify their art.' Duhem was wrong about the centuries: two, perhaps, and then Ptolemy and science take over. But Abu Ma'shar's arguments, largely Aristotelian, were intended to provide a philosophical basis for astrology. Duhem is also overstating his case when he says that Abu Ma'shar's arguments were taken 'almost entirely from the Peripatetics'. In this he is followed by Thorndike, and he by Lemay.[104] Really the great difficulty lies in deciding how much is from Aristotle and is deliberately Aristotelian and how much is commonplace and largely accidental. In almost any age and culture there is a set of ideas, of principles and of knowledge, which is common to most if not all educated people. In our own times the basic ideas of animal evolution, of man's place in nature and of at least early twenties physics, may be taken for granted in almost any company. In the Rome of the late Republic and early Empire, Stoicism provided the current philosophical background, as Neo-Platonism did for Late Antiquity. In the ninth and tenth centuries

---

[104] Richard Lemay, *Abu Ma'shar and Latin Aristotelianism in the Twelfth Century* (Beirut, 1982). The case is greatly overstated both for Abu Ma'shar's Aristotelianism and its influence. Lemay seems to work on the politicians' principle that if something is said often and emphatically enough it must be accepted as true; but his text contains more assertion than evidence. However, the summary of pp. 131–2 is pretty fair: there is no doubt that abu Ma'shar knew and used his Aristotle well, but he was much more eclectic and philosophically muddled than Lemay allows.

in educated Arab circles the mixture of Aristotelianism and Neo-Platonism common in the commentators such as Proclus – in some historical ways as important as the great philosophers themselves, just as Cicero with his *De Officiis* is one of the most influential of ancient 'philosophers' – formed the intellectual background to all scientific and philosophical thinking; and both late Aristotelianism and Neo-Platonism were influenced by and mingled with Stoicism and Neo-Pythagoreanism. So that sifting out of all this what is 'the philosophy' of a given author, unless he himself provides clear and unambiguous guidelines, is virtually impossible. Abu Ma'shar, at least in his astrological works, provides no such guidance, and his attributions to sources are not always to be trusted. The basic justification of astrology by reference to Aristotle's theory (in the *Physics* and the *De Generatione et Corruptione*) that all sublunar change is caused by motions in the heavens, could hardly be cited as evidence of great knowledge of Aristotle – a reading of al-Kindi would be enough. In an age of aids to teaching and study such as the epitomes and the *florilegia* much of Aristotle became the commonplaces of the schools, Arabic as well as Latin, and some of these schoolbooks may have existed in Greek first. A somewhat later but fairly representative example of such a book, the thirteenth century *Auctoritates Aristotelis*[105] quite baldly states the doctrine we are interested in, citing the *De gen. et corrup.*, (336–32): 'The movement of the sun and the other planets in an oblique circle is the cause of the generation and corruption of lower things.' The most one can say of the earlier Arabic astrology is that its background was that common Greek philosophical mixture of the age of the great commentators, and that Abu Ma'shar was at least consciously aware of the arguments derivable from Aristotle's *Physics, De caelo*, etc., and may have been the first, as Duhem says, to put them together.

He was born in 787 and died almost a centenarian in 886. The town of Balkh, in Khurasan, contained 'communities of Jews, Nestorians, Manichaeans, Buddhists and Hindus, as well as Zoroastrians'[106] – a mixture of Greek, Hebrew, Indian and Persian traditions, all found in his works. His most important astrological works were the *Flores Astrologiae*, a collection of brief, useful hints and aphorisms as a sort of rough guide to do-it-yourself interpretation, translated by John of Seville; the 'Little Introduction' translated by Adelard of Bath; the *De revolutionibus nativitatum*;[107] translated by both John of Seville and

---

[105] Jacqueline Hamesse, *Les Auctoritates Aristotelis*, Philosophes Médiévaux, XVII (Louvain/Paris, 1974).
[106] D. Pingree, 'Abu Ma'shar', in *Dict. of Scientific Biography*, I (New York, 1970).
[107] Greek text (of the tenth century) ed. D. Pingree (Leipzig, 1968).

Hermann of Carinthia in the first half of the twelfth century. There were many other minor works including two on 'elections' and a (lost) book of Tables.

Such books of tables of positions and rising times of heavenly bodies and signs were vitally important. Accurate observation was always difficult and, to labour a point already made, there were no clocks, no chronometers. The time might be fairly accurately learned from a clear sky by observation with an astrolabe, but the construction of an astrological chart, or 'figure', had to be done by finding the horoscope (the ascendant) and the positions of the planets from the tables, and working out the divisions of the twelve mundane houses, to say nothing of *caput* and *cauda* and the mansions of the moon. The accuracy of the tables depended not only on the expertise of the astronomer who constructed them but on the accuracy of copyists also; and the correctness of the figure on the competence and exactness of the astrologer setting it up. It was no easy task. An educated doctor of the thirteenth century, Robert le Fèbvre, using tables made by Henri Bate of Malines, nevertheless made a number of mistakes in his calculations.[108] What might not a half-educated quack do? Important fixed stars were included in these tables, for at least two reasons. First, those rising with a sign of the zodiac, the *paranatellonta*, might be observable though the sign itself was not. Second, the Arabs far more than the Greeks (or modern astrologers) made use of the stars associated not only with signs but even with degrees of signs in their interpretations. For example, one is warned in the *Flores* (fol. 64 of the 1488 Venice edition) to watch out that the Lord of the Year is not associated with any of a list of twenty-odd stars, each associated with one of the planets, beginning with two 'in the head of Aries' and ending with one in Pisces.

That the 'fixed stars' were not fixed, but moving – hence the long-term change in the position of the equinox, the 'first point of Aries', against their background – had been known from the time of Hipparchus, and the precession of the equinoxes given quantitative meaning in the *Almagest*. There were two schools of thought: that the equinoxes would eventually arrive back where they started after 36,000 years; or the 'trepidation' theory, that they first moved one way for a while and then moved back again, and so on. Ptolemy belonged to the first (correct) school, and worked out the amount of precession. His theory became the normal teaching of the Alexandrians. Origen refers to precession in his arguments against astrology (see p. 54 above) and mentions a ninth sphere outside the eighth (that of the fixed stars) to

---

[108] See Emmanuel Poulle, 'Astrologie et tables astronomiques au XIIIe siècle: Robert le Fèbvre et les tables de Malines', in *Bulletin Philologique et Historique*, (1964), pp. 793–831.

account for that motion; this ninth sphere must be the sphere of the ecliptic poles in the planetary hypotheses of Ptolemy. But Theon of Alexandria in the fifth century says that 'the ancient *astrologi*' thought it oscillated through eight degrees, what is later called *motus accessus et recessus*, 'a forward and backward movement', trepidation. Proclus refers to both theories. Ptolemy's view of precession became the accepted theory of Muslim and Christian astronomers in the Middle Ages, with 36,000 years the accepted period for the 'Great Year', with the suggestion of the obviously theologically difficult idea that everything would then be exactly as it had been before. The Indians, at least after the fifth century, seem to have preferred the trepidation theory, and since they knew that the equinoxes had moved more than 25° since ancient times, they allotted various values to the scope of the oscillation, 27° being common. Some writers managed to include both theories, which led to yet another, a tenth sphere, to account for the two movements, as in the Alfonsine Tables.[109]

It has been mentioned that medieval tables gave the positions of *caput* and *cauda draconis*, the ascending and descending nodes of the moon (see also pp. 126–7 above) along with those of the planets. By the time astrology passed in its Arabic dress to the western schools, *caput* and *cauda* had become 'bodies' treated as planets, given their exaltations and so on, and their periods of influence, as we shall see. They were known in late Greek astrology,[110] and so passed into the tradition, emerging in Jewish as well as Islamic writers.[111] Such 'materialisation' of the lunar nodes, mere points of the moon's crossing on the ecliptic, was quite contrary to the letter and spirit of Ptolemy; but it passed for a while into the western tradition, and the nodes are still important to some astrologers though not treated as planets as they certainly were in and after the twelfth century. Alcabitius, for example, says of *caput dragonis*:[112] '*caput dragonis* is masculine. Likewise it is beneficent and its nature is compounded of the natures of Jupiter and Venus. And it signifies kingly power and fortune and (worldly) substance. And some have said that its nature is to augment, because when it is with indicators of fortune it increases the fortune, and when it is with bad indicators it increases their badness.' And then *cauda* is described as the opposite.

Like the head and tail of the dragon the lunar mansions, which have been mentioned several times before, were ancient and Babylonian,

---

109 See P. Duhem, *Le Système du Monde*, II (Paris, 1914) 190ff.
110 See for example Neugebauer and van Hoesen, *Greek Horoscopes*, pp. 143f and 146f.
111 See the interesting Chapter 3 of A. Sharf's *The Universe of Shabbetai Donnolo* (Warminster, 1976).
112 MS Ashmole 158 (Bodleian Library, Oxford) f. 12v (= 1512 Venice edn).

known to Greek astrologers but never of importance to them. They were assimilated into Indian astrology and probably thence into Islamic, and it is reasonable to suppose that this ancient lunar zodiac became important to Muslim (and also to the Jews) for the same reason that Babylon produced it in the first place: all have or had the Semitic lunar calendar. There is no simple commensurate way of marrying the times measured by the moon's motions and those measured by the sun's in one calendar. The sun gives us a year fairly clearly marked in temperate regions by the seasons, and especially by the midwinter and midsummer solstices and the two equinoxes. The moon provides the month, from new moon to new moon. Alas, neither year nor month is made up of a whole number of days; nor are there a whole number of months in a year. So some adjustments must be made. Those with solar calendars must have leap years or the equivalent to give the year a whole number of days, and must work with a fictional month with which the moon gets out of step. Those with lunar calendars fix the number of months in a year – twelve gives a year of 354 days – and calculate by new moons like the Jews and Muslim, and then the sun and the seasons get out of step. This means that the Islamic year is different from and shorter than the Christian one; though the date of the greatest Christian feast, Easter, is still calculated by the lunar calendar. Dividing the lunar month has been done in various ways, the two commonest being into four parts and into three. The four parts familiar to us are the weeks of the twenty-eight day month. The three are the nine-day periods known from the eighth century B.C. Greek poet Hesiod (*Works and Days*, 810) and perhaps linguistically preserved in the Latin *nundinae*, market days, and *nones*.[113] The old lunar mansions, listed in many Arabic authors and in Indian and Syrian works, were the twenty-seven or twenty-eight star-groups, or asterisms, through which the moon passed in a synodic month of about 27½ days. Their chief use originally, in India, was for time measurement, length of time being measured by the moon's path against the stars and not by its phases. Instead of saying, 'I did such and such two days after the first quarter,' or whatever, one said, 'I did it when the moon was at so-and-so', naming one of the mansions.[114] They thus had a similar time-reckoning origin to that of the decans and the zodiac itself. Although they were of some significance in Hindu and, to a less extent, in Arabic astrology, the

---

[113] It makes sense to assume that the *Kalends*, the day of 'calling (the order of the days)' was the day of the priestly announcement of the new moon; the *Nones* were originally nine days later, and the *Ides* (the days of the moon's light – i.e. the full moon) were as always nine days after the *Nones*; all suggesting an original lunar calendar.
[114] R. Gleadow, *The Origin of the Zodiac*, pp. 142f.

difficulty of fitting them properly into the Greek solar astrology meant that they never really became part of the Western system.[115]

The twenty-seven of the lunar mansions suggests a link with the 'ninths', *novenarii* in the Latin. Al-Biruni explicitly says that they were Indian[116] in a section headed *Al-nuhbahr*: 'The Hindus regard the ninth part of a sign – 3°20' – which they call *nuvanshaka*, as very important. When a planet is in its own domicile and ninth, that ninth is called *bargutan* or most important. The table shows the ninths of all the signs; the lords of the ninths are the lords of the signs concerned ... This is an entirely Hindu method on which we are all argeed. My friends have altered the order of the lords of the ninths and have arranged them in the order of the spheres, but it is better that we abstain from using it.' This view of their Hindu origin is also, much earlier, that of Abu Ma'shar. Writing of 'divisions' in the *De rev. nativ.* III, c.9, he says: 'The division we have just described is used by the Babylonians and the Persians and the Egyptians; but the Indians and their neighbours seeing that in one division different things happen to men, do not calculate the division according to terms as the others do, but they calculate according to the ninths (τὰ νουπάχρατες) so that the interpretations come out more accurately.' And he adds that 'that word in the language of the Indians means "ninth", and it is of 200' or three and a third degrees; then there will be in each sign nine ninths, of which each has its proper ruler.' Abu Ma'shar then says that he has explained more exactly about ninths in his *Introductorium*; as indeed he did,[117] writing of the *novenae* which are called *noubhairat* by those 'who after dividing the signs into threes to which they allocate the lords of the trigons, at once divide each sign into nine parts and measure out three degrees and a third to each part.' And he explains the allocation of their lordships, e.g. in Aries the first ninth belongs to Mars, the second to Venus, the third to Mercury, 'and so on in order until the ninth Jupiter gains as lord.' The four trigons begin the lordships of the ninths with appropriate planets, 'as the fiery trigon has Mars first; the earthly, Saturn; the airy, Venus; and the watery, the moon.' But some astrologers distribute the lordships according to the order of the spheres. All of which gives a consistent picture, and

---

[115] In 1977, Sybil Leek published *Moon Signs: Lunar Astrology* (London), a kind of feminist counterblast to sun-sign masculinity. It begins: 'Sun-sign astrology is all moonshine'. The book is however concerned with the moon's position in the zodiacal signs from Aries to Pisces, with traditional detail of its power in each and in the houses, and its aspects and so on, all from the same old tradition. There is of course a brief chapter on the head and tail of the dragon, and it is all intended to make up for lack of attention to the moon by most astrologers.
[116] Wright's trans. §455.
[117] In Chapter 14 of Book 5; the 1489 edition is quoted but it is the same in later editions.

clearly the Arabs thought the ninths came from India.

But did they, originally? As to the name, Pingree[118] says the Arabic *nawbahrah* is the same as the Pahlavi *no bahr* or *navamsá*, and that this is the *doctrina partium novenaariarum Indicarum* added by the Persians at the end of the fourth or the beginning of the fifth century. Now chapter 14 of Abu Ma'shar's *Introductorium maius* is followed by a chapter *de duodenariis signorum*, 'on the twelfths of the signs'. The Indians not only had *navamsás*, ninths, but *dvadasamsás*, twelfths. These are, of course, the 2½° *dodecatemoria* familiar from Manilius on. This at least suggests that both ninths and twelfths came to the Indians from the Greeks. We have seen (pp. 121ff above) that among the muddle about *liturgi*, 'ministers', Firmicus had three *liturgi* per decan, which meant that each was three and a third degrees, exactly a ninth! It could be, and is perhaps most likely, that the ninths were originally Babylonian (they *look* lunar) and they edged into the Greek tradition, to get sideways into Firmicus, who would have accepted them even if he hadn't understood them, and possibly through the Greeks or probably independently were taken into the much more lunar Indian tradition.

Even less Greek-looking are the *ferdariae*. The Latin form is variously spelt *ferd-*, *fard-*, *fred-* and even *fridariae* (some modern astrologers refer to 'the fridaries'). The Greek is also variable in form and declension; and both Greek and Latin are clearly from the Arabic *fardar*, *fardariya* (the plurals are *fardarat* and *fardariyat*). Bouché-Leclercq says[119] Saumaise suggested that the word was from the Greek περιοδόριον, *periodorion*, 'a little period', but the word is unknown and looks wrong. On the other hand, περίοδος and περιόδιον, *periodos* and *periodion*, 'a period' and 'a little period' are known and could correspond to (but perhaps could not become, philologically) the *fadar* and the *fardariya* which are indeed great and smaller periods. They belong to a section of astrology always entitled 'On the divisions of times'. These divisions range from world-periods running to billions of years, to months and days in the lives of individuals. Abu Ma'shar's lost work, 'The Thousands', was on this subject of the divisions of times.[120] It belongs to the Islamic tradition of Masha'allah and those Arab astrologers influenced by the Indians, and Abu Ma'shar's source was probably Arabic and not ancient and Persian as he claims. The book is concerned with 'the problem of reconstructing

---

[118] Dorotheus, *Carmen*, praefatio p. xvi.
[119] *L'Astrologie Grecque*, pp. 491ff.
[120] See D. Pingree, *The Thousands of Abu Ma'shar* (London, 1968), from which (pp. 58ff) the quotations in this paragraph are taken.

past and predicting future historical events' (Pingree, p. 58), and although his methods are from Persian, Sasanian astrology 'their roots lie in methods of calculating continuous astrological influence upon a native in Greek genethlialogy', and are probably ultimately derived from the Greek of Hellenistic times.

For Abu Ma'shar, there are four sorts of *fardarat*, only the last of which really concerns late medieval astrology. The 'mighty *Fardar*' is a period of 360 solar years. The big *fardar* is 78 years, shared out among the twelve signs, 12 for Aries, 11 for Taurus, 10 for Gemini and so on down to one for Pisces. The middle *fardar* is 75 years; each middle *fardar* is ruled by one of the planets (planets taken to include the lunar nodes) in the order, round the zodiac, of their exaltations, so that the first is taken by the sun, exalted in Aries; the second by the moon, exalted in Taurus; the third by *caput dragonis*, exalted in Gemini, and so on – the pairs, planet and exaltation, being: Jupiter/Cancer; Mercury/Virgo; Saturn/Libra; *cauda dragonis*/Sagittarius; Mars/Capricorn and Venus/Pisces. The small *fardar* is also 75 years, which is divided into nine *fardariyat* and distributed to the nine 'planets' according to the same order of exaltations, Pingree says. But this is not in fact the order given by Abu Ma'shar in the *De rev. nativ.* IV, though he mentions it elsewhere as a method used by 'some astrologers'. The order in which Abu Ma'shar gives the *ferdariae* to the planets and nodes, and the periods he gives to them, are as follows: the first *ferdaria*, of ten years, to the sun; to Venus, the second, of eight years; to Mercury, thirteen; to the moon, nine; to Saturn, eleven; to Jupiter, twelve; to Mars, seven; to *caput*, three and to *cauda* two – a total of seventy-five. These periods seem to bear no relation to any other set of periods in Greek astrology and look neat enough to be arbitrary – seven to thirteen years for the planets and five to the nodes to make up the total. Abu Ma'shar says that *caput* and *cauda* follow the seventy years of the planets 'because they have no houses' and the others are in the order they are according to their dignities in the twelve signs; but the nodes do have houses, and no such relationship of dignities is discernible elsewhere. It is an odd but deliberate order – the *ferdariae* are explicitly called 'first, second' and so on by Abu Ma'shar.

This might be a convenient place to list for comparison the various orders of planets we have come across, and one or two more.

Old Babylonian (pre-fifth century B.C.): Moon, Sun, Jupiter, Venus, Saturn, Mercury, Mars.

Later Babylonian: Moon, Sun, Mars, Venus, Mercury, Saturn, Jupiter.

'Egyptian': Moon, Sun, Mercury, Venus, Mars, Jupiter, Saturn.

Mithraic: Saturn, Sun, Moon, Jupiter, Mars, Venus, Mercury.

Chaldaean = Greek (astronomical): Moon, Mercury, Venus, Sun, Mars, Jupiter, Saturn.

Greek horoscopes: Sun, Moon, Saturn, Jupiter, Mars, Venus, Mercury.

Hindu: Sun, Moon, Mars, Mercury, Jupiter, Venus, Saturn (= week days).

Fardarat: Sun, Moon, Jupiter, Mercury, Saturn, Mars, Venus.

ferdariae: Sun, Venus, Mercury, Moon, Saturn, Jupiter, Mars.

The order of the *Fardarat* is the order according to the planets' exaltations. The last, that of the *ferdariae*, is also the order given by al-Biruni for those divisions, with the same periods as Abu Ma'shar.[121] It was obviously received into Latin astrology and fixed, since it is quoted by Pico della Mirandola in his *Adversus Astrologiam*.[122]

There is a little evidence that all of this may be Greek in origin. Ptolemy only gives periods which he regards as 'according to nature' (*Tetr.* IV.10; see pp. 91ff above), that is, in years of life, four to the moon, ten (the commentator says that this is half its period because of its double nature) to Mercury, eight to Venus, nineteen to the sun, fifteen to Mars, twelve to Jupiter and the rest to Saturn. This is to take the planets in their astronomical, Chaldaean order. In the early fifth century Hephaistion of Thebes[123] repeats Ptolemy's list, but then goes on to another 'division of times' which he attributes to 'some of the ancient Egyptians'. He begins with a period of seventy-five years, which is then divided equally among the seven planets, giving each ten years nine months. Each planet's period of 129 months is then divided again among the planets according to Ptolemy's 'natural' division, but giving thirty months to Saturn (naturally!) and then twenty-five to the moon to make up the 129, with each planet coming first in its own group of 129. Within each of these secondary, shorter periods, the days are then allocated to the planets in a more complicated way. The number of months of each planet is converted into days, and that figure is divided by 129 to give a figure by which the planetary month-number is then multiplied to give the number of days in this last subdivision. So for example, Saturn's thirty months is converted to 913 days; that divided by 129 gives 7 as the nearest whole number; so Saturn has 7×30, or 210 days, Jupiter 7×12, 84 days, Mars 7×15, or 105 days and so on. Coming to Jupiter's period of twelve months, 365 days divided by 129 gives 2⅚: so Jupiter has 2⅚ × 12 or 34 days, Saturn 2⅚ × 30, or 85 days, and so on. Now the

---

[121] Wright, §§38–9.
[122] Book VII, c.6 (ed. Garin, p. 196).
[123] D. Pingree's edition (2 vols, Leipzig, 1973 and 1974); see I.2, 29.

complication is typical: the 75-year period is divided into 7 equal periods of years; each of these into unequal periods of months; and each of these into unequal but related periods of days; and all these periods are allocated to the planets. The result is that any given day could be under the primary influence of one planet, the secondary influence of another, and the tertiary influence of another, each modifying the other influences. There is a similar complication in Abu Ma'shar, who allocates each *fardariya* again in smaller periods to each of the planets. Of course, the more variables to be taken into account in judging a figure, the greater the chance of – and excuse for – error; but it was probably most of all a love of complexity and obscurity for their own sakes which led to such subdivisions, so sensibly avoided by Ptolemy. Two more small pieces of evidence might be added to the similarities in structure and ideas between late Greek divisions of times and Abu Ma'shar. First, a Byzantine astrologer giving very simple rules for finding the planet of the day just by counting from a particular date, gives the seven planets in the same *ferdariae* order;[124] and second, the first century A.D. Neo-Pythagorean wonder-worker and astrologer Apollonius of Tyana used the same order in his book 'On Planets'.[125]

It is very unlikely that Abu Ma'shar invented any of this; and his immediate sources were surely derived from Indian and Persian works, themselves heavily dependent on the Greeks. The system of Abu Ma'shar and other Arabic astrologers seems to be an amalgam of older traditions, and this it was that passed into Latin astrology. It was really late Greek astrology, from the first four or five centuries of our era, coloured by its passage through Persian and, to a lesser extent, Indian hands, which most filled the minds of the medieval astrologers, and only rather less the restrained art of Ptolemy's *Tetrabiblos*. Not only were they attracted by all the new and strange Arabic terms – they revelled in *hylegs* rather than 'prorogators' and so forth – and also by the fashionable names, but the differences in emphasis may have made the Arabs' astrology more exciting. In Greek astrology, from Dorotheus on, the answering of questions became more important than the analysis of character from a birth chart, the determinations of 'times', especially the length of life, more important than anything else. To some extent this was even true of Ptolemy, despite his avoidance of what he regarded as unnatural refinements, and his 'scientific' approach: he spends much time, and goes into detail, with examples, on the aphetic places and the length of life. And Arabs too

---

[124] See *CCAG*, X, Appendix, under Cod. 1265, fol. 3.
[125] So Ullmann, *op. cit.* (note 101 above) 346, note 2.

were interested in answering questions, such as 'When will be the best time to start on such and such – a journey, say, or some enterprise?' Or conversely, given the time and place of such a 'beginning', 'Will it have a good or bad outcome?' Three aspects of this sort of practice, still common enough in contemporary astrology, might be dealt with briefly here. They are progressions, elections and transits, the last two being really parts of the first. All of them are found in Greek astrologers, and were introduced to the Latin West through the Arabs.

A progressed chart is one in which there has been a 'revolution of the nativity': the elements of the chart – the planets, etc., and the Ascendant and the *Medium caeli* – are turned round through an angle corresponding in some way to the length of time from birth to the date for which prognostication is required, and then from that new chart's interpretation and from comparison with the natal chart, information is obtained about the subject now or in the immediate or distant future. If a person should wish to know whether the next year would be prosperous or the opposite, or whether next Thursday would be a good day for some particular act, it would not be very helpful simply to draw up a chart of the positions of the heavenly bodies for the beginning of the year or for next Thursday. Such a chart would bear simply a chronological and universal relation to the person concerned. In a progression, all really depends on and is derived from the natal chart, the person's own beginning. So now the question is, how far round to turn the natal chart to represent the passage of time between the subject's birth and the time under consideration? This clearly suggests that one of the commonest forms of enquiry will concern the subject's length of life: when is death to be expected? And also, what kind of death? In slightly more sinister vein, the enquiry might concern someone else's death; even the ruler's – which was of course a question rulers discouraged others from asking!

This sort of prognostication is a special kind of progression called a 'direction'. A point of the zodiac A is directed to another point B, and the number of degrees travelled to get from A to B is then converted into time, years, according to some rules. When the enquiry concerns length of life, A is the position of the *prorogator* or *hyleg* (the common Latin form of the Arabic *haylaj*). So first one has to find the aphetic place, the place of the prorogator. That might be the Ascendant or the *Medium caeli*, or the beginning of one of the houses – the tenth, seventh and ninth begin favoured. The planet in that place at the moment of birth is the *dominus vitae*, the lord of life, or the *dimissor*, *prorogator*, or *hyleg*, and is also called, from the Arabic again, the *alcohden*. The point from which the prorogator starts is the *aphetic* point, where life is 'unloosed' (the meaning of the Greek). Next we have to see how far it has to go, through what influences, until it meets with the *anairetic* point, the point of destruction. Then the number of degrees round the zodiac it has traversed must be converted into time as years and months and even days. This is the complicated procedure described in detail by Ptolemy in Book III.10 of the *Tetrabiblos* and by Dorotheus and then by most late Greek astrologers. The time-conversion involved first converting arcs of the zodiac, the ecliptic, into arcs of the equator; or in other words degrees of oblique ascension into degrees of right ascension. This process is described in the *Tetrabiblos* but needs the tables in the *Almagest* (II.8) for the calculations.

Other Greek astrologers than Ptolemy also spent much time on *katarchai*, 'beginnings'. Given that something began at such a time, what are its prospects? Or conversely, and these enquiries are 'elections', given that such and such an enterprise is to be undertaken, when will be the best time to start? This latter kind of enquiry became increasingly common in the courts of Renaissance princes and we shall see something of them in the next chapter. Both these problems require a turning of a natal or other 'beginning' chart – called a *radical* chart – that is, a progression. The commonest formula among modern astrologers for measuring the time round the zodiac is to take 'a day for a year': that is, to calculate the progressed chart for a date as many days ahead of the original birth date as the number of years the subject has lived. The new sidereal time is calculated to give the new Ascendant, *Medium caeli* and houses. This seems curiously arbitrary, but those modern astrologers who use the method simply say that it works, though no one knows why. Ptolemy might have been happier with what looks more like his 'natural' methods, counting 13½ days as a year, the figure being arrived at by dividing the year by the sidereal month, according to Edward Lyndoe.[126] The Greeks and the Arabs were just as arbitrary and confusing in their methods. One ancient way was to count each degree of right ascension as equivalent to one year of life; this is what Ptolemy describes in *Tetr.* III.10, after rejecting as simplistic and random the idea of simply taking into account the risings of each degree of the ecliptic. Abu Ma'shar describes the matter differently in the opening chapter of the *De rev. nativ.*: 'The sun being in a certain house at the moment of birth, and moving in the zodiac and passing through 360°, and returning through 365 and a bit days, the one born is then one year old and the second year begins. On the second return, the third year begins, and so on. So in the revolution of the year we must set up the Ascendant and construct the twelve

---

[126] *Everyman's Astrology*, rev. edn (London, 1970) 85ff. He says the method was invented by the German astrologer E. H. Troinski in 1951.

houses and set out the positions of the planets. For the Ascendants change in the revolutions of the times, as do the positions of the planets. The radical Ascendant and planets show us the first year, and then the second house signifies the second year, and the third house the third year, and the fourth house the fourth year and so on. Since the sign of the revolution and the Ascendant of the revolution and the houses of the planets all change, the things which happen to men differ.' So Abu Ma'shar is taking houses, or signs, since τόπος, topos is ambiguous, as years, so that once round the zodiac is twelve years. He says so explicitly in II.3, where he is following Dorotheus Book IV: 'In the revolution of the years you must look at the radical Ascendant and reckon each sign as one year, and where you arrive at, that is the sign of the revolution; and the lord of that sign is the chronocrator which is called in Persian salchodaes.' Then that sign and the radical Ascendant are compared in every possible way, including all that affects their decans, their terms, their ninth parts and even their degrees. In Book VIII of his Introductorium Abu Ma'shar lists no fewer than 97 degrees of special significance.

In the course of turning the radical chart to its progressed position, the planets, caput and cauda and so on will all be carried round, and thus pass through positions occupied in the radical chart by others. These entries into others' positions, ἐπεμβάσεις, 'entries upon', in the Greek and ingressus or ingressiones in the Latin, are transits, which are thus consequences and parts of a progression. These transits have the merit of being exactly calculable and having a sort of reality, since in a given period one planet will naturally pass through places in the zodiac previously occupied by another; so they remain of importance in all later theories of progressions. They are dealt with by Dorotheus in Book IV of the Carmen Astrologicum, 186–235 (see also the Greek at Pingree, pp. 379ff). Ptolemy has a mention of them in Tetr. IV.10:[127] 'We must also pay attention to the ingresses which are made to the places of the times ... particularly to the ingresses of Saturn to the general places of the times, and to those of Jupiter to the places of the year', and so on. Abu Ma'shar at the beginning of Book V of De rev. nativ., 'On the transits of the planets,' says: 'The entry of the planets, in the revolution of the years, upon their radical places and the radical places of the others, have certain ineffable[128] significations of good and evil consequences. Therefore we must look at their places. For a planet comes back many times in the revolution of the year to its own radical

---

[127] Robbins, 452–3. The footnote is surely wrong, and the interpretation there given makes no sense of the passage.

[128] The word in Greek is ἀπορρήτους; which can mean 'unspeakable, ineffable', or 'secret, esoteric', or of course, all of these.

degree and many times to its sign, if not actually to the degree. When in the revolution of the year it comes back to the degree in which it was in the radical chart, or into the term in which it was, then is significance will be complete (or: perfect); and if the planet in the revolution of the time is in a certain sign, and then recurs in its radical place, this too will have its signification. When it comes back into the place of another planet, it should be examined in three ways.' First one has to mix the significations of the two planets, or the same planet at different times and therefore differently aspected and so on. Second, one must balance the characters of the two, whether they are beneficent or the opposite, and whether in good or evil places. And third, 'one must look at the sign in which the planet was in the radical chart and treat it as the Ascendant and interpret accordingly.'

On the difficult and vexed topic of house division discussion is again postponed until the next chapter, since it was after the Renaissance that the modern methods and positions were established. The problem is fairly easily stated. The houses – the mundane houses, to give them their proper name, to distinguish them from the planetary houses, for example – are the framework within which the zodiac and all the stars and planets revolve.[129] Twelve in number from antiquity, the first house is the house of the Ascendant; houses I to VI are beneath the horizon, with the signs which are rising in turn; VII to XII are above the horizon, containing the signs moving round east to west to the setting point. Now these are in effect 30° divisions of the ecliptic, along which lies the zodiac circle of the twelve signs, turning once every twenty-four hours. Since the ecliptic is inclined to the equator, at any latitude between the equator and the Arctic (or Anarctic) circle the signs will take unequal lengths of time to rise and set. These unequal periods are listed in tables of 'rising times' for given, different latitudes, or 'climes' (*climata*) as the Greeks called them.[130] Now the problem of house division is this: two points, the Ascendant and the setting point, are fixed since they are the points where some point of the zodiac is rising above and another is setting beneath the horizon, which of course varies with the latitude. So three circles are involved, the equator, the ecliptic and the horizon, each with its own poles. To divide any of these one can draw lines, great circles, through the poles – longitudinal lines. One must run through the Ascendant to give the first house, and one through the setting point to give the seventh. But what about the five in between, to give the six houses above the horizon and the six below? By what rule does

---

[129] See pp. 25ff above.
[130] See Neugebauer and van Hoesen, *Greek Horoscopes*, in the list of terms under *climata*.

one draw those? And which reference system of the three is the one to use? If any, indeed, for one can use none of those three, but instead divide the Prime Vertical, the circle through the observer's zenith and the east and west points of the horizon. Obviously any set of longitudinal divisions will cut all three circles, equator, ecliptic and horizon; and houses are divisions of the ecliptic. Their beginnings, or cusps, have some significance, and it also matters a good deal in which house planets find themselves. So since different systems of house division may alter the locations of planets in the houses, consistency at least if not uniformity of practice would seem to be desirable. Unfortunately there is not nor has there ever been a universally accepted method of house division.

The ancient and medieval world was as confused over the question as the present. To add to the confusion, Vettius Valens in Book II calculates his houses not from the Ascendant but from the Lot of Fortune, and some of the horoscopes he quotes are constructed in this way; in which odd practice he appears to have been following Critodemus. Ptolemy gives no indication of how to make the division, though he refers to the houses as quite understood, and he puts the cusp of the first house five degrees before the Ascendant. A number of ancient and medieval astrologers do the same, including Rhetorius, according to the horoscope of 428 A.D. quoted by Neugebauer and van Hoesen;[131] this horoscope is a little curious, in that it has an unequal division of the second and fourth quadrants (houses IV to VI and houses X to XII) but equal division of the other two. Al-Biruni seems to have the same five 'dead' degrees at the beginning of the house; and his method of determining house division on the astrolabe produces unequal houses (Wright, p. 205): 'Place the degree of the ascendant on the east horizon, the point of the ecliptic on the west horizon is the cusp of the seventh house. Then look at the meridian; what has arrived there is the sign and cusp of the tenth house (the *Medium caeli*). If what you find is also the tenth sign from the ascendant, the angles are erect.' This means that the quadrants are 90° divisions. 'When they (*sc.* the angles) are succedent, the point indicated on the astrolabe will be in the eleventh sign from the ascendant, although it must be written down as the cusp of the tenth house. E.g. if the cusp is in Aquarius, the house will be formed of Aquarius and so many degrees of Pisces, while if the cusp is in the ninth sign, the angles are cadent, and the house is formed of Aquarius and so many degrees of Capricornus.' Alcabitius also has unequal houses, as appears from his *Introductorium*:[132] 'Now that with God's

---

[131] *Ibid.*, p. 138; using CCAG, VII.1, pp. 221ff.
[132] Bologna, 1473, in the chapter *De esse zodiaci accidentali*.

help we have been through the essential nature of the zodiac, let us now go over the accidental nature also. For the zodiac is every hour figured thus: it is divided into four parts by the equator and the meridian, and each quadrant is divided into three unequal parts according to the ascension times of the ascending sign. In this way the circle is divided into twelve parts which are called houses. They are also called cusps. This process is set out in *Achaziz*, that is, the *Book of the Course of the Stars*. Now the beginning of the division is the Ascendant, the start of which is on the equator in the east.' The book he refers to has not survived. So, there were ways of constructing mundane houses with unequal divisions, and there seems to be little evidence in late Greek or medieval astrology for much use of a simple 'equal house system', despite the statement of Koch and Knappich[133] that it was commonly used because it demanded no mathematics, and the belief of many modern astrologers (among whom it is the commonest method used) that it was the most ancient method.

The differences in the ways of calculating the division of the ecliptic into the mundane houses are typical of the variability which character-izes the art at every stage of its history. At no point is there a clear body of accepted learning with generally acknowledged rules. The reasons for this are no doubt many. Astrologers might claim, as many have, that in a subject so vast, with so many – almost countless – influences at play, and such complexity of people and things influenced, certainty is never possible and differences of method and interpreta-tion are inevitable. There is certainly no simple and clear description possible of 'late Greek astrology', only a collage of pieces of pictures, sometimes with obvious connections, but often seemingly uncon-nected. The same is true of the body of astrology possessed by the Western schools in the thirteenth century. What was passed on to them by the Arabs was essentially late Greek astrology. It is very difficult to determine the contributions to the tradition actually made by the Arabic astrologers. One way might be to look at modern astrological books and sift out what clearly came from the Arabs. But examination of a number of textbooks and dictionaries yields little or nothing,[134] especially if one removes from the haul Arabic names for older, Greek ideas. It seems likely that whatever their origins and their connections with Greek astrology, the 'ninths' and the lunar mansions

---

[133] Walter Koch and Wilhelm Knappich, *Horoskop und Himmelshäuser*, Teil 1 (Göppingen, 1959) 49.
[134] Besides M. E. Hone's textbook, already used several times, there were considered: John and Peter Filbey, *Astronomy for Astrologers* (1984); H. E. Wedeck, *Dictionary of Astrology* (1973); J. Mayo, *Teach Yourself Astrology* (1964); Sepharial, *A New Dictionary of Astrology* (1931); Charles E. O. Carter, *Principles of Astrology* (1925); Maurice Wemyss, *The Wheel of Life*, 5 vols (n.d.; late 1920s); and older works by Alan Leo.

were introduced (though not invented) by the Arabs; and the emphasis on certain aspects of astrology rather than others was altered to some extent, though the Latin astrologers followed their own needs and interests too. The liberal use of Arabic terminology in the early years was restricted as acquaintance wth the Greek grew in the thirteenth century. Nevertheless it remains true that the transmission of that whole body of astrological lore which was developed from Greek times through the Middle East and India, was the work of the Arab scholars and their translators; and that by the thirteenth century it was all in the hands of Western astrologers in Latin for the first time in some seven centuries. It is however most important to remember that this astrology was received at the same time as and as an integral part of a whole scientific corpus, including the astronomy of the *Almagest*. We shall return to this point at the end of the chapter, for it may be that the seeds of the apparent death of astrology in the late seventeenth century were contained in the very movement which gave it its second birth.

Those who read and assimilated this newly received science, including *astrologia*, were mostly churchmen; not priests necessarily, though many were, but at least in minor orders.[135] They were *clerici*, 'clerics'. Our words 'clergy' and 'clerk' are both derived from this same Latin word, since in the Middle Ages all clerks were clergy: 'clerical' still preserves both senses. Almost all medieval scholars were church-men; in the long line of Christian philosophers of the Middle Ages the only layman was the Irishman Erigena in the ninth century. Before the twelfth century, most learned clerics were monks, but by the time the city and cathedral schools had grown and been formalized and the universities begun in the thirteenth century, most were secular clergy or belonged to one of the two new orders of friars, the Franciscans or the Dominicans. So it was the Church, in a sense, which received and accepted the new science, including astrology. Why was not astrology rejected as it had been in late antiquity?

In the earlier centuries the Church was fighting superstition and idolatry, and concerned to differentiate its beliefs and practices from the religion and, until and except for St Augustine, the philosophy of the pagan world about it. By the thirteenth century the ancient and superstitious practices of ordinary folk had been absorbed into Christian patterns of living, and differences very much blurred, as some intelligent contemporaries saw and deplored. Paganism had officially disappeared; society was Christian. Of course, these divi-

---

[135] There are seven orders: the first four, from *ostiarius* to *acolyte*, are the minor orders and they were preliminary grades as it were, not subject to all the rules, including celibacy, applicable to the three major holy orders of subdeacon, deacon and priest.

sions are simplistic and somewhat unreal. Paganism and Christianity had lived together in the fourth and fifth centuries, often in the same individual's life and mind. Paganism only disappeared by vanishing into Christianity. The antique gods survived not only in the heavens but as literary figures, and, as both, as art forms – of this there will be more to say when we come to the Renaissance. But at least in the thirteenth century the Church did not feel separated from a secular world of a different sort: it was the world. Nor was it called upon to cope with problems like those of late antiquity, which had been a world of turmoil, of transition, in which nothing appeared firm or unalterable save the Church itself. The western world of the high Middle Ages was, or appeared to be, a firmly established Christian world: Christendom, in which men did not need to seek refuge in ideas of Fortune or in astrological Fate, since their safe home was the Church.

For the centuries of the growth of this Christendom the philosophical background of the West was Augustinian and hence Neo-Platonist. The Platonic tradition was challenged by the discovery of Aristotle in the twelfth century. For the early Middle Ages, Plato and Aristotle were only the revered names of the two great ancient philosophers. Apart from the minor logical works of Aristotle, the writings of neither were directly known. The story of the absorption of Aristotle by the western schools does not belong to this book,[136] but it is fairly common knowledge that the great philosopher-theologians of the thirteenth century – Bonaventure, Aquinas, Scotus and Ockham were the most important – were all Aristotelians. Aristotle's ideas on what constituted *scientia*, that is, knowledge, were generally accepted in the schools, and for two hundred years or more Aristotelianism was the background philosophy of educated men. And Aristotle, as we have seen, said that all sublunary change was the result of and dependent upon motions in the heavens.

All of this meant that astrology could be and would be accepted as part of *astrologia*, as a science properly belonging to the Aristotelian scheme of things, to the whole scientific picture. It played an important part in medicine, and meteorology and alchemy, as well as in such semi-magical pursuits as all forms of divination and the making of amulets, for example. What had to be preserved through all this was the freedom of man's will, his responsibility to God. His physical make-up might be subject to the influences of the heavens, but never his personal being, his will. This was not always an easy distinction to preserve, and there were those in the Church who felt

---

[136] The best short introduction to the history of medieval Christian philosophy is F. C. Copleston's *A History of Medieval Philosophy* (London, 1972), which has a good bibliography.

that 'a non-Christian philosophical naturalism' (Copleston, *op. cit.*, p. 207) was abroad in the schools, and in 1277 Bishop Stephen Tempier of Paris over-hastily issued a list of 219 condemned propositions, not in any particular order,[137] and anathematized all who held any of them. They included teachings of Aristotle, Avicenna, Averroes and even Aquinas, and six of the errors were clearly concerned with astrology. The six condemned propositions are (the first number is Mandonnet's and the second that of the original list):

94 (195) That fate, which is a universal disposition, proceeds from the divine providence not immediately but by the mediation of the movement of the heavenly bodies ...

104 (143) That by different signs in the heavens there are signified different conditions in men both of their spiritual gifts and of their temporal affairs.

105 (207) That in the hour of the begetting of a man in his body and consequently in his soul, which follows the body, by the ordering of causes superior and inferior there is in a man a disposition including him to such and such actions and events. This is an error unless it is understood to mean 'natural events' and 'by way of a disposition'.

106 (206) That anyone attribute health and sickness, life and death, to the position of the stars and the aspect of Fortune, saying that if Fortune is well-aspected to him he will live, and if not, he will die.[138]

154 (162) That our will is subject to the power of heavenly bodies.

156 (161) That the effects of the stars on free will are hidden.

The desire to avoid the error contained in these last two possibly led to the creation of a dictum which became a universally used conscience-saver: *sapiens dominabitur astris*, 'the wise man will be master of the stars'. This saying, in various forms, is usually said to come from the *Centiloquium*, and is sometimes attributed to the *Almagest*; it is to be found, in fact, in neither.[139] A fair illustration of

---

[137] They were edited in a more logical arrangement by P. Mandonnet, *Siger de Brabant, IIe Partie: Textes inédits* (Louvain, 1908) 175ff.
[138] The Latin here is: *quod sanitatem, infirmitatem, vitam et mortem attribuit positioni siderum et aspectui fortunae, dicens quod si aspexerit eum fortuna, vivet, si non aspexerit, morietur.* I have taken the language to be technically astrological and *fortuna* and *aspexerit* to refer to the Lot of Fortune and to aspects.
[139] There is an interesting discussion of the maxim in Appendix 4, 'Homo sapiens dominatur astris', in G. W. Coopland, *Nicole Oresme and the Astrologers* (Liverpool, 1952) 175–177.

the normal educated churchman's attitude to astrology, perhaps, is given in a letter of Berthold of Regensburg, written about two years before his death in 1272. In it he says:[140] 'As God gave their power to stones and to herbs and to words, so also gave he power to the stars, that they have power over all things, except over one thing. They have power over trees and over vines, over leaves and grasses, over vegetables and herbs, over corn and all such things; over the birds in the air, over the animals in the forests, and over the fishes in the waters and over the worms in the earth; over all such things that are under heaven, over them our Lord gave power to the stars, except over one thing. Over that thing no man has any power nor any might, neither have stars nor herbs, nor word nor stones nor angel nor devil nor any man, but God alone. And he will not exercize his power, nor have any authority over that thing. It is man's free will (*friu willekür* = *liberum arbitrium*, "free choice"): over that no man has any authority except thyself.'

But it was an uneasy arrangement. In the thirteenth century churchmen varied in their attitudes to astrology, from more or less full acceptance to a qualified rejection. It is very important to remember that no one questioned the validity of astrology. It could be criticized as too complicated and too difficult to be possible, and parts of it, notably 'judicial' astrology – genethlialogy and the attendant judgments of the affairs of men – might be rejected as wrong. But that it was all possible, everyone accepted. In particular, what might be called scientific or natural astrology was more or less universally acceptable: that is, the uses of astrology in medicine and in meteorology and in alchemy. Since the changes of the sublunary world were caused by heavenly movements, physical changes like chemical reactions and bodily diseases, and the weather (like the tides, always accepted as caused by the moon's movements) were clearly linked to the movements of the stars and planets, and no one could expect to alter the natures of metals (with their ancient links with the planets) or to cure diseases or to understand and forecast the weather and related phenomena, storm and flood and earthquakes and so on, without a knowledge of astrology. This was not superstition; it was good science. So far as meteorology was concerned, it was probably entirely academic. The two classes of men most concerned in practice, farmers and sailors, went on forecasting (at least in the Middle Ages: things may have changed in the seventeenth century) by their old, empirical

---

[140] F. Pfeiffer, *Berthold von Regensburg: vollständige Ausgabe seiner Predigten* (Vienna, 1862) I.50.

and more or less successful methods. Scholars argued over meteorology, including the causes of earthquakes and the aurora borealis, for
example, though they never experienced the one nor saw the other. It
was all in books, written by and for academics.[141] This was of course
no more than typical of medieval patterns of thought and behaviour in
science as in most spheres. What was in books was always more real,
and more important, than what might be seen in the world; the
universal always more true than the particular.

Robert Grosseteste, the great scholar who was Bishop of Lincoln
from 1235 to his death in 1253 – in his vast diocese lay the University
of Oxford, of which he had been a member and chancellor – fully
accepted astrometeorology and the use of astrology in alchemy and
medicine, even if in his later years he became more strongly hostile to
judicial astrology. In his early work 'On the Liberal Arts'[142] Grosseteste
had written: 'Natural philosophy needs the assistance of *astronomia*
more than that of the rest; for there are no, or few, works of ours or of
nature, as for example the propagation of plants, the transmutation of
minerals, the curing of sickness, which can be removed from the sway
of *astronomia*. For nature below (*natura inferior*) effects nothing unless
celestial power moves it and directs it from potency into act.' There
are, it seems, three legitimate, even necessary, kinds of astrology:
meteorological, alchemical and medical. Just before he became Bishop
of Lincoln he wrote the nearest we have to a summary of his thinking,
his *Hexaemeron*.[143] In that work his arguments on astrology are
thoroughly Augustinian. He says (c.9) that even if for the sake of
argument we posited that 'the constellations have a significance and
an effect on the works of free will and on events called fortuitous and
on man's behaviour, yet it would not be possible for an astrologer
(*aliquem mathematicum*) to judge concerning these things.' First,
because sufficient accuracy of observation and calculation is not
possible, and second, because of the impossibility of distinguishing
between twins (cf. Aug., *Civ. Dei.* V.3–9). But in fact free will is not
under the stars, but only under God (c.10), and all, freedom, providence, prayer, would have to be rejected 'if the stars held sway, as
astrologers pretend' – but notice the Latin: *si valerat constellacio, sicut*

---

[141] See Stuart Jenks, 'Astrometeorology in the Middle Ages', in *Isis*, 74 (1983),
pp. 185–210.
[142] *De artibus liberalibus*, ed. Ludwig Baur, 'Die philosophischen Werke des Robert
Grosseteste, Bischofs von Lincoln', in Cl. Bäumker's *Beiträge zur Geschichte der Philosophie des Mittelalters*, IX (1912). The edition includes his *De sphaera* and the later very
popular *De prognosticatione temporum*, 'On weather-forecasting'.
[143] *Robert Grosseteste: Hexaemeron*, ed. Richard C. Dales and Servus Gieben, O. F. M.
Cap, *Auctores Britanninci Medii Aevi*, VI (London, 1982). A *hexaemeron* ('six-day period')
was a commentary on the Genesis creation story.

fingunt astronomi: astronomus is clearly synonymous with *mathematicus*. His summary is (c.11) that 'judges such as these are misled and misleading, and their teaching is impious and profane, written at the direction of the devil.' Robert Kilwardby, the anti-Thomas Dominican Archbishop of Canterbury, took a similar line in his *De ortu scientiarum*, written about 1250.[144] He accepts the Isidorean division of *astrologia* and rejects the *superstitiosa* part, judicial astrology, while accepting natural astrology, which deals with the effects of the stars on health, the weather and so on. He quotes Gundissalinus on the same division, and then realises that he has misquoted, since Gundissalinus used the names the other way round; so he added the interesting note (§76): 'It should be noted that although what we have said is different, and the proper way of taking *'astronomia'* and *'astrologia'*, yet sometimes the name of the one is used for the other, just as happens with *scientia* and *sapientia*, which are taken properly different, but sometimes one is used for the other.'

In contrast, one of the great thirteenth century thinkers, Roger Bacon, wholly accepted astrology. What he says of the subject is to be found especially in Part IV of the *Opus Maius* and in the *Secretum Secretorum*.[145] His editor Bridges says (p. lx) that 'the influence of the stars over human life was a belief almost universally held by all instructed men from the thirteenth to the sixteenth century; and abundant traces of it are visible throughout the seventeenth, not to speak of still later times,' and he remarks in a footnote to a passage where Bacon more than hints at the possibility of foretelling when Antichrist would come (pp. 268–9): 'It may be said on the whole that so far from belief in astrology being a reproach to Bacon and his contemporaries, to have disbelieved in it would have been in the thirteenth century a sign of intellectual weakness.' Over-strongly put perhaps, but Bridges was broadly correct. Bacon's use of the terms *astronomia* and *astrologia* is much that of Gundissalinus: he defines *astronomia* as 'practical *astrologia*', and says (p. 242): 'The true *mathematici*, which is what we are here calling *astronomi* and *astrologi*, because they are so called indifferently by Ptolemy and Avicenna and many others ...' He explains the ambiguities of the term 'house', *domus*, and also the difference between the 'fixed' zodiac, the 30° divisions from the 'first point of Aries', and the moving zodiac, the signs in the sky. He adds a note on the usefulness of the mansions of the moon ('A

---

144 Ed. Albert C. Judy, O.P. (London & Toronto, 1976).
145 *The 'Opus Maius' of Roger Bacon*, ed. J. H. Bridges (1900; 2nd edn reprinted Frankfurt-am-Main, 1964). *Roger Bacon: Opus Maius*, Vol. I, trans. R. B. Burke (Philadelphia, 1928). *Opera hactenus inedita Rogeri Baconi*, fasc. V, *Secretum Secretorum*, ed. Robert Steele (Oxford, 1920).

mansion is the space of the zodiac which the moon crosses in a day', p. 384) for astrometeorology and for critical days in medicine. In his introduction to the *Secretum Secretorum*, he dabbles in geomancy's connections with astrology. He has an interesting note on the planets' natures and effects: 'It should be known, of the signs and of the planets, that they are not in their natural substances hot or cold, dry or wet, but they have the ability to heat or cool, to dry or to wet; just as wine is not naturally hot and dry, but cold and wet, yet it heats and dries; and it makes drunk but is not itself drunken; and so with countless other things.'

The Dominican Albert the Great, *Albertus Magnus*, of Cologne, like his contemporary Bacon, fully accepted astrology into his scientific world-picture.[146] His 'prescribed texts' for astronomy included the *Almagest* with Gerard of Cremona's translation of the commentary of Geber, Latin translations of Masha'allah and other Arabic writers, and books on the astrolabe; and for astrology, the *Quadripartitum* (the Latin for *Tetrabiblos*) and John of Spain's Abu Ma'shar, etc. He clearly also knew his Firmicus Maternus. His greatest pupil was Thomas Aquinas, whose views on astrology were clear and consistent, as might be expected. In *Summa Theologica* Ia, q.115, a.4, the question asked is, 'Whether the heavenly bodies are the cause of human acts.' It is known that they affect the body (and hence the organs of the soul, such as the eyes), and therefore the intellect is affected indirectly and by accident (*indirecte et per accidens*). In the response to the third objection Thomas writes: 'Very many man follow their passions, which are motions of the sensitive appetite, alongside which passions the heavenly bodies can work; few men are wise enough to resist passions of this kind. And therefore astrologers, as in many things, can make true predictions, and this especially in general; not however in particular, for nothing stops any man from resisting his passions by his free will. Therefore the astrologers themselves say that "the wise man is master of the stars" (*sapiens homo dominatur astris*), inasmuch as he is master of his passions.' He says much the same in the *Summa contra Gentiles* III.84; and in his commentaries on Aristotle's *De caelo et mundo* and *De generatione et corruptione*, he is purely Ptolemaic in his astronomy and has the same attitude to astrology. He also explains that pure circular motion would not produce change, it is the obliquity of the ecliptic which does that.

Henri Bate of Malines, who lived in the second half of the thirteenth century and died some time before 1310, took a similar but slightly more sympathetic line – sympathetic to astrology, that is. He translated the *De revolutionibus annorum mundi*, 'On the revolutions of the

---

[146] See *Albertus Magnus and the Sciences, Commemorative Essays 1980*, ed. James A. Weisheipl, O.P. (Toronto, 1980).

years of the world', of Abraham ibn Ezra and was translating astrological works for the papal court in Orvieto towards the end of the century.[147] He wrote his own introduction to and commentary on ibn Ezra, who incidentally thought very little of Abu Ma'shar: 'If you come across a book of Abu Ma'shar on the conjunction of the planets, don't take any notice of it; no sensible man would agree with it.' About 1302 Henri Bate wrote a *Speculum*, a sort of *summa*, including a Book XII on Fate, for the Bishop of Utrecht, Guy de Hainault. His authorities for that book included Calcidius, Augustine, Boethius, 'Hermes' and Firmicus; and specifically on astrology, Ptolemy, Avicenna and Abu Ma'shar. The scientist and clock-designer Richard of Wallingford[148] clearly accepted astrology as a science, as is shown in his *Exafrenon pronosticacionum temporis*, which 'is an exposition of basic astrological principles', written before 1326; it 'shows no taint of the astrological determinism which the theologians feared would undermine the doctrine of free will', and 'no suggestion of respect for the pagan deities associated with the planets in the literature and iconography of the time.' Wallingford was obviously influenced by Grosseteste, but his chief source is John of Seville's translation of the *Maius introductorium* of Abu Ma'shar. The *Exafrenon* was translated into English by a contemporary of Chaucer in the late fourteenth century.

On the other, anti-astrological side, the Mertonian mathematician Thomas Bradwardine, who was called to be Archbishop of Canterbury during the ravages of the Black Death in 1349 and died a few months later, in his large work *De causa Dei*[149] aimed to show that 'it would perhaps be very fitting and most profitable if Theologians and good Catholics were not ignorant of Astrology and other such sciences', because they were necessary for the explanation of Scripture, and also for demonstration of their errors and the defence of man's freedom. He uses *astrologia* in a general way, mainly to refer to astronomy; he seems to accept natural astrology, he nowhere discusses genethlialogy or elections, and he generally takes an Augustinian line as on, for example, the Star of Bethlehem. He knows, however, his Ptolemy and his Abu Ma'shar. Later in the fourteenth century Henry of Langenstein[150] thought in much the same way, accepting medical and

---

[147] See G. Wallerand, *Henri Bate de Malines* (*Les Philosophes Belges XI*) (Louvain, 1951).
[148] See J. D. North, *Richard of Wallingford*, 3 vols (Oxford, 1976); the *Exafrenon* is in Vol. II (*Exafrenon* apparently means a work in six parts; it has six chapters). North includes (III.277ff) an extremely valuable glossary of Latin words. The quotations in the text are from North.
[149] *Thomae Bradwardini Archiepiscopi olim Cantuariensis De Causa Dei . . . libri tres*, etc., ed. Henry Savile (London, 1618).
[150] Nicholas H. Steneck, *Science and Creation in the Middle Ages. Henry of Langenstein (d.1397) on Genesis* (London, 1976). It is actually an account of the *hexaemeron* part of Henry's commentary on *Genesis*.

meteorological uses of astrology, but writing a number of anti-astrological tracts (probably sparked off by the discussions of the comet of 1368) the arguments of which very much recall those of Grosseteste.

The general acceptance of 'natural' astrology – the use of planetary influences in medicine, alchemy and meteorology – is not surprising, given the universal belief in Aristotle's physics. It would have been unscientific to have rejected such *astrologia*. We shall not here be concerned with alchemy, the story of which is interestingly parallel to that of astrology, though in some ways simpler. The emergence of chemistry from alchemy and the disappearance of the latter are more simply accounted for than the apparently analogous emergence of astronomy and the (at least temporary) disappearance of astrology. Alchemy had always been more a practical than a theoretical science despite many magical and quasi-religious accretions: hypotheses not only could be but had to be tested in the crucible. *Astrologia* was a wholly theoretical science until very modern times; the only test of a hypothesis was observation and measurement to see whether it fitted what was seen, whether it 'saved the phenomena', in the ancient Greek expression. It is true however that alchemy and astrology both disappeared from the educated world (and alchemy had never be-longed to any other) at about the same time and many of the causes were common; of this more will be said in Chapter VI. For now, it need only be noted that the associations of planets and metals established in Alexandrian Egypt ensured astrology's close links with alchemy, the main object of which was the transmutation of base metals into precious, and one aspect of which was the whole science of alloys and the like, including of course the rather shady business of fakes and counterfeits. It was all very scientific with a basis in ancient doctrines of the elements which also formed part of Aristotelian physics; so on one in the later Middle Ages or Renaissance ever questioned the validity of the association, whatever his views on the whole.

Astrometeorology, or the forecasting of the weather and of natural disasters by reference to events in the starry heavens, was and is almost the oldest and surely the most persistent part of astrology. From the earliest days of 'proto-astrology', the omen-literature of the first millenium B.C., certain conjunctions or eclipses or occultations of planets, and especially comets, were associated with storm and flood, drought and burning heat, and earthquakes. The development of the science of *astrologia* made possible long-term forecasting of such starry events and their consequences, and such prognostication became and remained part of astrology not only in times when astrology was favoured and widely practised; even in ages of its disrepute popular almanacs always contained, as they still do, weather forecasts. It is true that apart from the almanacs of later times this was, in and before the Middle Ages, largely a bookish exercise, practical weather prediction being the province of those most concerned, country men and seamen. Tales were told of most *astrologi* no doubt, as certainly of Bonatti, about their failures in forecasting the immediate weather prospects and their ensuing, usually soaked, discomfiture, though not many went so far as the innkeeper who told the eighteenth century almanac writer Partridge that he could always rely on the weather being precisely contrary to what was predicted in Partridge's almanac. But it must be remarked that farmers and sailors included, as they still include, much 'astrological' lore in their weather forecasting, and many would swear more by the state of the moon than by the satellite pictures of anticyclones. That the heavens, and especially the sun and the moon, are connected with the weather is obvious, if it be only in the calendrial, seasonal sense. And it may be that before very recent times of satellites and computers, astrological weather-forecasting was no less accurate, or no more inaccurate, than any other way of attempting the near impossible.[151] Comets were and remain special cases. The extraordinary weather-spasms of this spring (1986) have by many been set down to Halley's comet. Comets' influence spread itself much more widely than the weather, of course, to include disasters of most kinds, both personal and general, including wars and the deaths of princes.[152] Comets were carefully but variously classified and given curious names, and allocated to planets, whose natures they shared, and their effects in the different signs were listed. Ptolemy has little or nothing to say of them, but the Pseudo-Ptolemy of the *Centiloquium* had nine types, and the commonest source-book for the thirteenth century was 'Haly's' commentary on the *Centiloquium* (according to Steinschneider actually written by Ahmed ibn Yusuf). Comets had effects on the air and produced vapours, dry or wet, hot or cold, according to their natures. Almost all their effects were noxious: war, pestilence, famine, flood or drought and above all death. The treatises on comets are generally speaking more 'scientific' than astrological

[151] Perhaps Britain particularly, and even N.W. Europe, was the most difficult area to cover accurately with such forecasts as were possible. Dr G. Herdan, the late medical statistician in the University of Bristol (better known, perhaps, for his *Language as Choice and Chance*), once argued from a statistical analysis that one could forecast tomorrow's local weather in three ways: it will be as it is today; it will be as it was on the same date last year; or it will be as the Meteorological Office says it will be; and the error would be the same in all three cases.

[152] See *Latin Treatises on Comets between 1238 and 1368 A.D.* edited by Lynn Thorndike (Chicago, 1950). It is curious that Mark Twain was impressed that he was born in November, 1835, with Halley's comet in the sky; he died in April, 1910, with the comet back again. But then so did thousands of others.

and indeed the late thirteenth century one of Gerard (of 'Silteo') is very critical of judicial astrology in ways which point forward to Oresme and Pico, while asserting the values of 'natural' astrology – an ambivalent attitude met with in many later authors.

Without a comet to account for it, the Black Death, which arrived in Europe in 1347 and swept across the continent for three years,[153] while it was most commonly seen as God's wrath visited on a depraved world, was also provided with astrological credentials. The official statement of the Medical Faculty of the University of Paris presented to the king in 1348 reported that 'on 20 March 1345, at 1 p.m., there occurred a conjunction of Saturn, Jupiter and Mars in the house of Aquarius. The conjunction of Saturn and Jupiter notoriously caused death and disaster while the conjunction of Mars and Jupiter spread pestilence in the air (Jupiter, being warm and humid, was calculated to draw up evil vapours from the earth and water which Mars, hot and dry, then kindled into infective fire). Obviously the conjunction of all three planets could only mean an epidemic of cataclysmic scale' (Ziegler, p. 38). Ziegler is surely right (p. 22) when he says that 'the monstrous dimensions of the disaster ... forced its victims to seek some proportionately monstrous explanation', so that normal medical explanations of epidemics from Galen or the Arab Razes were largely irrelevant. But the natural tendency was to look for astrological causes of changes in the atmosphere since astrology and medicine were joined before Ptolemy's time, and corruption of the air was the most commonly suggested immediate cause of the Plague and its spread. A treatise of 1348 states the principle plainly: 'all corruptions of the air are reduced to celestial causes'.[154] Various conjunctions, and an eclipse of 1345, were alleged to be causes, and it seems that only Gentile da Foligno and Konrade of Megenberg rejected such explanations and tried to suggest physical and physiological causes. Gentile was best known for his *consilia*, his 'case-books', which were truly in the

---

[153] The best single work on the Black Death (with an excellent bibliography) is Philip Ziegler's *The Black Death* (London, 1969) cited here from the Pelican Books edition of 1970. He makes a finely pertinent observation on contemporary ideas of the causes on p. 24: 'Enjoying as we do the immense superiority of a generation which has devised means of mass destruction more effective even than those afflicted by nature on our ancestors, it is easy and tempting to deride their inability to understand the calamity which had overtaken them.' Anna Campbell said something similar earlier in her important *The Black Death and Men of Learning* (New York, 1931) 8. Her book has a good general account of the fourteenth century treatises and of the attitudes of and effects on men of learning. See especially Chapter V for astrology; but notice that while the author recognises the lack of distinction between astronomy and astrology at that time, she herself nevertheless divides her scholars in a modern fashion.

[154] See K. Sudhoff, 'Pestschrift aus den ersten 150 Jahres nach der Epidemie des "schwarzen Todes" 1348', in *Archiv für Geschichte der Medizin* (Leipzig, 1911) V.42.

Hippocratic tradition. His was one of the six treatises on the Plague written in 1348.

More typical of medieval medical theorists, perhaps, was Arnald of Villanova, who died in his seventies in 1313. His works, in the Basle edition of 1585, are classified as *Medica* and *Exotica*, and the *exotica* are subdivided into *Chymica*, *Astronomica* and *Theologica*. The one book on astrology is 'On judgments of sicknesses, according to the movement of the planets, for the not inconsiderable assistance of doctors'. Earlier in the volume (823C–E), in a medical work 'on preserving one's youth', Arnald claims that Hippocrates showed that astrology was a significant part of medicine; and although there was no necessity involved in stellar influences, these influences did dispose and 'habituate' everytything. Yet 'the wise man will master the stars by his rationality': *vir sapiens dominabitur astris sua rationabilitate*. The twin and related sciences of astrology and medicine are both needed by the doctor, under the grace of God. The work *De iudiciis infirmitatum* contains an outline of astrology, with explanations from Aristotle's physics of, for example, the natures of triplicities; he rather glosses over terms, as needing more effort than is justified by their importance; his houses are unequal, but it is not clear what system he is using; and, not surprisingly for a doctor, he has two chapters on the moon. As an example of the kind of use to which it was all put, he says in c.10: 'If the Ascendant should be in a "obile" sign, and the moon in the same sort of sign – namely Aries, Cancer, Libra or Capricorn – and the Lord of the Ascendant likewise, the sickness will be over quickly, for good or ill.' Astrologers were also needed to advise on times to carry out operations, and on the gathering and uses of herbs. Medicine was the only truly empirical science invented by the ancient Greeks, and despite the growth of theories and schools of thought, in all ages, must remain empirical at the bottom. Since doctors needed to be as exact as they could in their applications of astrology, especially in their timing, medical men played an important part in the technological developments of the later Middle Ages.[155] Not only, perhaps, of the Middle Ages: astrological influence on medicine persisted until the nineteenth century.

The links between medicine and astrology were nowhere more obviously stressed than in the University of Bologna, one of the oldest universities and medical schools in medieval Europe. Italy then as for centuries later was a collection of city states, with more or less unbroken tradition links with antiquity; and an educated laity,

---

[155] Lynn White Jr, 'Medical astrologers and late medieval technology', in *Viator*, 6 (1975) 295–308; the introduction is very wide of a number of marks, and grossly exaggerates the importance of Martianus Capella.

including city governors, whether oligarchic and mercantile or aristocratic, played a much greater part in society than north of the Alps.
The Italian universities were different in their origins and constitutions from those of north-west Europe, and much more independent
of the Church, though none of course was wholly so in an age when all
learning came under the Church's scrutiny and guardianship. Their
function was to educate men for the professions, especially law and
medicine. A student of medicine was bound to study physics; the
understanding of physiology (the 'study of nature') demanded it. So
the doctor was bound to be a 'physician' – un physicien, in French, a
physicist; the French for the English 'physician' is médecin. He also
had to study astrology. The Professor of Astrologia taught a four year
course.[156] His duties included answering, free, enquiries from students
within a month of being asked, and publishing his almanac for each
year, with planetary movements and conjunctions etc., particularly for
the use of doctors of medicine. In the early fifteenth century, for which
we have details, the course was a curious one, including the somewhat
difficult Theorica planetarum, 'Theory of the Planets', in the first year,
and the introductory Sphaera in the second. The Almagest waited until
the fourth year, with 'the rest of the Quadripartitum'. From the reaction
of the Medical Faculty of the University of Paris in 1348 to the request
from Philip IV for a statement on the Black Death, and the slightly later
and similar statement from Montpellier, we may assume that astrology
played the same part in French medical schools and there too, as at
Bologna, alongside of Euclid the student read Sacrobosco's Sphaera
and Ptolemy (including of course the Centiloquium) and their commentators. The subject was astrologia or astronomia, without distinction. In
Bologna the professor taught astrologia until the middle of the
fourteenth century, and thereafter astronomia, according to the statutes,
but as Bartolotti says (p. 11), 'the material was always the same'. The
seventeenth century professor Bonaventura Covalieri published in
1639 a Nuova pratica astrologica on Keplerian lines, and even in 1799
the professor was still required 'Conficiat tacuinum astronomicum ad
medicinae usum' – to make an annual almanac for medical use.

Naturally, in the study of astrologia, the mechanics of the universe
have to be understood at least in outline before astrology can be
described or practised. The description of the universe in astronomical
terms was done, as it had been in antiquity, in a Sphaera, a book 'On
the Sphere'. By far the most popular textbook in the schools was for
centuries – despite would-be rivals by such scholars as Grosseteste,
Peckham and Campanus – that by John of Holywood, usually known

---

[156] See the early pages of Ettore Bartolotti, La Storia della Matematica nella Università di
Bologna (Bologna, 1947).

as John Sacrobosco. His *Sphaera* was traditional, largely Latin in its sources, fairly simple, and clear. As Thorndike says,[157] he 'welded together Macrobius and Ptolemy and frosted it over with Alfraganus, and his book stayed in style for five centuries.' It was written in the first quarter of the thirteenth century. What it covered is described in the Proemium (Thorndike's translation): 'The treatise on the sphere we divide into four chapters, telling first, what a sphere is, what its centre is, what the axis of a sphere is, what the pole of the world is, how many spheres there are, and what the shape of the world is. In the second we give information concerning the circles of which this material sphere is composed and that supercelestial one, of which this is the image, is understood to be composed. In the third we talk about the rising and setting of the signs, and the diversity of days and nights which happens to those inhabiting diverse localities, and the division into climes. In the fourth the matter concerns the circles and motions of the planets and the causes of eclipses.' Since chapter 4's matter on 'the circles and motions of the planets' takes up only forty-three lines of Thorndike's Latin text, one can see why students needed the *Theorica planetarum* at least with, though scarcely before, the *Sphaera*. Sacrobosco's book is wholly astronomical, in the modern sense, though he does refer, having described the zodiac, to the fact that 'by Aristotle, in *On generation and corruption*, it is called the "oblique circle", where he says that, according to the access and recess of the sun in the oblique circle, are produced generations and corruptions in things below.' Commentators might remain within the purely mathematical limits of the original, or enlarge into astrology as the writer pleased. One anonymous commentary of the late thirteenth or early fourteenth century[158] uses *astrologia* and *astrologus* as the generic terms, and then distinguishes the *communia* of a science which must be known to understand the *propria*. The *Sphaera* covers the *communia*, that is, what we should call astronomy and the '*propria* of the art are the things which are known through those things which are common, or which follow on the knowledge of those things such as are the conjunctions of planets and the culminations of *centra* and the wonderful effects following from the aspects of the planets and many other things which need deeper discussion in their special places.' So the 'common ground' is astronomy and much that is described as 'proper' is astrology. The earliest commentaries in Thorndike, which

---

157 Lynn Thorndike, *The Sphere of Sacrobosco and its Commentators* (Chicago, 1949). The book contains the Latin text of the *Sphaera* and an English translation as well as texts of the commentators.
158 Thorndike, 456ff.

are late thirteenth century, contain a good deal of astrological matter, and clearly an elementary textbook needed very little explaining on the astronomical side. The provenance and the dates of the commentaries testify to the lasting and widespread influence of Sacrobosco; and it did provide an entirely astronomical basis for expansion by any teacher interested in mathematical astronomy rather than astrology.

The professors at Bologna were of course committed by the statutes of their appointment to the practice of some astrology. The first name in the list of professors given by Bartolotti is that of Guido Bonatti, one of the best known of thirteenth century astrologers. Alas, much that is 'known' about him is guesswork or apocryphal; in particular, he may or may not have studied and taught in Bologna in the 1230s – there is no firm evidence beyond tradition. He was born at Forli some time before 1220 and died towards the end of the century. He wrote a twelve-book treatise *De astronomia* which dealt with astrology, with 'revolutions' (progressions) and elections and so on. The astrology is purely traditional, with the common confusion over house-division, for example; all in the same thirteenth century Arabic-Latin mould. Bonatti seems to have been in a number of Italian cities, including Florence and Bologna, and to have been attached to more than one prince, including Guido de Montefeltro, if Villani's *Life* is to be believed.[159] Villani, quoting Benvenuto de Imola's *De divinatoribus*, c.20, is the only authority for the story of the tentative reconciliation of the feuding Guelfs and Ghibellines at Forli about 1282. The Guelfs were the supporters of the Pope against the Emperor, whose supporters were the Ghibellines, to which party Montefeltro and hence Bonatti belonged. The idea was that Forli should be solemnly re-founded and new walls built, and that at an astrologically determined auspicious moment a leading Guelf and a leading Ghibelline should cast in the first stones for the new walls. All was ready, and the two parties assembled, but when Bonatti gave the signal that the crucial moment had arrived, the Ghibelline cast in his stone but the Guelf hestitated and then refused to co-operate because Bonatti was a Ghibelline and was obviously 'fixing' it for his own side's advantage. Bonatti is to be seen in Dante's *Inferno*, Canto XX.118, but very much only in passing. In describing the diviners who were being punished for wanting to pry into a future belonging only to God by having their heads turned on their shoulders to face backwards, Dante simply says: *Vedi Guido Bonatti, vedi Asdente*, 'I saw Guido Bonatti, I saw Asdente'. The latter was a notorious soothsayer of Parma. It looks very much as

[159] In *Rerum Italicarum Scriptores*, XXII, ii, ed. Mezzatinti (1903). Villani it is who says that Guido of Montefeltro 'used the advice of this very skilled astrologer in all his actions'. Villani also remarks of Bonatti's book that 'in it he treats the subject of astrology so clearly that he seems to be desirous of teaching it to women'.

though the Florentine Guelf Dante has Bonatti in Hell rather because of his attachment to the Ghibellines than because of his astrology.

Three lines earlier Dante had introduced an even more notable, and earlier, astrologer: Michael Scot: 'That other, who is so small about the flanks, was Michael Scot, who truly knew the game of magic frauds'; and certainly he was concerned with geomancy among other forms of divination. There is no knowing why he was thin-legged! Again however there are more fables than hard facts. He was a fairly typical thirteenth century savant, interested in more or less anything 'scientific'. He was probably born in Scotland toward the end of the twelfth century – in 1217 he translated al Bitrugi's *Sphaera* in Toledo – and in the 1220s he was well enough established and known at the papal court (not, it seems, only as an astrologer) to be appointed to the Archbishopric of Cashel, which he declined because he knew no Irish, and to be recommended in 1227 to the Archbishop of Canterbury by Pope Gregory IX as a scholar and one who had 'added a knowledge of Hebrew and Arabic to his wide familiarity with Latin learning'. From about that time until his death about 1236 he was attached to the court of Frederick II in Sicily, where he wrote his few astrological works, which seem really to be all one work[160] including the widely read *Liber introductorius*. Both Frederick and Michael Scot appear to have been more interested in all kinds of scientific questions than in astrology, but both of course would accept astrology as an established part of contemporary science, practically useful and even necessary. The evidence for Frederick's interest is thin, however. Two things link the emperor with astrology: his marriage and his foundation of the new city of Victoria, and only the first rests on good authority. In 1235 Frederick married Isabella the sister of Henry III of England but, Matthew Paris informs us under that year, 'he refused to know her carnally until the fitting hour should be told him by his astrologers . . .', which caused a little offence. It may indeed have produced a son, Jordanus, but the only certainly known son was Henry, born in 1238. Since Matthew Paris, though not the most trustworthy of historians, was in fact intimate with both King Henry and his brother Richard, Earl of Cornwall, the story has to be believed. There is however no overt connection with Michael Scot.

In 1247 Frederick besieged Parma, and decided to build a new city over against Parma, which he called Victoria. The chronicler Rolandino of Padua, who had been a Bologna student, says:[161] 'He built over against the city (of Parma) almost before the gates another city, which

---

[160] See c.XIII of C. H. Haskins' *Studies in the History of Medieval Science* (Cambridge, Mass., 1924).
[161] *Rolandini Patavini Chronicon*, ed. P. Jaffé, *MGH Scriptores*, XIX (1866; repr. 1963) 85.

he named Victoria. And because he knew that the great men of ancient times had regard to the Ascendant when they wished to found cities, and themselves drew the perimeters of the cities with a plough, which is why they are called 'cities' (*urbes*; Varro is the authority: the boundary was marked with the curved tail of the plough, called *urvus* or *urbus*), he began himself to mark out his new city when Aries was in the Ascendant; both because that is the sign of Mars, said to be the god of war, and because in its setting it was in opposition to ascendant Libra, the sign of Venus, which was said to be the planet of Parma and its good fortune. So he seems to have thought that the fortune of the citizens of Parma, opposed to him, would begin to set. For in astrology and other such subtle arts the first house is given to the doer of a deed, the seventh to his opponent. But I think that he did not remark that the fourth sign from the Ascendant was Cancer, and the fourth house denotes buildings, houses and cities, and so his city, begun under such an Ascendant, would necessarily be cancerous.' Rolandino may have studied astrology at Bologna, and it does look as though he is here showing off his knowledge. What is significant is that there is no mention of astrology or astrologers in seven other sources for the story of the founding of Victoria, including the generally reliable Ghibelline *Annales Placentini* and Salimbene, gossipy and anti-Frederick though that author was. It is of course certain that Frederick believed and was interested in astrology, and Michael Scot's astrological work was written for him, and although it may be going too far to say 'he would undertake no important enterprise without first consulting the stars',[162] he certainly used both Michael and his successor Theodore as his astrologers, as the same Rolandino else-where tells us.[163] And as Haskins says (*op. cit.*, p. 290), Scot's account, in his *Liber Introductorius* 'of the wealth and position of the astrologer and his mode of life reflect the influence and position of the profession in the Italy of the thirteenth century'.

That book, Michael Scot tells his readers at the beginning, was written by 'the *astrologus* of the Emperor Frederick' – the astronomer royal, as it were – 'for student beginners and those not over-burdened with intelligence.' It is a large work, full of detail, well illustrated in the manuscripts and wholly traditional.[164] He says, interestingly, at f. 41v of Bodley 266, that 'there are in each sign many images and

---

[162] Thomas Curtis van Cleve, *The Emperor Frederick II of Hohenstaufen* (Oxford, 1972) 308.

[163] *Rerum Italicarum Scriptores*, VIII, i, *Rolandini Patavini Cronica Marchie Trivixane*, ed. A. Bonardi (1903), Book IV, c.xii. (Also in *MGH*: see note 161 above.)

[164] References here are to MS Bodley 266, a fifteenth century copy of the fourteenth century Munich MS 10268.

mansions, not only of the moon but of the other planets.' If *mansiones* is to be taken with *ceterorum planetarum* (as well as *ymagines*), are they mansions in the same sense as lunar ones? That is, are they distances covered by planets in a given unit of time? Or is it just a reference to decans, dodecatemories and so on, all allocated to planets? He lists some of his authorities (f. 65r) as Ptolemy, Alexander, Demetrius, Theodosius, Dorotheus, Ja'far, Thebit ibn Qurra, al Fargani, Empedocles (?; the MS has *eppedotes*),[165] Euclid and Aristotle. The *horologium* and the astrolabe are necessary, he says, to the astrologer to establish the hour and the Ascendant, and also to calculate the houses: Scot gives directions for these on f. 183r. The *horologium* was certainly not a clock (clocks were not known until the late fourteenth century) but was probably a sundial: portable sun-'dials' – some were cylindrical – were made from the ninth century on. So a dial would be used to establish the time of day, and the stellar positions found from tables; and the astrolabe would be used at night. The work is a completely integrated mixture of what we should call astronomy and astrology, since there was absolutely no distinction within the science of *astrologia* for Scot or his readers. The account of the *saltus lunae*, the 'moon's leap', the adjustment of the moon's nineteen-year cycle to keep it in step with the sun, ultimately taken largely from Bede, is followed by a section on calendary intercalculations, mnemonic verses on the signs of the zodiac (obviously regarded as calendar markers, their original and continuing use, as is shown in so many pictorial representations), descriptions of constellations and the planets, and then, logically enough, an account of the planetary houses, their exaltations, their terms, and by association the divisions of the zodiac, and so to the mundane houses, and so on. The lists of planets and their effects generally include the head and tail of the dragon, and the lunar mansions are introduced more than once. It is a long work, but it does cover a good deal of the ground.

Roger Bacon thought very little of Michael Scot as scientist or linguist, but he had a great respect for another thirteenth century astrologer, a contemporary of Bonatti, Campanus of Novara, to whom he refers in 1267 as one of the few good mathematicians of his time. Campanus, who died in 1296, was really a mathematician and astronomer first, and his interest in astrology seems to have been in that aspect of the subject. He wrote a *Sphaera* and a *Theorica planetarum*, 'Theory of the Planets' (not the one commonly used in the

---

[165] At f. 8r Scot has the 'definition' *Deus est intellectualis spera cuius centrum est ubique, circumferentia vero nusquam*, 'God is an intellectual sphere whose centre is eveywhere and whose circumference is nowhere'. This is given in Hamesse's edition of the slightly later florilegium, *Auctoritates Aristotelis* (p. 299) under the name of Empedocles.

schools after the 1240s to supplement Sacrobosco; that was probably Gerard of Cremona's, as Regiomontanus said). Campanus' *Theorica* includes instructions for making an *equatorium*, a simple armillary sphere used in teaching. He was and is best known for his edition of Euclid and his commentary on the important mathematical work of Leonard Fibonacci of Pisa. Campanus' works were unoriginal, perhaps, but important for late medieval education. The editors of his *Theorica planetarum*, Benjamin and Toomer[166] have doubts about the authenticity of astrological works ascribed to Campanus. Toomer in his biographical article says that 'a method of his for dividing the heavens into the twelve "houses" is mentioned by Regiomontanus and others, but no such work survives that can definitely be assigned to him.' There seems to have been a manuscript with a Latin title which means, 'A little work on the twelve signs of the zodiac, with a special method of erecting a chart of the heavens by division of the prime vertical,' in the eighteenth century, but if so, it has not yet turned up.[167] It is the kind of subject that would have interested Campanus, who seems fairly aloof from judicial astrology. He quotes the Isidorean distinction, and accepts that astrologers need first to study the theory, which is what interests him, before proceeding to 'judgments'. Whatever Campanus' ideas on house division, in the next generation Andalò di Negro, Boccaccio's teacher, who died in 1334, wrote yet another *Introductorium* in which the horizon and the meridian are the framework, and the houses are equal in unequal quadrants. Andelò is much more an astrologer than an astronomer, and deals with such purely astrological matters as the Lot of Fortune, for example, and lists of lucky and unlucky hours and their association with the planets.

At this time, early in the fourteenth century, when popes and bishops and the courts of princes all had their astrologers, one of them, astrologer at the court of Florence, who had lectured at Bologna on the *Sphaera* and on Alcabitius, was burnt at the stake as a heretic on 16 September 1327: Cecco d'Ascoli.[168] Cecco may have been the son

---

[166] *Theorica Planetarum*, ed. F. S. Benjamin and G. J. Toomer (Madison, Wisconsin/London, 1971); see also Toomer's article in *Dictionary of Scientific Biography* (New York, 1971), III.

[167] *Histoire Littéraire de la France* (Paris, 1847), XXI. P. C. F. Daunou refers to eighteenth century bibliographers, but no reference is given for the manuscript.

[168] What follows is largely based on two works of Giuseppe Boffito: 'Perchè fu condannato al fuoco l'astrologo Cecco d'Ascoli?' in *Studi e documenti di storia e diritto*, XX (1899) 357–382; and 'il "De principiis astrologie" di Cecco d'Ascoli, novamente scoperto e illustrato', *Giornale storico della Letteratura Italiana*, Suppl. 6 (Turin, 1903). Lynn Thorndike, 'More light on Cecco d'Ascoli', in *Romanic Review*, XXVII (1946), 293–306, adds very little, in fact; he uses Ernst Mehl, 'Zum Prozess des Cecco d'Ascoli', in *Festschrift für Georg Leidinger* (1930) 179–186, but that, like most of the earlier work considered by Boffito, is largely informed guesswork.

of a Salernitan doctor. He was certainly much concerned with medicine and begins his commentary on the *Sphere* of Sacrobosco thus: 'A doctor must of necessity know and take into account the natures of the stars and their conjunctions ...' He studied and taught in Bologna, lecturing there from 1324 on the *Sphaera* in the second year course and on Alcabitius in the third year and writing commentaries (incomplete) on both. The first is in Thorndike's book already cited, and the second is the *De principiis astrologiae* (a title a little difficult to translate, since *principia* are principles, foundations and beginnings). On 16 September 1324 the Dominican Inquisitor in Bologna, Lambertus de Cingulo, found Cecco guilty of offences against the faith, and sentenced him to acts of penance, fined him heavily and confiscated his astrological books, and forbade him to teach astrology. In 1326 he was in Florence with the duke, but was burnt the following year, apparently for teaching the same errors, and his works were condemned on 15 December of that year. So much is fairly clear from later (seventeenth century) manuscript evidence. Marsilio Ficino, Pico della Mirandola and Villani, closer to Cecco's time, are all agreed that Cecco, known as a magician as well as an astrologer, applied his astrology to the birth and death of Christ, and to the coming of Antichrist and the end of the world; and perhaps also implied that astrological necessity ruled not only men's wills but all the future.

What is the evidence of Cecco's works? There is no other contemporary evidence. Apart from his astrological works he also wrote a long satirical poem in the vernacular, *L'Acerba*, which Boffito uses to support his interpretation. There were other works lost or not yet traced such as two he refers to in his commentary on the *Sphere*: a commentary on Hippocrates' *Airs, Waters and Places*, and a book on 'Wonders in Nature' which might, as Thorndike suggests, be the *De mirabilibus mundi* ascribed to Albertus Magnus. To return to the extant works, one great difficulty is that it is impossible to be sure that the texts of Cecco's commentaries as we have them are not emended texts altered to satisfy the ecclesiastical authorities. There are places where it certainly looks as though Cecco has added a note of conformity to what remains a very provocative text. For example in the commentary on the *Sphere* the text in Thorndike reads (pp. 180–181): 'Another thing you must know is that according to our faith, the true faith, that circle made in the zodiac by the rays of the planets, although it is the cause of life, yet it is not the cause of our will nor of our intellect except by a disposition (*dispositive*: shades of Tempier and 1277!), and this I hold and truly believe, although other astrologers hold the contrary, saying that all things generated and corrupted and renewed in this lower, generable and corruptible world have efficient causes in the higher, ungenerable and incorruptible world, and they prove it thus ...' And there follows a syllogistic proof of their position, followed by the sentence: 'I shall destroy that argument in my commentary on the *Centiloquium*, first proposition, where is the place for it.' Similarly in the discussion on the eclipse at the Crucifixion, briefly dealt with by Sacrobosco at the end of the *Sphaera*, Cecco states the question formally as a *quaestio disputata* or *quodlibetalis*:[169] 'Whether (*utrum*) the eclipse which happened during the Passion of Christ was natural or (*an*) miraculous; and it seems that (*videtur quod*) it was neither natural nor miraculous.' Cecco shows on good astronomical grounds (as did Sacrobosco) that it could not have been natural, at the time of the full moon. He then argues that it was not miraculous either, for then there would have to have been a change in the heavenly workings, or their complete overthrow, 'but if the universe cause were changed or overthrown, all that is caused would be universally wrecked and changed.' But neither of these things seemed to have happened, therefore, etc.[170] Then, after much discussion of others' explanations of the eclipse he writes: 'Therefore I say in reply to the question that the eclipse at Christ's death was miraculous and against (or: beyond – *praeter*) nature, and occured only because of God's absolute power, because God when he wishes can alter the order of nature; "wanting" and "being able" are the same for him (*velle et posse convertitur in ipso*).' Which is all good scholastic argument but leaves one wondering what the actual discussion in the classroom was like!

There may have been complicated political motives behind the execution of Cecco, compounded with city rivalries. It is possible that his second judge, the Franciscan Bishop of Aversa, Accursius, regarded him as a supporter of Louis of Bavaria and the breakaway Franciscans insisting on the absoluteness of poverty, under Michael of Cesena and, later, William Ockham – Cecco is said by Villani to have assisted Louis. But it is probable enough that his teaching at Bologna was heretical, and the combination of causes brought about his death rather than his imprisonment. Or like others later, he may have been what the Church called contumacious: Villani says he was a vain man and 'of worldly life', *di mondana vita*. The same authority also suggests personal motives of Accursius and of Dino of Florence, who was 'the great cause of the death of Cecco, falsely condemning his said book ...

---

[169] Masters in the medieval university had, on occasions laid down in statutes, to 'dispute' questions before their fellows and students. The set occasions when the master produced the questions he intended to dispute produced *quaestiones disputatae*, 'disputed questions'. On a number of other days he had to argue on questions 'from the floor', as it were – 'any question at all', which is what *quaestio quodlibetalis* means.

[170] Cecco is using the old scholastic *modus tollendo tollens*, from the Aristotelian logic taught in the Arts faculties: if *p* then *q*; but not *q*, therefore not *p*.

per invidia, through jealousy'; but as Villani adds, this does not prove Cecco innocent of heretical teachings.

Whatever the truth of it, it cannot now perhaps be known. And whatever the heresies in his attitudes and his comments, the actual astrology of Cecco's works is very much in the late medieval tradition and he was, it seems, also acquainted with various forms of magic and divination, all of which he believed could give information on the future, though astrology was the most reliable way. It is such a marvellous way of knowing the future that it makes man divine, and like the angels, and it enables the doctor, 'if he knows the beginning of the sickness rightly to judge whether it is caused by hot, cold, wet or dry matter, and whether it will be a mortal illness or the patient will recover, and this without even examining the sick man himself!' Cecco's commentary on Sacrobosco is mainly astronomical, and the astrology is extraneous; but the notes on Alcabitius are of course largely astrological, with a good deal of medical matter included. His sources include all the great names of thirteenth century astrology, but include also Dorotheus, presumably at second hand through Masha'allah or Firmicus Maternus. His medical interest leads him to list the planets and their plants, which are very much in the ancient Greek tradition: Sun and heliotrope; Moon and paeony; Saturn and sempervivum, or houseleek; Jupiter and agrimony; Mars and fennel (?); Venus and all-heal (panacea); Mercury and verbena (?). Cecco has an interesting note on *caput* and *cauda*: 'Caput* and *cauda* are intersections of circles and are not stars positioned in the heavens like Draco itelf ... They are called nodes, and move 3'2" westwards each day. *Caput* is composed of the natures of Jupiter and Venus, and *cauda* of Saturn and Mars. They have the same sorts of effects here below as the seven planets.' The objection is raised that the planets affect us by their light, but the nodes have no light, therefore etc. To which Cecco replies: 'I say to this argument that the secrets of the heavens are hidden in the particular but the astrologer argues from the actual effect', which is exactly the argument of modern astrologers in similar circumstances. Lastly, it is interesting that Cecco apparently preferred trepidation (of 10°) to regular precession of the equinoxes, though otherwise he is traditionally Ptolemaic.

By the end of the fourteenth and the early years of the fifteenth century, the courts of Europe, lay and ecclesiastical, were fairly thickly strewn with astrologers. They were consulted by everyone; but how much notice was actually taken of them, how many princes or bishops actually altered course on the advice of such pilots, it is very hard to say. One gets the impression that their function was not so much to answer the questions 'What?' or 'Whether?' but rather 'When?' The task was generally to discover the favourable time for some enterprise;

and of course to cast the natal charts of princes and their offspring. As G. W. Coopland writes in his edition of Oresme's *Livre de divinacions*,[171] commenting on a French scholar's remark that the Emperor Charles V made Thomas de Pisan his favourite astrologer, and always consulted him and always obeyed him: 'It is precisely of the last point that we are in inevitable ignorance; of the consultation we may have knowledge, but scarcely of the obedience.' It was however a period in which the lay nobility were as interested in and as convinced of the validity of divination of all kinds, including astrology, as any of the credulous masses of the uneducated; and certainly no one doubted the value of astrology to medicine. It is true, as Coopland says (p. 6) that superstition 'was clearly widespread and mischievous. We need not stress too heavily evidence drawn from the titles of the books collected by Charles V in the great library installed by him in the Louvre. The lines of demarcation as between the various provinces into which the study of the universe was later to be so profitably divided were not yet laid down, and a work whose title would appear to indicate a treatise on magic might include much that we should call physics and mathematics. More significant is the fact that such men as Oresme and the great Gerson thought it urgent to write in condemnation of the dependence on soothsayers that existed in the highest places.' One might legitimately wonder at that 'profitable division', but the wholeness of late medieval learning, it cannot be stressed too often, included much magic and divination and astrology without distinction. When men like Oresme or Peter d'Ailly wrote of astrology, even when they were critical, they used the astrological writers as authorities exactly like the rest and treated their works with exactly the same respect.

Nicole Oresme, who taught theology in Paris from 1358–1361 and died in his sixties as Bishop of Lisieux in 1382, wrote, in Paris, both a short Latin *Tractatus contra judiciarios astronomos* and a longer work in French substantially the same as the Latin book, the *Livre de divinacions*; the texts of both are in Coopland's interesting work. Oresme classified astrology under six heads. First, what we call astronomy, which is 'speculative and mathematical, a very noble and excellent science'. Second, 'the qualities, the influences and the powers (physical or natural) of the stars, the signs, the degrees' etc., such as heat and cold, wetness and dryness. This is a speculative but natural science which can be known, though predictions are made on an

---

[171] G. W. Coopland, *Nicole Oresme and the Astrologers* (Liverpool U.P., 1952), p. 184, footnote 27. There is also interesting matter in Oresme's *Livre du Ciel et du Monde*, ed. Albert D. Menut and Alexander J. Denomy, and translated by Menut (Wisconsin U.P., 1968).

out-of-date basis since precession has altered the state of things and their effects. Third comes 'the revolutions of the stars and the conjunctions of planets' and so on, and here there are three kinds of predictions. One, from major conjunctions, of great events, as plagues and famine, floods, great wars, deaths of princes, the appearances of prophets and the beginnings of new religious sects; these can be and are known, but only in general, and details cannot be known. Two, weather predictions – very unreliable; Oresme suggests that farmers and seamen are better at it. And three, medical predictions and information on humours and so on, which is fine so far as concerns the sun and the moon, but less reliable when the other planets are involved. The fourth division of astrology is genethlialogy, the fifth interrogations and the sixth elections. These belong to Fortune, as the first three to Nature; and they constitute, of course, judicial astrology. Of the fourth, Oresme says (Coopland's translation, p. 57): 'The fourth part, of nativities, is not in itself beyond knowledge, so far as the complexion and inclination of a person born at a given time are in question, but cannot be known when it comes to fortune and things which can be hindered by the human will.' And since it is so often wrong in practice (he obliquely refers to Augustine on twins) 'I say that this part of astrology cannot be known and the rules written down on it are not true.' Likewise, but more shortly, he rejects the last two divisions as having no rational foundation and no truth in them.

Which all looks very clear and rational; but there is less certainty and clarity than there seems to be. In chapter 15 Oresme says, commenting on the idea that the heavens are a book of God's creation, 'wherein are written the fortunes of kings', that 'what is to happen in the future is not written in the sky, except in so far as from congruent movements we may know future constellations which are, or will be, cause or signs of various inclinations and diverse fortunes', which seems to open the astrological door pretty wide, 'saving always the freedom of the human will'. And he goes on to write of the three 'noble ends' of astrology: to know 'great matters'; to learn of the Creator; and, less important, 'to ascertain certain dispositions of this lower and corruptible nature, whether present or to come, and nothing beyond that.' The same doubts and ambiguities are found in the writings of his follower Peter d'Ailly who, like Oresme, taught at Paris and thus became very much involved in the attempts to heal the 'Great Schism' in the papacy (at one time there were three 'popes') which was ended only in 1417 with the Council of Constance and the election of Martin V. In the process d'Ailly became Archbishop of Cambrai and a cardinal, but in 1417 he retired to carry on with his astrology for the three years remaining to him. The astrological section of his *De falsis prophetis* is derived from Oresme, but in his *Vigintiloquium*, a book showing 'the agreement of astronomical truth with theology', written about 1410, he grants that since the stars alter the atmosphere and so on, and these things influence men's characters and behaviour, astrology has its uses; saving, of course, man's free will. But even of this he says in his prologue, 'although the will is not compelled, yet the body is altered by the powers of the heavens, and then the soul which is united to the body is strongly disturbed and effectively moved, though it is not compelled.' Astrology becomes *superstitiosa* when it is used to foretell 'free' future events. It is the errors of superstitious and bad astrologers which bring astrology into disrepute. Neither Oresme nor d'Ailly, nor indeed Jean Gerson, who wrote a tract against judicial astrology for the Dauphin in 1419, made any distincton between astrology and astronomy, or questioned the validity of astrology – only whether it worked, or whether it was licit. But at the beginning of the fifteenth century there are more doubts around, and more criticisms being voiced, even within the framework of superstition and magic which formed the general background.

It is true that men were, throughout the Middle Ages, all over Europe (and beyond), more open to beliefs in what now would be regarded as superstitious, or fanciful, or even nonsensical ideas, at the same time as they advanced rational thought in theology and philosophy and even in mathematical science. They did not make the kinds of distinctions we are so educated to make that we do so without thinking, and without realising how modern and how local and perhaps how tentative they are: between science and fantasy, facts and theories, books and experience, between, even, religion and superstition. Not that we do this all the time or very well or consistently, nor that some of us never do it at all; politicians generally, and arguably many of their electors, confuse these and other such categories most confoundedly. But although history is always written from the point of view of the victors, in the history of ideas there ought to be no such concept as victory, which smacks of arrogance. At any rate, the understanding of the history of ideas demands that one approach each time from the preceding age. Knowledge of what comes after is needed to appreciate the movements, the directions, to see the small beginnings as significant. But one must always then make the effort to see even those beginnings in context, as their contemporaries saw them. Otherwise there is no understanding how they ever occurred then and there among those thinkers, unless one is to believe in some directing Spirit of Progress. For the thousand years of this chapter and for most of the time covered by the next, astrology, in our sense, was as it had been for Antiquity an integral part of the Liberal Art of *Astrologia* – or *Astronomia*, whichever one cared to call it. What happened to or was said about astrology in this period was never a consequence of anyone anticipating modern attitudes.

The Middle Ages began with the rejection and virtual disappearance of astrology in the West, and closed with its almost universal acceptance. It disappeared partly because of the disapproval of the Church. Only partly, because ecclesiastical disapproval could not have achieved it alone. The Church disapproved of the pagan Liberal Arts, which in the *quadrivium* included *Astrologia*. They survived, not because of Boethius or Cassiodorus, much less because of Martianus Capella, but because they were bound to: there was no substitute. Of course, what really survived was the late antique form of education, consisting for almost everyone simply of Grammar and Rhetoric. So much was essential for a Church with Scriptures and a Latin liturgy. Essential though it was, it all but disappeared in the West, north of the Alps at least, in the seventh and eighth centuries. It was this collapse of education, and in particular the collapse of higher education, of the *quadrivium*, which really made the survival of astrology impossible. The faint memory of astrology was preserved in the works of those very churchmen, Augustine and Bede and others, who condemned it; but little more than the name and the memory. There was no astrology in Western Europe from the early sixth to the late twelfth century. It is striking that in all G. G. Coulton's works on medieval life and the medieval church there is no mention of astrology of sufficient importance to be noticed in the (very full) indexes. Nor is astrology referred to in early medieval admonitory or minatory sermons, though demons and their evil misleadings of men are there. The thirteenth century Caesarius of Heisterbach, in his long *Dialogue on Miracles*, has much to say of superstitions and demons and necromancy, including the information that there were 'many scholars from different countries studying the art of necromancy' in Toledo (Book V, c.4), and that some religious houses had resident necromancers who, having of course given up the wicked practice, could nevertheless be prevailed upon to use their art for good purposes (e.g., Book V, c.18); but nowhere does he mention an astrologer. If he knew anything about astrology at all, he regarded it as a science and nothing to do with miracles.

It returned to the West from within *Astrologia*. *Astrologia* could only be reintroduced from and through the Arabs, since there were no Latin textbooks. The desire and search for the *quadrivium* were older than the translations from the Arabic, and then the Greek; the beginnings lie in the ninth and tenth centuries with the slow revival of the schools and the growth of the numbers of scholars who might be interested. But the first 'renaissance' was wholly Latin: Gerbert d'Aurillac went to Catalonia for the *quadrivium*, not for Arabic learning, and the revival of philosophy which culminates in the great precursor and maker of Scholasticism, Peter Abelard, sprang from Priscian and Boethius, not directly from Aristotle. When the translations of works of medicine, mathematics, science and philosophy began to be used in the Latin schools from the late eleventh century on, they were received by a scholastic world which was ready and eager for them. Among them came *astrologia*, received and accepted in the thirteenth century because it was, as it had always been, a Liberal Art, a science, part of the late antique Aristotelian-Stoic-Neo-Platonist world picture, which became the world-view of Islam and of Christendom. The Church found astrology included and, provided God's omnipotence and man's freedom were preserved against the fatalistic determinism of some astrologers, had no reason to reject it. The later thirteenth century and the fourteenth was a time when men were interested in anything and everything, in all strange new sciences, real or pretended (a distinction then impossible to draw). It was also a period of more widely spreading education among laity as well as clergy, and of growth of the importance of the vernaculars alongside of Latin, as is shown both in literature and in the numbers of vernacular chronicles. Men's attitudes changed, for a great number of reasons. The 'rationalism' of the schools (and of political thinking) – Ockham and Wyclif are among the great names – changed men's ideas on the Church. So did the Black Death, which left the Church in a very exposed and far from easy relationship to its flock. And perhaps above all the towns became more important: *Stadtluft macht frei*, 'city air makes you free' was not only socially true, but to some extent intellectually also. By the late fourteenth century there was in all educated centres a greater spirit of critical adventurousness than at any time for over a thousand years. Within *astrologia*, as within alchemy, really lay two subjects, overlapping and merging: what we would call sciences – astrology and chemistry – which were the preparatory ground for the others, the arts of astrology and alchemy. It may be that the separation of these sciences from the arts, and the gradual disappearance of the latter were due to the exercise of the new critical spirit on the practices in the two fields, and that the crucial point was that the development lay in the sciences because that was where the *results* were achieved, while the 'arts' seemed still to be no more successful than they ever had been. The widening of this separation, its effect on astrology and the attempts of astrologers to make their art respectably scientific, are part of the matter of the next chapter.

IVa Vézélay, tympanum over the west doorway showing the zodiac

IVb Detail of Cancer from the Vézélay zodiac

VI

Renaissance and Enlightenment:
The Second Death of Astrology

This chapter could begin with as simple a fact as the last. The Renaissance happened when and because the Turks captured Constantinople in 1453. The Greek scholars then took up their beloved manuscripts and fled to Italy, and so the West became aware at first hand of the Ancient Greek World, for the first time. They then rejected the wasted years between, the Middle Age, and the modern world was born. Alas for so neat an explanation, the Greek Manuel Chrysoloras returned, after having visited Italy on an embassy from Constantinople, to take up a municipally paid lecturship and teach Greek in Florence in 1396; and between 1404 (the *Phaedo*) and 1435 (part of the *Symposium*), Bruni translated five of Plato's works and his Letters. Mussato and Petrarch and the early Humanists take us back to the early fourteenth century, and in the thirteenth there were proto-Humanists north and south of the Alps with changing attitudes to the ancient classics. Indeed, it was because the Florentine scholars were avid for classical learning already that Chrysoloras was tempted back as a teacher, to be followed by others, including his nephew. It is possible to argue that there was so much continuity between the late medieval thirteenth century and the 'Renaissance' fourteenth, that there was really no Renaissance at all, just continuous change proceeding at different rates in different fields of activity and in different places. Yet something did happen. The Europe of the late sixteenth century is different in fundamental ways from that of the late thirteenth; and we did end up with a threefold, not a twofold, division of European history.

The last fact, the fact that we can have a chapter entitled 'The Latin Middle Ages', is indeed very significant. No medieval man, however great his admiration for the ancients in comparison with those of more recent times, but only a new man of the Renaissance could have invented the term *medium aevum*, the 'Middle Ages'.[1] The ideas that

---

[1] R. R. Bolgar, *The Classical Heritage and its Beneficiaries* (Cambridge, 1954) 240–1, quotes Richard of Bury (1281–1385) on the ancient authors and 'their successors' who 'are barely capable of discussing the discoveries of their forerunners, and of acquiring those things

the writers of antiquity formed a world – a pagan world – which it was possible to penetrate and with the great men of which one could 'converse' through what they wrote; that then there was a period when that world was largely lost, or only parts of it assimilated; and that only now can we, not humbly but proudly, associate with them and recreate that cultural world; these ideas are at the core of the *literary* Renaissance from Petrarch's time on. It is very important to realise that it is true of this movement, and of all those that followed or accompanied it down to but not including the scientific movement in the North Italian universities in the sixteenth century, that it concerned only an élite: a never large number of men in a handful of Italian cities; and many of those scholars, philosophers and artists were peripatetic, attracted by patronage or driven by politics from city to city. The same is perhaps less true north of the Alps, where there was a different kind of continuity. If the Italian cities and their education had always been more secular, and so their attitudes to literature, and indeed to paganism, different from those of the North, it was nevertheless the North which produced those fourteenth century movements gathered under 'Nominalism' which led to the separation of theology from philosophy, and metaphysics from science, which made room for that individualism in theology and in science that is so fundamentally important in the sixteenth century.

The philosophical movement of the Italian scholars was in a different direction. With the exception of Pomponazzi the return to antiquity meant the return not only to Plato, but to the Neo-Platonists and the Neo-Pythagoreans, and to the Stoicism of Seneca. It also meant a return to the Fathers, Greek and Latin, to Augustine perhaps especially, but also to the Neo-Platonic theology of the Pseudo-Dionysius. Just as the Fathers had found in Platonism and Stoicism congenial philosophical ground, so too did these fourteenth and fifteenth century thinkers. Such influences naturally led to the integration of theology and philosophy, so that discussion of the nature of man meant establishing his position in the Creation with relation to God and the angels and not just in the 'chain of being'; and also to a sometimes overt Platonic rejection of the reality of the physical world

---

as pupils which the ancients dug out by difficult efforts of discovery.' Yet it is true for Richard as for his twelfth century predecessors that the awareness of 'modernity' (from *modo*, 'now') and even of inferiority is merely the awareness of the newness of what is happening, and the sometimes only literary modesty of the dwarfs on the giants' shoulders. The *veteres antiqui*, 'old ones, ancients', who included the Christian Fathers as well as the pagan authors of antiquity, still began, not at some theoretical time in the past, but a few years ago. Compare particularly Chapter 14, 'Classicism', of Ernst Robert Curtius' *European Literature and the Latin Middle Ages*, trans. Willard R. Trask (London, 1953).

of sense. The introduction into this sort of picture of man and the universe of Hermetism and the Cabalah produced the extraordinary world-picture of Pico della Mirandola, which was – quite under-standably – to get him into serious difficulties with the Inquisition, and as naturally led to his vast anti-astrological work. His criticism of astrology was criticism of it as a false science, within his scheme of things: astrology implied that man was within and part of and even in some way subservient to the sensible world, which was anathema to one who set man alongside God, above and potentially beyond all the rest of Creation. We shall look in detail at his *Disputationes*, but it is important to notice that his attacks on astrology are not those of a modern, rationalist, humanist, but arise out of convictions that no one now would wish to defend.

It was of course possible to accept the newly arrived Platonism and keep astrology. As we have seen, Platonism was one of the roots out of which the Greeks' acceptance and development of Middle Eastern protoastrology grew, because of Plato's late attitudes to the heavens and the planets and their permanence and beauty and divinity. The first of these Renaissance Platonists, who was indeed responsible for the most important early translations of Plato and the Neo-Platonists and of the *Corpus Hermeticum*, was Marsilio Ficino. Before Ficino, the chief philosophical influences on the Humanists were the Latin authors Cicero and Seneca, which meant a strongly ethical, rhetorical and Stoic outlook emerged, as indeed in Coluccio Salutati (1331–1406).[2] Incidentally, Salutati divided the Senecas into two, as brothers, but gave the prose, including the philosophical Letters, to the elder, and the poetry, the Tragedies, to the younger. His *De nobilitate* shows his relatively low opinion of medicine and indeed of *Physica* in general. 'One of the reasons seems to have been that he associated *physica* with the schoolmen' – quite correctly, as we shall see. Consequently he had little time for astrology; and in any case his reading of Augustine would have put him off. Nevertheless, his reading included Abu Ma'shar, the Alfonsine Tables, Bonatti, Campanus' *Theorica Planetarum*, Peter of Abano's *Conciliator*, and Ptolemy's *Geography*, *Almagest* and *Quadripartitum*, and the *Centiloquium*, so he was not uninterested in *astrologia*.

Ficino's attitudes were ambivalent, and changed during his lifetime time (1433–1499), but in general he may be said to have been against superstitious, judicial astrology, while still much interested in astro-logical medicine. His philosophy was Augustine-Platonist, and much else, but this meant that for him 'Philosophy' or wisdom was a

---

[2] See B. Ullmann, *The Humanism of Coluccio Salutati* (Padua, 1963). The quotation is from p. 89.

seamless garment, inseparable from theology. So man's knowledge of God and himself and truth and reality was all of a piece, in which a judicial astrology that subordinated man to the heavens could have little part, except at the purely physical level. Hence he could be and was interested in *iatromathematica*, and 'he regarded his work on this "astrological science" as a serious problem, if difficult to succeed in; but not failing in his science for which he should feel ashamed. Both, opposition to traditional astrology and work on a new iatromathematical method, surely belonged inseparably to his life's work.'[3] For Ficino the planets might physically determine at birth the abilities, strengths and weaknesses, of a man's body, but it was then entirely up to the individual what he made of those possibilities and became.[4] Ficino's philosophy made room for a very great deal in his typically Renaissance eclecticism. He could and did draw on 'Thomism, Augustinianism, Ockhamism, Epicureanism, Ciceronian humanism, the *Hermetica*, Plato, the Neoplantonists, the *Orphica*, the *Chaldaean Oracles*, the Platonising Arabic and Jewish thinkers who had been translated in the Middle Ages, particularly Avicenna and Avicebron, but also including Averroes and many others, and not to forget the Scriptures.'[5] It is scarcely surprising that he vacillated in attitudes to astrology!

The impact of Giovanni Pico della Mirandola's *Disputationes adversus astrologiam divinatricem*,[6] and indeed the influence of Pico, were very great, despite the shortness of his life: he died at thirty in 1394. But as Robert S. Lopez says:[7] 'Pico was outstanding thanks to his prodigious learning, his noble birth, his inherited wealth, his celebrated handsomeness, all enhanced by the most desired aspect of that age – youth!' His twelve-book attack on judicial astrology came, in 1394, at the time when astrologers were really in their heyday in the Italian Courts. There existed then 'a kind of contest for the confidence of princes; a contest in which were brought into play all the subtle intrigues of which the courtiers of that time were capable. The apparition of a comet, the terror aroused by an earth-tremor, were occasions for getting oneself noticed, occasions when the most

[3] Hans Baron, 'Willensfreiheit und Astrologie bei Marsilio Ficino und Pico della Mirandola' in *Kultur – und Universalgeschichte: Festschrift für Walter Goetz zu seinem 60 Geburtstage* (Leipzig/Berlin, 1927) 147–170; p. 150.

[4] *Cf.* Ernst Cassiser, *Individuum und Kosmos in der Philosophie der Renaissance* (Leipzig/Berlin, 1927) 120.

[5] Charles Trinkaus, *In Our Image and Likeness: Humanity and Divinity in Italian Humanist Thought* (2 vols, London, 1970) 504.

[6] Edited with an Italian translation and notes by Eugenio Garin (2 vols, Florence, 1946, 1952).

[7] *The Three Ages of the Italian Renaissance* (Charlottesville, 1970) 24.

reputable astrologers might fall into disgrace, and the most obscure find their fortune.'[8] They were occasions, of course, when an astrologer, whose normal tasks were to produce birth-charts for princely offspring, cast election-figures for important occasions, and in some courts to publish annual prognostications, really had to take a chance. Any such striking event, not only in the sky, but in the weather, for example – a freak and devastating storm, perhaps – called not only for explanation but more importantly for prognostication: what did it mean? It had to mean something: throughout the period, at least until the late seventeenth century, the physical world was still seen as having layers of meaning, as signifying more than appeared to the senses. It might be possible for academic *astrologi* to write later about such things, and show by their charts that it was, of course, all foreseeable; but actually getting the foreseeing right at the time, before the events, was to say the least more difficult. The errors of astrologers, excused so entirely plausibly by Ptolemy in the *Tetr.* (I.2), bulk very largely in Pico's attack.

Pico's own philosophy was developed out of that of his most important teacher, Ficino. One tradition that Ficino could not draw upon was the Hebraic. Pico was a good Hebraist, and interest in the Jewish Cabalah was, according to Trinkaus (*op. cit.*), one of the two additions made to Ficino's thought. The other was the 'Neo-Platonic and mystical nature of the so-called Averroist doctrine of the possible intellect as universal rather than intellectual', which he assimilated from the Paduan teaching of Elia del Medigo. These together with Ficino's Platonic synthesis aided him in his construction of an integrated vision of God and man and the world, in which all was animated from God, through the angels and the heavens to man, whose potentialities, explicitly presented to him by God, were virtually infinite, divinity itself seeming scarcely beyond his grasp. There was little doubt of a very Platonic rejection of the reality of the body: 'Nor should we measure our condition according to weak body, for this man is not that weak and earthly thing which we see, as is written in the *Alcibiades*, but he is soul, he is intellect, which exceeds every circuit of heaven, every course of time' (*Heptaplus* c.7). It follows that a materialist astrological determinism had to be rejected, and since it was so universally accepted, rejected firmly and convincingly and finally. Hence the twelve books of the *Disputationes*.

---

[8] Benedetto Soldati, *La Poesia astrologica nel Quattrocento* (Florence, 1906) 76. Modern authors write of 'the apparition of a comet' in this way, I suspect, because they are discussed at such length by astrologers; but were they really so common and so striking in those days? The few comets I have seen in more than 60 years have been disappointing objects, in binoculars.

What Pico attacks in these books is not all *astrologia*, but 'that which foretells things to come by the stars' (Proem).[9] The work is against divinatory astrology, for the reasons explained; and consequently what we have referred to as 'physical astrology' is scarcely referred to – it would have been as acceptable to Pico as to any of his contemporaries. Divinatory astrology includes judicial astrology of all kinds: natal charts, progressions, elections, 'interrogations' (the answering of questions, finding lost people or things, and so on), all the uses of astrology to discover what is hidden, the stock in trade of every astrologer of the period. Pico puts all these practitioners together, from the most professional to the merest quack, and attacks indiscriminately: he frequently asserts that they are only really interested in wealth and self-advancement. It is, of course, the scorn of the aristocrat with great inherited wealth, and scarcely an accusation against astrology. Commoner, and much more justified, is the argument from the disagreements among astrologers themselves: some consensus on important matters of method might be expected among those who practice an ancient art, even if there might be differences of interpretation. Pico reverts to this, relevantly and rightly, again and again, and sums it up briefly in VIII.2, which begins: 'from this various and manifold variety of opinions, it can easily be perceived how uncertain divinatory astrology must become'.[10] On the consequent errors of astrologers, their frequent mistakes in interpretation, Pico rejects Ptolemy's excuses from complexity and simply asserts – entirely properly within his own scheme of the universe – that the reason they are wrong so often is that 'the astrologer consults signs that are not signs, and examines causes that are not causes' (III.19). That these astrologer's 'signs and causes' seem to make sense of chance events (a perennial problem for those with an all-embracing picture of the world, including the Christian) is of course explicable on different principles in Pico's own system for dealing with freedom and determinism (*cf.* IV.4).

Naturally Pico attacks the whole apparatus of minute and not so minute divisions of the zodiac – decans, dodecatemories, terms, *fridariae, novenarii*, and so forth – partly as artificial divisions of the natural wholeness of the heavenly circle and partly as areas where astrologers obviously disagreed so much among themselves. Of

---

[9] All references are to Garin's edition. Despite the apparent clarity (and modernity) of Pico's distinction between *astronomia* and *astrologia* in the Proem, he uses the terms, and *astronomi, astrologi*, with all the usual ambiguities throughout the work; but the beginnings of the modern difference are there – one can at least see which word is going to mean what.

[10] '*Ex hac autem tam varia tamque multiplici opinionum varietate quam incerta reddatur astrologia divinatrix facile est perspicere*'.

course, he knew that Ptolemy too had rejected most of these sub-divisions: but one of his accusations is that astrologers are often such bad astrologers on their own grounds, in that they rely on muddled Latin sources instead of the comparatively scientific Ptolemy (*Proem.* and elsewhere). And it is true that the most popular authority in astrological matters in the fifteenth century was probably Manilius, after his rediscovery by Poggio in 1416, with Firmicus Maternus always there also. We shall see that the more learned astrologers were themselves worried about this, and reacted into attempts to become more 'scientific', more Ptolemaic. But Pico's attacks on the divisions of the heavenly circle into houses and so on, and his arguments on the impossibility of regions of the sky affecting issues below – even if celestial bodies could: they were at least there, as bodies – have some vagueness about them, for neither Pico nor his contemporaries were yet sure what *was* 'up there': they had not yet reached the very sophisticated notion that these bodies were simply moving in an empty and possibly infinite space. However, the undoubted artifici-ality of the degree – why should there be 360 of them? – enabled him, with other reasons (III.7), to reject progressions of all kinds: 'a degree for a year' was obviously arbitrary and therefore nonsense; and as we have seen, astrologers still have to admit that the only reason they can adduce for it is that (as they claim) it works.

Book V is concerned to show that the idea of the 'great conjunctions' signifying major historical events is wrong. Partly, he argues on the same ground as that on which he rejects houses and aspects. Why should different regions in the sky produce different effects, since all the sky is the same? And how is it that 'rays' are presumed to affect one another? Rays might affect things below on which they fall, but they cannot affect other rays. If rays have always the same powers whatever part of the sky they come from, and cannot affect one another, then aspects are irrelevant and no aspect can be weaker or stronger than another, much less vary in benevolence or malevolence. And since all the planets and all the stars are always present in the heavens at every moment, why is one nativity different from another, or one conjunction considered 'great'? It is not difficult for Pico to show that astrologers have in practice differed widely on the interpre-tations of the great conjunctions, and mostly been wrong (he would have enjoyed the disarray of the optimistic astrologers after the outbreak of war in 1939). And how, he asks, can the effects of these conjunctions persist for such long periods, when the actual coming together of the planets – even in 'great' conjunctions involving the slow-moving Saturn and Jupiter – occupies so short a time? How can astrologers indulge in their common practice of explaining important historical events, in retrospect, as due to this or that conjunction years earlier? Book VI follows these objections with the very plausible *a fortiori* argument that if astrologers cannot get the large things right, how are they to be trusted in the little? If indeed events in the sub-lunary world are determined, or at the least signified – pre-signified, indeed – by celestial movements and positions, one would expect important events involving cities and nations, famine and war, to be clearly signed. But from what the astrologers have to tell us the clarity is not there; so why should one expect the tiny details of individual lives to be as clearly sign-posted in the heavens as the natal chart suggests? Of course, they are not, and it is easy for Pico to deploy all the ancient arguments against the inconsistencies of the astrologers.

More important, perhaps, and just as traditional, are the objections based on astrologers' disagreements on three matters, to be added to those on house division. They cannot agree on the relative importance of conception and birth. Pico misrepresents Ptolemy on his question (VIII.3) but his arguments are ancient and often repeated. He adds that in any case the seed is already formed before conception, and if there is an important moment it is that of the formation of the seed, whenever that is. Second, astrologers are far from unanimous on the influences of the fixed stars, even the *paranatellonta* (VII.9). It is an objection that goes back to Seneca (see p. 53 above). And incidentally there is the matter of unseen, and therefore unknown planets, and their possible influences (VIII.1), an idea Pico derived, according to Garin, from Favorinus (*apud* Aulus Gellius XIV.1; and cf Seneca, *Quaest. Nat.* VII.13). Last, there is the difficult problem of the fixed or moving zodiac (VIII.2). The precession of the equinoxes means that 'the first point of Aries', the point where the sun crosses the equator on its·way north, the spring equinox, is no longer in Aries at all. Now does the division of the zodiac begin at that point, into twelve 30° sections, the first section being called Aries, whatever the constellations which actually occupy those 30°; or does one give the 30° around the constellation to each of the signs, and accept that the zodiac is moving round the heavens? It is a question that still exercises astrologers, as it always must those who hold to the zodiac at all; and it is difficult to see that there can be any other ground for decision other than experience – which works better?

Which is true for all the ambiguities Pico rightly fastens upon – rightly, though of course to perceive and state an ambiguity is not logically to refute the system which includes it. At the beginning of Book IX, however, he launches an attack on divinatory astrology as a whole. 'Three things,' he says, 'must necessarily be grasped if true forecasts are to be made about the future.' Notice that he writes 'are to be made' not 'were to be made': *si vera ... praedicenda sunt,* not *sint.*

'The first is this, that the hour of the beginning of whatever matter is being considered is reliably ascertained (*ut hora ... fideliter teneatur*). The second, that we grasp the exact condition of the heavens and position of the stars at that hour. The last, that what that position of the heavens and stars effect, we should understand by arguments that are true, or at least not fallacious, from being observed in experience'. The rest of the book shows without much difficulty that the required accuracy is virtually impossible anyway, and that astrologers have always been content with the inaccuracies of their Tables, unsupported by observations. There was, of course, a vicious circle from which the astrologer could not escape: the only way to establish the time at all accurately was to observe the heavens, and assume the Tables to be correct. Having used the state of the stars to establish the time, one could scarcely then use the time so found to establish accurately the state of the heavens. When a picture shows an astrologer holding up his astrolabe to the stars, is he finding the time, to look up the ASC and the MC and the houses in his Tables, or finding the Ascendant and so on, to look up the time and discover the positions of the planets and the nodes from the books? It need hardly be added that the modern astrologer could safely answer all Pico's charges on this score, were he properly equipped. Book X shows that the *rationes* of the astrologer are not true, that the art is not properly rational; and Book XI that it is not based on experience and observation. It is worth remembering that at this time as for centuries before, *experimentum* meant 'experience', which of course included experimentation – but *astrologia* could only be observational, never experimental. The last book goes back to a point made at the beginning of the work, and produces what for the Renaissance humanist was the damning argument that astrology was not derived from the Classical Greeks and Romans but from the Egyptians and Chaldaeans. The Greeks themselves provided this ammunition, though they were in this, as we have seen, mistaken; mathematical *astrologia* was a Greek creation.

Although many of Pico's arguments are the traditional ones, used over and over again from Augustine onwards, the whole was indeed a massive attack, and its great value as a storehouse and summary is shown by the use made of it by all later controversialists on both sides. Its effect was restricted of course to those in his own world and to the astrologers. It had no effect on the common beliefs of men – nor even, perhaps, of popes and princes – and there is no evidence of its converting any astrologer from his creed. But then, whenever have such controversial books had such effects? The best they can achieve is to clarify and sharpen up debate, and it can reasonably be argued that Pico's *Disputationes* did that.

The effect of Pico's work can be seen as late as the beginning of the seventeenth century in the textbook of the only interesting astrologer to emerge from Renaissance Italy, the Dominican Tommaso Campanella (1568–1639). His work is thus entitled in the 1629 edition (given as from Lyons on the title page, though the British Library Catalogue says 'probably not Lyons'): 'The six books of Astrology of Campanella of the Order of Preachers, in which Astrology, from which all the superstition of the Arabs and the Jews has been eliminated, is dealt with on physical principles (*physiologice*), according to Holy Scripture and the teaching of Saints Thomas and Albert and the great Theologians, in such a way that it may be read with great profit without coming under suspicion from the Church of God.' He takes further precautions in the heading to the table of contents: 'In the Preface we show how scientific Astrology (*Astrologiam physicam*) is to be separated from the superstitious; by it neither are divine providence and power to be overthrown, nor the freedom of the human will; and we shall show that Astrology is partly true knowledge (*scientia*), partly conjecture, and partly supposition (*suspicio*), like medicine; and how one should proceed in it, and that the stars work in lower things in a fourfold manner; and what authorities should be used.' The 'fourfold manner' is explained on p. 9: 'The stars work in lower things by heat, light, motion and aspect.' Campanella's good sense is shown in his attitude to the 'terms' of the zodiac (p. 41). They are the last and least of the 'dignities' (decans and so on), and are too small to have been discovered in experience, so there is much argument about them among astrologers. Although he gives a table of 'Egyptian terms,' he says, 'I confess I am not sure about them.'

When he comes to deal with the *horoscopus*, the Ascendant (p. 118), he says, 'Although it is extremely difficult (so much so that it is regarded as impossible by Pico, and by Saint Ambrose) nevertheless it is absolutely necessary to be sure of the degree and minute of the horoscope.' This major problem makes the erection of a birth-chart very difficult, since all the rest depends on the establishment of the Ascendant. The second problem is of course, how to divide the zodiac into mundane houses. Campanella is brief, though far from clear; he claims it is Alcabitius' method, which seems to be 'rational enough'. He settles on equal quarters of 90°, it seems, though it cannot have worked as he describes it. The first runs from the Ascendant 'to the zenith or *Medium Caelum*' including what are presumably equal houses XII, XI and X; the 'or', *seu*, must surely mean that the zenith is taken, which can be the *Medium Caelum* – one cannot simply identify the two, as Campanella must have known. The second, however, he says runs 'from the *Medium Caelum* to the setting point', with houses IX, VIII and VII; the third from the setting point to the *Imum Caeli* (VI,

V and IV) and the last the three remaining houses between the *IMC* and the Ascendant. The houses are described, as traditionally, as angular, those next to the ASC and so on, succedent, those in the middle, and declining, those adjoining the next, setting-end cardinal. But he says (p. 32) that 'astrologers are by no means yet agreed on the way in which a figure should be erected'. All these difficulties lead to what is still called 'rectification', though now it is only needed when there is much doubt about the date and time of birth. The known dates of accidents, illnesses, journeys and so on are 'calculated backwards', as it were, to reach a figure which accommodates them all. He is clear enough on precession and the zodiac (p. 22): 'So the equinox does not begin as it once did at the beginning of Aries but in Pisces, so that now it is marked as 2° Pisces.' And he adds that *astrologi* call the vernal equinox 'the first point of Aries'. Lastly, and very importantly, he expresses simply the astrologers' answer to those who thought (and indeed think) that Copernican Heliocentrism was bound to give the death-blow to Astrology (Book I, c.2, art. 1, 3): 'Whether the sun moves or stands still, it is to be supposed a moving Planet by us, considering the matter from our senses and our description; for the same happens whether it moves or the earth.' In other words, what matters to the astrologer is their *relative* position, as with all the planets; their angular distances seen from here.

There is magic in Campanella's other works, based on Ficino's, and there is magic in Pico as well as Ficino. One of their sources was a curious work called *Picatrix*.[11] This became 'the book of magic'. It circulated widely in the fifteenth century, when magic and astrology and religion and various occult sciences were inextricably mixed in the minds and practices of men.[12] As D. P. Walker says, the two streams of magic, the 'natural, spiritual' kind, which shades off into psychology and musical and poetic theory, and demonic, which became overtly so in Agrippa of Nettesheim, for example, separated to some extent in the fifteenth century to come together at the end of the sixteenth 'in the planetary oratory of Paolini and the magic practised by Campanella' (*op. cit.*, p. 75). *Picatrix*, or 'the *Picatrix*' as it is also known, was an Arabic compilation probably of the late twelfth century, which was translated into Spanish in 1256. From this Spanish version, it seems, the Latin version circulating in the fifteenth century was made. It was introduced into the West in the work of Ibn Khaldun, who died in 1406: all the Latin manuscripts are fifteenth century or later. It is

---

[11] A number of reconstructions have been suggested of the possibly Greek name lying behind this strange word, but it does not matter here. There is no edition of the work, but there is a long extract edited by V. Perrone Compagni in *Medioevo*, I (1975) 237–337.
[12] See, as well as Keith Thomas, *op. cit.*, D. P. Walker, *Spiritual and Demonic Magic from Ficino to Campanella*, Studies of the Warburg Institute 22 (London, 1958).

described in those manuscripts as 'a book of ancient secrets of the philosophers intended only for the wise to use for good' (Compagni). It is divided into four books and is very largely concerned with astrological magic. Book III describes, along with many other necromantic ideas, 'how it is possible to converse with the spirits of the planets'. After much astrology it states clearly 'these are the things without which it is impossible for anyone to come to the practice of this *scientia*, and all are found in the books of *astronomia*.' There is no reason here to follow the story of astrology's involvement in magic in succeeding centuries,[13] though it is an interesting story in its own right. The object of all this is stated by Nauert (*op. cit.*, p. 234): 'Writers on magic and astrology regarded the *magus* not as an ordinary man, but as one of a small elite of wise men, able to become (as Francis Bacon later wrote of the scientist) "masters and possessors of Nature". For the making of a magus astrology was universally acknowledged to be necessary, since earthly things such as images and talismans and all potent substances were intimately bound up with the states of the heavens, and the sky was now peopled with spirits and very much of the antique apparatus of gods and demigods.'[14]

If Ficino's and especially Pico's 'philosophy' – which included all knowledge – lifted men out of the world of sense as far as or even further than was possible, and set him in a spiritual world of gnosis and mystery, the philosophy, sharply separated from theology, of Pico's almost exact contemporary Pietro Pomponazzi of Mantua (1462–1524), set man firmly in the physical world. Pomponazzi taught at Padua, Ferrara and Bologna, and belonged to the North Italian Scholastic, Aristotelian tradition. Trinkaus (*op. cit.*, pp. 53ff) attributes to him 'the remarkable assertion of an autonomous, naturalistic vision of man.' His sort of 'humanism' has a considerably more modern ring to it than that of the literary and Platonist Renaissance; though of course the word 'humanism' is not misused as it is now to mean a narrow, rationalistic atheism. As Peter Laven says[15] 'It must be

---

[13] See Charles G. Nauert Jr, *Agrippa and the Crisis of Renaissance Thought* (Illinois, 1965); and also the works of Frances Yates, especially *Giordano Bruno and the Hermetic Tradition* (London, 1964). Frances Yates correctly describes *Picatrix* as 'A most complete textbook for the magician, giving the philosophy of nature on which talismanic and sympathetic magic is based together with full instructions for its practice.' And add the fascinating *La Zodiaco della Vita: la polemica sull' astrologia del trecento al cinquecento* (Bari, 1976). Translated as *Astrology in the Renaissance: the Zodiac of Life*, by Carolyn Jackson and June Allen (London, 1983).

[14] It may be worth a note, since some readers may look for his name in a book such as this, to say that Nostradamus (1503–1566) is irrelevant to any history of astrology. He did practice astrology, it is true, but only as a quack and among other forms of occultism. He is now really only known for his 'quatrains', a series of nearly nonsensical verses some of which can be 'interpreted' to seem relevant to later ages and even our future: but nonsense is always capable of any interpretation.

[15] *Renaissance Italy* (London, 1966) 197.

remembered that even the Popes were Christians.' Pomponazzi derived from Aristotle and Cicero more than Plato (though there may have been influence from *Republic IV* and *Protagoras*) the idea that 'it is the moral life, rather than the life of the intellect or the life of the producer' (these are the three intelligences classified by Aristotle) 'that is distinctively human.' On such Aristotelian views, with a separation of *philosophia* from theology which recalls Boethius, man is a physical, mortal being, and personal resurrection, the reunion of soul and body, impossible according to philosophy, though known for certain by revelation. If man was as the Christian Aristotelian saw him to be, natural magic and astrology were both parts of a reasonable view of the world, with the usual Christian reservations; which was in the tradition, of course, of Albert the Great and Aquinas. From this standpoint the burden of Pomponazzi's criticism of Pico was that Pico was unscientific; as indeed he was. After expressing the almost universally accepted *caveat* about man's freedom – 'that is what Ptolemy meant when he said, the wise man will lord it over the stars' – he goes on to defend the astrologers against Averroes and Pico, who either misunderstood them or simply got the subject wrong: 'and certainly in their books I have found nothing but a haughty and impudent presumption (*arrogantiam et petulantiam*): they contain nothing good but their style.'[16] According to Pomponazzi, and the same is true of Girolamo Cardano (1501–1573), another Pavia-Bologna teacher and mathematician, whom we shall notice further when we come to house division and its problems. Nature acts like a god – indeed, God acts in and through nature, and it is argued that what is good, including good magic and so on, is produced by God as efficient cause, and what is evil, including demonic magic and superstitious astrology, is produced by ourselves as deficient causes. Clearly, while looked at from where we are, the views of Pico and Pomponazzi may seem to have very much in common, to be of their time, not ours, the differences between them are fundamental. In particular, while Pico' view of the world has no need, almost no room, for physical science, Pomponazzi's contains it as an essential ground.

Those engaged further south in the literary, humanist Renaissance of the fourteenth century had little understanding of and not much respect for the late medieval universities of the North, despite the travels of many of them. Much has been said then and since, by antipathetic and not too well informed critics, of the sterile logic-chopping of the schools. But for the last half-century or more it has been known that the origins of what is now (with some vagueness) called 'scientific method' go back not to Francis Bacon, not to Galileo,

---

[16] *Petri Pomponazzi philosophi et theologi . . . opera* (Basileae, 1567) 264, 267.

but beyond, into the Middle Ages, and ultimately to such works as Cicero's and Boethius' *Topics* and thence to Aristotle, especially to the *Posterior Analytics* – a work recovered in the West in Latin in the twelfth century. It was precisely the apparently dull medieval method of teaching by the *lectura*, the 'reading' (hence the title 'Reader') of *auctoritates*, ancient or even contemporary authorities, and commenting on them, which produced the *Commentaries*: the great theological works of the thirteenth century either were or grew out of commentaries on the *Sententiae* (the 'Sentences', i.e. opinions) of Peter Lombard, a collection of excerpts from theological authorities. Discussion of methods of arriving at *scientia*, knowledge, arose out of commentary on the logical works just mentioned – the more advanced fare of the better Arts faculties. Roger Bacon had already in the thirteenth century emphasized the necessity for the use of mathematics in all enquiry into the physical world; and mathematics belonged also to the Arts as well as to the medical faculty. It belonged to the medical faculty by its attachment to *astrologia*: we shall return to medicine later, but for longer than the period covered by this book no one would have studied medicine without including some study of *astrologia*. And it must always be remembered that even when it appeared most dominated by *auctoritates* medicine had always to be an empirical science. Given all this, it is really in these late medieval universities that one would expect the beginnings of modern science to be perceptible. And indeed thus it is.

Near the beginning of the fourteenth century Peter of Abano had described in his *Conciliator*, 1310, the two kinds of demonstration, or proof, derived from the Aristotelian tradition.[17] There is demonstration of effects through causes, *demonstratio propter quid*, 'because of what?', and demonstration of causes from effects, *demonstratio quia*, 'this because'. Both are, of course, really the same and inextricable, but facing different ways, as it were; 'the way up and the way down are one and the same', as Heraclitus wrote. Now the way in which we try to understand and explain the world we live in is to note effects, to abstract to causes – since we do not know causes in any direct or occult way – and then to explain the effects, to describe them anew and differently, because of and in the light of the now understood cause. And then we can subordinate causes to one another and form a kind of hierarchy, and our understanding and power of explanation, and hence our power over nature, grow. It follows from all this that, in opposition to the Thomist tradition, the mind must know particular,

[17] What follows is mainly dependent upon: Peter Laven, *Renaissance Italy* (London, 1966) and J. H. Randall Jr, *The School of Padua and the Emergence of Modern Science* (Padua, 1961).

singular things directly, in order to abstract to causes. This is, of course, the Nominalist, Ockhamist, position, and one which is bound to separate scientific philosophy, *philosophia naturalis*, from theology and even metaphysics: an essential 'liberation', perhaps, for the development of modern science, though it might now with hindsight be argued that the separation became too wide for comfort. The process just described is a kind of elementary sketch of the 'scientific method', and Randall says (p. 21) that 'the transformation of the demonstrative proof of causes into a method of discovery is precisely the achievement of the Paduan theory of science', or knowledge. The same problems of method were bound to and did arise in the medical faculty, especially in the context of diagnosis. It was one of the greatest achievements of the ancient Greeks that the Hippocratic schools of medicine invented the only truly empirical science of antiquity. Theoretical discussion of its methods was advanced at the beginning of the fifteenth century by such men as Jacopo da Forli (died 1413) and Ugo Benzi of Siena (died 1439), and arrived at much the same conclusions as the physicists. They, in the fourteenth and fifteenth centuries, along with military engineers with their new and very practical interest in ballistics, transformed ideas on motion from the curious (mistaken) qualitative notions of Aristotle to quantitative ideas of velocity, acceleration and (almost) inertia, *vis insita* among other terms, and most important perhaps it was all based on observation of what happened, experimentation, and measurement (*cf.* Laven, c.8).

For two centuries and more the University of Padua became the centre of this development of empirical science. It was a slow process since it involved the rejection of Aristotle, and emancipation did not come suddenly. In accordance with the medieval tradition, reinforced as it was now by Renaissance respect, Classical authorities could really only be rejected when accommodation ceased to be possible ('When X said such-and-such, what he really meant was . . .') and demonstrably false statements had been exposed: for example, the notion that a missile such as a cannon-ball moved in a straight line so long as the 'push' of the air kept it going and then dropped by its 'natural' downward motion to the ground. It took a long time to show that it was from the start subject to both its *impetus* forward, diminishing because of resistance, and its constant *gravitas*, its heaviness, its downward movement, in varying proportions. Towards the end of the sixteenth century the description of the 'inductive method' had become explicit at Padua in the work of Zabarella, and he influenced Galileo, who arrived at the university in 1592. All that was lacking from this picture was the mathematics. Number-mathematics, *arithmetica*, led in Italy largely from Neo-Pythagoreanism into theosophical speculation with no connection with science. The rediscovery of the great Greek mathematicians of the Hellenistic age led to the geometrical, Pythagorean-Platonist mathematics of Kepler, for example. It is sometimes a surprise to those who actually look at what Newton wrote to discover that the *Principia Mathematica* is very largely in geometric terms. The ancient Greeks of course were driven that way by their extremely cumbrous system of writing numbers; and real mathematical development in physics had to wait for the transfer of geometry to algebra in Descartes' coordinate geometry and the Leibniz-Newton invention of the calculus, to deal with continuous change algebraically. But the need for mathematics and mathematical development was felt in the sixteenth century.

It may seem strange to have got this far without serious mention of the Reformation, which was a Northern movement and which indeed increased the division of Europe into North and South, still so very evident. The relationship of the Reformation to currents of ideas, especially those which concern us here, is far too complex for anyone yet to have seen their way even moderately clearly through it. But it can be said that Reformed theology widened, from the other side, the gap between empirical science and theology, between this world and the other, between physics and metaphysics. It must be added that no-one in these centuries (and few perhaps ever since) believed that truth, certain truth, could ever be established and known from 'facts': Truth remained as it had been since Plato and Augustine, metaphysical or revealed.

Of the relationships between the new science and astrology some instances may be given. Johannes Peuerbach, the teacher of Regiomontanus, published in Nuremberg in 1474 his *Ephemerides ad XXXII annos futuros*, 'Ephemeris for the next 32 years'. *Ephemeris* merely means 'daily', and an ephemeris is a book of tables of the positions of sun, moon and planets each day for so many years. In the case of slow-moving bodies positions might only be given for longer intervals, and calculation is needed to establish all the positions for a given date. So Peuerbach sets out an introduction on how to use his tables, in the course of which he explains how to work out the retrogradations of planets. He also explains that the 'superior' planets, Saturn, Jupiter and Mars are 'oriental' when the sun is moving away from them after conjunction. Venus and Mercury are oriental when they precede the sun in the morning, and occidental when they follow the Sun in the evening. 'Accidents of this sort,' he goes on, 'are noticed by two syllables *or* and *oc* placed at the heads of the five columns. So much then for their motions and the effects that follow them.' Now all of this introduction is purely astronomical and scientific; but he immediately goes on: 'What great benefits these matters provide for doctors' practice in so many ways, and for nativities of men, and their "revolutions" (i.e. progressed charts), for alterations in the weather, for beginnings of undertakings, commonly called "elections", and for innumerable other civic uses, will be fully explained later in appropriate commentary.' 'Civic' uses because the *Ephemerides* are meant, perhaps largely, for mariners; and the 'innumerable other uses' presumably refers to the making of talismans and other less reputable pursuits. At any rate the one-ness of *astrologia* is still very evident.

One of the great names in the history of science is that of Francis Bacon, first Baron Verulam and Viscount St Albans. Born in 1561, Cambridge educated and a Gray's Inn lawyer, a Member of Parliament for 34 years until he became Lord Chancellor in 1618, he was disgraced for bribery in 1622 and died in 1626. His most important works were his *Essays*, the last edition of which he published in 1625; the *Advancement of Learning* (1605) and the *Novum Organum*, 'New Instrument' (1620). His *New Atlantis* was published posthumously in 1660. He has often been likened, from his *Essays* and his life, to his favourite, Seneca; but in our context he is rather Boethius. He was an immensely learned man, who absorbed not only the ideas of his age but also the currents of thought. Like Boethius he perceived the needs of the time, and putting all this through the mill of a fine mind he produced much to satisfy the needs and direct the currents. He ordered and refined and made explicit much of the theory of attaining to knowledge of the physical world, the ultimate aim of such understanding being mastery of the natural world for the good of man. How, then, did he stand with regard to astrology?

In the *Historia vitae et mortis*[18] he says (Vol. V, p. 221): 'Inquire into the length and shortness of men's lives according to the time of their activity; but so as to omit for the present all astrological and horoscopical observation.' Which, apart from that 'for the present', seems fairly unequivocal. But the works to look at are the *Advancement of Learning* (Vol. IV), and the *Novum Organum*. (The name means 'new instrument' and refers to the *Organon*, the collective name for Aristotle's logical works, since they were for Aristotle not philosophy, but the necessary tool or instrument of the philosopher.) In Book III of the *Advancement of Learning* (pp. 349ff), Bacon wrote: 'As for Astrology, it is so full of superstition, that scarce anything sound can be discovered in it. Notwithstanding, I would rather have it purified than altogether rejected.' Purified, that is, of all 'tradition' that is 'not based on reason or physical speculations.' He goes on: 'I do not hestitate to reject as an idle superstition the doctrine of horoscopes, and the

[18] *The Works of Francis Bacon* ..., ed. Spedding, Ellis and Heal (14 vols, London, 1857–1874).

distribution of houses; which is the very delight of astrology, and has held a sort of Bacchanalian revelry in the heavenly regions ... The doctrines of nativities, elections, inquiries, and the like frivolities, have in my judgment for the most part nothing sure or solid, and are plainly refuted and convicted by physical reasons.' Again notice the slight mitigation of a sweeping judgment, 'for the most part'. The 'purification' is then explained, the ground rules, as it were. Five things are listed. 'Let the greater revolutions be retained, but the smaller revolutions of horoscopes and houses be dismissed.' This really follows as a consequence of the next three. His second point is that the heavenly bodies affect the more tender, the more sensitive bodies, as humours, air and spirit. To which another editor[19] adds in a footnote, 'But if celestial bodies act upon humours, air and spirits, and these in turn affect solid bodies, it follows that they also act on solid bodies.' Third, they affect masses, large numbers, rather than individuals; the amount of 'influence' on an individual is so small as to be negligible. Fourth, this influence works over long periods, rather than short, obviously for the same reason; 'and therefore predictions of the temperature (i.e. weather) of the year may possibly be true; but those of particular days are rightly held of no account.' Perhaps not by every purchaser of almanacs! Fifth, 'that there is no fatal necessity in the stars; but that they rather incline than compel.' That so much is admitted is explained by what he says next: 'I hold it for certain that the celestial bodies have in them certain other influences besides heat and light; which very influences however act by those rules laid down above, and not otherwise. But these lie concealed in the depth of Physic, and require a longer dissertation.'

Astrology thus purified and restricted is called 'Sane (i.e. healthy) Astrology'. It would contain, within the limitations just set out, the following:[20] firstly, 'the doctrine of the commixture of rays'; that is, conjunctions, oppositions, and at least the major aspects. Secondly (and thirdly, but they can be run together), the distances, and hence the relative strengths of influence, of the planets; and their positions – culminations, and so on. Fourthly, the retrogradations and the stations (the points where they stand still in changing their direction) of the planets, and eclipses of heavenly bodies. Fifthly, the natures of the planets and the stars, and hence their differences. And lastly, the traditional interpretations of all these things where they seem to accord with sound sense and are not contradicted by or inconsistent with what is scientifically known. The uses of such sane Astrology

19 *The Works of Francis Bacon* ..., ed. Basil Montagu (17 vols, London, 1825–) III.130.
20 References now are to Montagu's edition. What immediately follows is still from III.130.

would be for the prediction of 'comets, ... meteors, inundations, droughts, heats, frosts, earth-quakes, fiery eruptions, winds, great rains, the seasons of the year, plagues, epidemic diseases, plenty, famine, wars, seditions, sects, transmigrations of people; and all commotions or great innovations of things natural and civil' (p. 132). It could also be useful with much less confidence and with no pretence as to exactitude of times, for a restricted number of 'elections': for example, for horticultural and agricultural actions like grafting and sowing and planting, the moon is particularly important. And he generalises into the open-ended statement that 'perhaps there are more of these instances to be found in civil matters than some would imagine'. The practical way in which one arrives at this sane Astrology is fourfold: by experiments in the future, and by checking on past experience, by sifting traditions, and by the use of 'physical reasons'. Lastly, Bacon dismisses as 'wild astrology' all the semi-magical uses connected with seals and talismans and amulets and so on.

In the *Novum Organum* Bacon appears more dismissive. In the first book, of Aphorisms, XLVI says that 'all superstition is much the same, whether it be that of astrology, dreams, omens, retributive judgment, or the like, in all of which the deluded believers observe events which are fulfilled, but neglect and pass over their failure, though it be much more common.' And at the end of LXII he says, 'There are, therefore, three sources of error and three species of false philosophy; the sophistic, empiric and superstitious.' But the following aphorism makes it clear that (as the 'retributive judgment' above suggested) superstition includes theology and religion, where mistaken, and such philosophy as Platonism. The distinctions between what is 'science' and what is not are still not clear, and there is still plenty of room for astrology even in the scheme of things described so influentially by that arch-prophet of modern science, Francis Bacon.

There is one aspect of 'natural astrology' not mentioned by Bacon in all of this: medicine, *iatromathematica*. Medicine, or physic, as it was called in the seventeenth and eighteenth centuries, has been astrology's oldest and most constant associate. Astrologers always regarded the doctor as their nearest point of comparison, because of the fundamental similarities of the two 'arts' – *artes*, that is, 'skills'. They had virtually begun together, in Greece, and their history was, from the astrologer's point of view, similar. They were both arts depending on the observation of what actually happened in experience (*experimentum*), and the framing of hypotheses to explain and interpret those experiences. In both cases, the numbers of 'facts' and the complexities of man and human life were both an embarrassment and explanation of error. The greatest distinction between them, and it contributed greatly to astrology's decline, was that in medicine it was possible actually to handle the 'subject', the patient. Operations on the living, sometimes of an almost modern character, and dissections of dead animals and, early and late, humans, told the doctor a great deal about how the body worked, and physiology and anatomy developed greatly from the early seventeenth century onwards. In *astrologia* hypotheses were never verifiable: they could merely be shown to be more, or less, preservers of what was observed – for example, any idea of concentric spheres had to be rejected almost as soon as it was formulated in Plato's school, because it could not 'explain' the variations in the apparent brightness of the planets, at a time when any change in the heavens, in their real luminosity, for example, was wholly unaccept-able; or, if they were astrological hypotheses, such as that the conjunction of Saturn and Mars was evil, then appeal had to be made to the traditions of astrology distilled from the past experience of astrologers. This was neither easy in ages when records were ill-kept or not kept at all, nor always very convincing. Nevertheless, medicine and astrology remained closely associated, and to the seventeenth century at least some knowledge of *astrologia* was a necessary part of a doctor's training.

No doubt there were various kinds of astrological medicine; one outline is given by Carroll Camden, Jr, who also gives a list of sixteenth century supporters of the art.[21] According to astrologer-doctors, there were two kinds of diseases, acute, which never lasted more than a month and were usually of less than a week's duration; and chronic, which went on for much longer than the month. The first kind were to be judged according to the positions and aspects of the Moon; the second depended on the Sun. There were four classes of 'critical days': decumbitures, that is, the date and time of the patient's taking to his bed, marked on the chart by the position of the Moon at that instant; the crises, familiar from fevers, especially malaria; and the judicial and intercidental days, found astrologically. When the Moon moved into the same degree as the decumbiture, in the next following 'house', that was a judicial day; and when the Moon was in the degree sextile to the position of the decumbiture, that was an intercidental day. The 'houses' in this scheme were eight (memories of the octatopus?), each of forty-five degrees, beginning with the degree of the Moon's position at decumbiture. Each of the cusps of the houses, as the Moon moved through them, also marked a crisis; at least, four of them were important crises, the cusps of the third and fourth houses, the cusp of the second house quartile to the decumbiture, and the decumbiture itself; the other four gave the doctor judicial days. All this seems pretty detailed, without any observation of what is actually

---

[21] 'Elizabethan Astrological Medicine', in *Annals of Medical History*, NS II (1930) 217–226.

happening to the patient. Indeed, H. G. Dick,[22] says as much: 'The astrological Physician would diagnose the disease, predict its course, and prescribe for it on the basis of his prediction – often merely by casting a horoscope for the patient unseen.' England's 'greatest exponent of mystical, magical and astrological medicine' was Robert Fludd (1574–1637), and 'today the best compendium of the pseudo-science' is W. Lilly's *Christian Astrology* (1647) (Dick, pp. 306, 310). Fludd was a considerable figure. His controversy with Mersenne was rightly described by Frances Yates as the first major confrontation between the Renaissance 'naturalists' and the new Mechanical Philosophy, and Kepler took very seriously the difference between his own and Fludd's mathematical philosophy.

The transition from belief in an ancient geocentric universe – the universe of our senses: which was why the mathematical hypothesis of heliocentrism was rejected in antiquity and later – to the acceptance of a Copernican heliocentric one took a very long time. (I have serious doubt about whether my grandfather, who was born in 1870 and schooled only until he was nine, really believed the earth went round the sun.) In 1556 Robert Recorde (c.1510–1558), who wrote the first arithmetical textbook in the vernacular, *The Ground of Artes*, published his *Castle of Knowledge*, a textbook of the mechanics of astronomy. It is wholly geocentric; but then elementary textbooks of mathematical astronomy still are. What is interesting to us about this book is the Address to the Reader, or preface, in the course of which he writes:

So was there never anye greate chaunge in the worlde, nother translations of Imperies, nother scarse anye falle of famous princes, no dearthe and penurye, no death and mortalitie, but GOD by the signes of heaven did premonish men therof, to repent and beware betyme, if they had any grace. The examples are infinite, and all histories so full of them, that I think it needeles to make any rehersall of them more; especially seeyng thei appertain to the Iudiciall part of Astronomy, rather than to this part of the motions, yet shall it not be preiudiciall anye waies, to repeat an example or twoe ... But who that can skyll of their natures, and coniecture rightlye, the effect of them and their menacynges, shall be able not only to avoide many inconveniences, but also to achieve many unlikelye attempts; and in conclusion be a governoure and rulare of the stars accordynge to that vulgare sentence gathered of Ptolemye:

---

[22] 'Students of Physic and Astrology', in *Journal of the History of Medicine and Allied Sciences*, I (1946) 300–315; the quotation is from p. 303.

Sapiens dominabitur astris
The wise by prudence, and good skyll,
Maye rule the starres to serve his will.

And later he adds '... without it (*sc.* Astronomy) physicke is to be accompted utterlye imperfecte.' There is no more astrology in the book, which is wholly concerned with the mechanics of the heavens, but the object of the exercise is clear.

Two of the important names in the process of introducing Copernican cosmology into England were Thomas Digges (died 1595) and Thomas Bretnor (fl 1607–18). According to Francis R. Johnson[23] Digges' addition of Copernicus to his father's *Prognosticon* in 1576 included for the first time the idea of an infinite, star-filled universe. 'He was the first modern astronomer of note to portray an infinite, heliocentric universe, with the stars scattered at varying distances throughout infinite space.' The change from a finite, geocentric world to an infinite universe with a heliocentric planetary theory, however difficult conceptually, was generally made in the sixteenth and seventeenth centuries; the first Copernican *Tables* were those of Erasmus Reinhold in 1551, and such tables had soon replaced those which had been used for four centuries before. But as has already been mentioned, this 'scientific revolution' made no difference to the astrologers. An astrologer's chart or figure is always centred on the subject, individual or otherwise, and what it pictures, and what is interpreted, is the positions round the subject of certain points in the heavens – the ascendant, the setting point, the houses, *caput* and *cauda Draconis*, for example – and the locations of Sun, Moon and planets in that scheme. This is to set out a figure, nowadays usually circular but in our period almost always square, with all these things at the correct angular distances from one another round the subject at the centre; and this picture is the same whether one's cosmology is Ptolemaic or Copernican. Johnson quotes (p. 252) an example from Bretnor of a 'Copernican' astrological prognostication; it begins: 'This Brumal Season, commonly called *Winter*, and usually taken for the first quarter of our Astronomical yeare, tooke its beginning the 11 of December last: for then (according to old dotage) did the Sun enter the first scruple of the cold and melancholicke signe *Capricorne*, or rather according to verity this earthly planet entering the first minute of Cancer, and furthest deflected from the Sunne's perpendicular raies, did then receive least portion of Sunshine, and greatest quality of shadow.' And in another place Bretnor points out that 'the Sun in Aries' and 'the earth in Libra' are equivalent, though the second is the right way to put it.

---

[23] *Astronomical Thought in Renaissance England. A Study of the English Scientific Writings from 1500 to 1645* (New York, 1963) 164f.

The best-known name – and deservedly so – among these late sixteenth century astronomer-astrologers is that of the Elizabethan polymath, John Dee. W. C. Dampier rightly wrote of him in 1929:[24] 'The prevailing confusion between magic and science is well seen in the person of John Dee (1527–1608), who spent much time in astrology, alchemy and spiritualism, but was also a most competent mathematician and an early supporter of the Copernican theory. He wrote a learned preface to an English translation of Euclid, published by Billingsley in 1570. When Pope Gregory XIII corrected the erring calendar by ten days in 1582, Dee was employed by Elizabeth's Government to report on the means of adopting the reform, and it was only the adverse opinion of some Anglican Bishops that caused a delay in England of 170 years.' This reminds us that *astrologia* was one of the most practical sciences of the age. Apart from the astrology, the almanack forecasts and so on, it was essential for calendar making and time-keeping, for medicine and all uses of herbs, and rules of health, for horticultural and agricultural practices, for navigation and for cartography. A man like Dee was of great importance in society, quite apart from any personal reputation he might establish as a *magus*; it has much less to do with magic than one might imagine. It also meant that instrument-makers were an essential element in the development, since greater accuracy was always demanded. Dee stands early in the process. He travelled on the Continent, and between 1547 and 1550 is thought to have visited Louvain, Brussels and Paris, and this 'made him acquainted with the foremost Continental mathematicians, among whom the designing, description and use of instruments in the service of geodesy, cartography, dialling, gunnery etc., was taken for granted as part of their work.'[25] Apart from this, Dee was a considerable scholar with wide interests, as is shown by his enormous library.[26] 'Dee was not merely an alchemist and spiritualist, but a really learned man, and one who had done his best, by petitions and otherwise, to stimulate interest in the rescuing of MSS from the dissolved monastic libraries and to induce the sovereign to establish a central national collection of them' (James, p. 3). His library was sold some time after

[24] Sir William Cecil Dampier, *A History of Science and its Relations with Philosophy and Religion* (Cambridge, first edition 1929; last revised edition 1948; repr. 1966). The last (paperback) edition has a valuable postscript and reading list by I. Beernard Cohen. It is still a valuable as well as a very readable work, even as having 'an evil career which did not end even with Copernicus and Newton'. The quotation in the text is from p. 144.
[25] E. G. R. Taylor, *The Mathematical Practitioners of Tudor and Stuart England* (Cambridge, 1954) 170.
[26] See Supplement 1 to the *Translations of the Bibliographical Society* (Oxford, 1921): 'List of manuscripts formerly owned by Dr John Dee. With Preface and Identifications by M. R. James.' Dee's 1583 catalogue was published in his diary by J. O. Halliwell, *The Private Diary of Dr John Dee* (Camden Society XIX, 1842).

1625, and among the purchasers were Ussher, Cotton, Selden, Digby and Ashmole. As James says (p. 10), 'had it survived intact it would have been a first-class repository of medieval science books excluding medicine'. Not entirely: five of the MSS listed by James are wholly or partly medical. 'Alchemy, astrology, astronomy, physics, geometry, optics, mathematics are all very copiously represented; and Dee appears to have given special attention to collecting the works of two great writers, Roger Bacon and Raymond Lull ... History, British and English, is perhaps the subject best represented next to Natural Science. One Welsh MS occurs.' In his catalogue are to be found, among nearly fifty astrological works, all the great names of the history of the subject, including the Greek of Vettius Valens, and at the other end, as it were, Nicolas Oresme's *Liber divinationum*.

A scholar-scientist indeed; and a practising astrologer, for his sovereign and others, much consulted. His astrology was part of his *astronomia*, and 'improved' by science in a manner that much recalls Ptolemy's attitude.[27] His system was based on rays emanating from the planets, etc., which implied the relevance and importance of astronomy – for planetary distances, for example – and optics. A good deal was derived from Roger Bacon. 'Astronomical and physical principles serve Dee's astrology chiefly by making possible a computation of the strength of the rays or species emitted by celestial bodies at divers times and places' (*op. cit.*, note 27, p. 88). For example, the *mora*, the time above the horizon, of a planet is greater than that of the paranatellonta, the stars rising at the same time, because of the planets' eastward motion; but the *morae* of retrograde planets are of course shorter, and therefore their influence is diminished. In Aphorism XXI Dee says (the translation on pp. 130–131 of Shumaker is slightly inaccurate; I give my own): 'Every seed (*semen*) has potentially in itself the whole and unchanging order of each act of generation, to be unfolded in the way in which the nature of the place of the conceiver and the power of the surrounding heaven which falls upon its work and conspire together.' Which is almost a one-sentence summary of the second chapter of Ptolemy's *Tetrabiblos* I! In the thirteenth Aphorism Dee makes an impossible demand: 'The true sizes not only of the earth's globe, but also of the planets and of all the fixed stars should be known by the astrologer.' But the attitude is there, though he does often support even what are recent original discoveries by quotation from old authorities, because innovation is still felt to be wrong!

[27] See *John Dee on Astronomy: Propaedeumata Aphoristica (1558–1568), Latin and English*, ed. and trans. with general notes by Wayne Shumaker, with an introductory essay by J. L. Heilbron (Los Angeles, 1978).

Among the men who were purchasers of Dee's books were men who belonged to that circle of savants from which emerged the Royal Society – Sir Kenelm Digby, for example, was a founding member. In the first half of the seventeenth century there arose a number of groups of men who gathered, very often in private houses, round particular learned men to discuss the latest intelligence in a large number of fields, including the new science. It happened across Europe, not only in the capitals, but in provincial cities also, as far east as Poland, and from Sweden to Italy.[28] Alongside and overlapping these groups went constant correspondence: 'Mersenne, Boullian and Gassendi had correspondents everywhere in Europe, with whom they discussed eclipses, longitudes and the length of the meridian' (Mandrou, p. 185). Geographically, the correspondents of Nicolas Peiresc of Aix-en-Provence covered from Madrid to Schleswig-Holstein, from London to Aleppo. Some of the groups, all of which met often and regularly, called themselves 'academies', such as the Accademia dei Lincei, which called itself that, in Rome, in 1609, but suffered from the condemnation of Galileo in 1632 and soon disappeared. One of the interesting things about these groups is that their members came from all the professions, and they were outside the universities. Their chief problem was censorship. It was a period of increasingly oppressive orthodoxy, both political and religious – Protestant and Catholic. Only two countries really offered anything like freedom for the new thought of the age and new uncensored publication of it, Holland (the United Provinces), and England. But in France the rise of the Jansenists and the Port-Royal from the 1630s gave some opportunities for opposition to the Jesuit-State alliance and for the exchange of ideas and for publication; the Port Royal *Logique* of 1650, for example, is quite clear about the illogicalities and the unscientific nature of astrology, as clear as Diderot and the *Encyclopédistes* of the early eighteenth century.

The first truly scientific society, which early placed itself under royal patronage, was the Royal Society in London, which received its Royal Charter in 1662. It was actually founded two years earlier, and grew out of a group of men who had met for some years at Gresham College, in London; so it too was apart from the universities, though it soon included university men, and most of its early fellows were professional men – perhaps the least likely, from the viewpoint of its later membership and activities, was Sir Christopher Wren. It was the

---

[28] For a general sketch of the 'republic of letters' in the early seventeenth century see the most interesting *From Humanism to Science 1480–1700*, by Robert Mandrou, trans. Brian Pearce (First French edition, 1973; trans., Hammondsworth, 1978) pp. 183f. If it is somewhat parochially French, it is an excellent corrective to the strong English bias of most that has been written here and in the United States.

model for the French Académie des Sciences, founded in 1666, but it had three great advantages: it was free to pursue its multifarious interests without interference from Church or State and it regularly published, as it always has, its Proceedings. These gave it continuity and public standing, and its membership and presidents gave it prestige; and the fact that there was a subscription for membership, largely to pay for its publications, gave it economic independence of patronage. Philosophical and literary pursuits were excluded from its aims, which were from the beginning firmly anchored in practical and profitable technical arts and skills, such as architecture and navigation and mechanical invention. 'Among the founders the first place was held by chemists, physicians and astronomers. Locke, a physician, joined the society in 1668. The mathematicians and astronomers Robert Hooke and Edmund Halley were accompanied, from 1671, by Newton, who soon came to occupy an important position in the society' (Mandrou, p. 269). Despite the Royal Society's explicitly Baconian programme for science, there was another side to it: it was not only concerned with 'improving the useful arts, ... (but) also to reviving ancient skills and secrets of which had been lost and the virtues of which would be tested by experiment' (*idem*, p. 268), such as, obviously, alchemy. Charles Webster truly writes, in a more general context:[29] 'From the historical point of view it is impossible to disregard the sources of evidence suggesting that non-mechanistic modes of scientific expression remained intellectually challenging to natural philosophers of all degrees of ability into the age supposedly dominated by the mechanical philosophy. It is therefore questionable whether the rise of science was associated with a total decline of magic as it was understood in Western society in the sixteenth and seventeenth centuries.' 'Such figures as Aubrey, Ashmole and Plot preserved to a remarkable degree the outlook of the natural magicians of the Renaissance, and central to their scientific activities were alchemy and astrology' (*idem, ibid.*, p. 64). These men, and other early members of the Royal Society like Beale and Henshawe and Boyle all privately practised astrology, and all were dead before 1700, to be succeeded by unbelievers.

It is well-known that Newton was much concerned with the investigation and recovery of ancient Egyptian-Chaldaean esoteric understanding of the universe, and spent much time on it – regarding it, probably, as being as important as his scientific work or his work at the Mint. But his attitude to astrology is easily summed up: he evinced no interest in it whatever, either of support or rejection. We know

[29] *From Paracelsus to Newton: Magic and the Making of Modern Science* (Cambridge, 1982) 11. A fascinating book.

nothing of his attitude. A favourite story of present-day astrologers has been exposed as a canard by I. Bernard Cohen.[30] The astrologers say that when Halley spoke disparagingly of astrology, Newton mildly rebuked him: 'Sir, I have studied these things – you have not.' Quoting David Brewster's *Memoirs of the life ... Newton* (Edin., 1855, vol. II, p. 408), Cohen writes '... when Dr Halley ventured to say anything disrespectful to religion he invariably checked him with the remark, "I have studied these things, – you have not." '

To return to the Continent of Europe, there were very few lasting scientific societies to emerge from this period; the French *Académie des Sciences* survived after it began regular publication of proceedings from the later 1660s – an essential condition of continuity, divorcing the life of the Society, which is long, from those of its members, which are short. But there were of course growing numbers of scientists and mathematicians, some great – the greatest by far, and arguably the greatest of his or many generations, being Leibniz, who, like Newton, ignored astrology. As did, of course, free-thinkers and rationalists like Diderot and the *Encyclopédistes*: 'Astrology' does not feature in their great work, nor is it mentioned under 'Astronomy'. But there are three other reactions relevant to us: Gassendi's science, Kepler's new, mathematical approach, and that of Morin the French astrologer, who attempted to turn out the traditional Ptolemaic art in a new dress to suit the new age; and failed. All of which involves juggling a little with our times, but it seemed more logical, and it is all within that indefinable period of 'Enlightenment' which produced the modern world.

Gassendi's Franciscan friend and correspondent, Marin Mersenne, seems to have taken what was probably a very common seventeenth century attitude. He did not write on astrology but in his *La Vérité des Sciences*[31] Book II, c.1, is headed: 'Of the division, and diverse species of Mathematic: of their usefulness, and necessity, and that Philosophy, jurisprudence and the other Arts cannot attain their perfection without them.' In the course of this chapter he writes (p. 243): 'Doctors, Chymists and Cabalists also need Mathematics, for Paracelsites would not be able to understand the book which Paracelsus wrote *de ente astrorum* (On the nature of the stars) nor his great Astrology which is in the tenth volume of his works, nor the Astronomy of *infernal* things ("*choses infernales*", second word italicized: what are they? Does it simply refer to "these lower regions" as in Gassendi below? But it is *infernales* not *inferieures*.), if they had not studied Mathematics.' Which

---

[30] *Isis*, XXXIII (1941) 60–61. 'Query No. 99: Isaac Newton – an advocate of astrology?'
[31] Marin Mersenne, O.F.M., *La Vérité des Sciences: Faksimilie-Neudruck der Ausgabe Paris 1625* (Stuttgart-Bad Canstatt, 1969).

is all he says here of astrology, but the way it is referred to suggests he regards it as among the normal and respectable activities of a scientist.

Gassendi himself produces for the first time what looks like a truly modern 'scientific' attitude; perhaps not surprisingly – his same attitudes and ways of thinking led him both in right directions in science and in what many in the contemporary Catholic Church thought were wrong directions in religious matters. Pierre Gassendi,[32] as he was and is known, though apparently he always signed himself 'Gassend' in the French style, b.1592, d.1655, was a canon of Dijon, and taught at Paris, as Professor of Mathematics (= astronomy) in 1645. His principle of knowledge made him an anti-Cartesian; a principle he shared with Mersenne and indeed Hobbes. It was that no-one could know anything beyond his own capabilities: *ut suas ultra facultates nemo sapiat*. 'When men move from this, let them not trust that they can penetrate the secrets of nature, because they lack the capability of knowing them no less than the capability of creating them.' (*Opera Omnia*, Book I, p.xi). So metaphysics as a clear, deductive science is impossible. He was a Copernican, as might be expected, whose science included right ideas on inertia, and weight and pressure, for example.

He knew his astrology and all the main sources, ancient and medieval, very well, down to the fine details of numbers and nomenclature. He asks, in Book VI of his *Syntagma philosophicum*, t.I, pt. 2a, Sectio II, which is entitled 'On the effects of the stars', 'what effects do the stars produce in these lower regions, and how?' It is agreed that the first effect is light, especially the Sun's; and then warmth and dryness – cold and wet come from the earth. And these produce secondary effects such as times and seasons. And these are obvious: but they are also indiscriminate and general, so what happens here and now rather than then and there is purely accidental. The future may be known from causes – spring means flowers will bloom – or signs – dawn light means the sun will rise. If astrological prediction is neither of these it is not *praenotio* (foreknowledge) but *conjectio* (guesswork). True knowledge of the future is God's alone. He suggests three reasons why the stars are not *causes*. The precession of the equinox has altered the rising times of the signs and relations with the Sun, and so on, but the seasons remain the same even under the new heavens. Second, for example, Sirius which is said to be a great cause of heat for us (the 'dog days') is for our Antipodeans a cause of

[32] See *Dictionary of Scientific Biography*, V (New York, 1972) 284ff; and *Opera Omnia: Faksimilie-Neudruck der Ausgabe von Lyon 1658 in 6 Bänden mit einer Einleitung von Tullio Gregory*, Band I (Stuttgart, 1964).

great cold! And what about regional variations in general? And lastly, if the stars were causes they should always be right: but ... astrological predictions are mostly wrong and always unreliable.

This is followed by a full and accurate description of traditional astrology mainly from ancient sources down to and including Firmicus Maternus, and that by objections, from the usual authorities, including Pico della Mirandola, of course. Here he asks, what about Thales cornering the oil market from predicting the weather? The answer is that Thales was scientist enough to do it without astrology, that there wasn't enough exact astronomy about at that time for him to do much forecasting, and 'that anyway it was well-enough known that Thales was laughed at for his Astronomy not only by others but even by his own servant-girl', and astrologers don't *observe*, like Thales, they rely on *Tables*. He says pithily at one point astrology is not a true art but pure gambling. He even rejects medical astrology, on the grounds of the universality and general effects of the heavens. He then spends some time rejecting all genethlialogy, progressions, transits, revolutions and so on. One of his chief grounds for objection is Pico's, the *arbitrariness* of it all: the degree is arbitrary as a division of the circle, so what of 'the degree for a year' theory? 30° is an arbitrary space, not a 'house' in the heavens. He sums up the reason for astrology's continuance thus: 'In no age have men not been greedy to know the future, and in none have there been wanting imposters to boast that they know it.' There is an interesting and sympathetic reference to an idea (of Lucas Guauricus) that there might have been *two* Ptolemies, one who wrote the *Almagest* and one who wrote the *Quadripartitum*, so strongly is the contrast beginning to be felt. There are, of course, causes why men are as they are and do as they do, but they lie in men themselves and in this world, not in the stars. The only way to discover what influences there are on the earth from the heavens is the scientific way, through *Observantia nempe sive Experientia*. Gassendi is anti-Morin throughout, of course: Morin had foretold that Gassendi would fall ill and die at the end of July or the begining of August in 1650 – a prognostication Morin refers to in his (posthumously published) *Astrologia Gallica* (1661; p. 747b). Gassendi died in 1655, a few years before Morin. But first another, great scientist.

The superficial view of Kepler, derived from hundreds of popular histories of modern science or astronomy – even highly reputable ones – is of the great modern astronomer who took Brahe's and his own and others' observations, and by dint of hard mathematical thinking untrammelled by Ptolemy and Aristotle and the Past hammered out his laws and came to the shocking and conceptually revolutionary conclusion that heavenly movements were not all circular, as Authority had always insisted, but that the planets moved round the sun in ellipses. Which is in a curious way true yet a travesty of the truth. To move from Gassendi to Kepler is to move from the ambience of a modern mind to that of Renaissance man, even to the early period of Ficino, despite the fact that Kepler was only twenty-one years Gassendi's senior, but removed by a century from Ficino.

To begin with, and most important, Kepler (1571–1630) was not really an astronomer at bottom, certainly not an observer, but a mathematician.[33] Not a mathematician of the modern, Leibniz-Newton kind, but a Ficino-mathematician, of the Neo-Platonist, Cabalistic type. His aim was really to produce a closed, coherent mathematical world that would allow for almost *a priori* demonstration of the Copernican theory and of heavenly changes, including of course, the *novae* which were so important in the late sixteenth and early seventeenth centuries in showing that the superlunary world was not unchanging. The basis for all this construction really lay in theories of harmony ultimately going back to Pythagoreans and Plato and the Neo-Platonists, and set out with all its musical and many of its cosmological ramifications and details in Ptolemy's *Harmonicorum libri III*.[34] One of his own most important works, particularly from our point of view, is his *Harmonica Mundi* (Frisch, vol. V, 1864).

He first studied at Tübingen University from 1591 where he first became interested in *astrologia* under Maestlin. Then he taught at Graz, and existed largely on his astrological practice – in which he was no charlatan; he fully accepted astrology, and it was the mathematics of it that fascinated him: hence all his work on aspects. From 1598–1601, when Tycho Brahe died, he studied with that great observer – a somewhat reluctant instructor of a curious young mathematician, to begin with at least. His interests in astrology became more and more in its mechanics, and in how it all fitted in with the rest of his world. The bases for his work were twofold, theological and mathematical. In the *Mysterium Cosmographicum* (Frisch, vol. I, 1858) he noted that God created *quantity*, and hence the regular solids, the day before He made the heavens: 'For quantity was created in the beginning, with body, the heavens on the second day.' On which he noted in 1621: 'Rather, the ideas of quantities are and were coeternal with God, and indeed God himself; and they are still there in our minds (souls: *animis*) as exemplars, made in the image of God (even his essence), on which gentile philosophers and the doctors of the Church agree' – a truly medieval attitude! He goes on in

[33] There are several editions of his works: I have used *Johannis Kepleri astronomi Opera Omnia*, ed. C. Frisch (Frankfurt, 1858–).
[34] Publ. Oxford, 1682, ed. Johannes Wallis; facsimile (New York, 1977) as vol. LX in the Second Series – Music Literature, in *Monuments of Music and Music Literature in Facsimile*.

Mysterium Cosmographicum: 'What plane figure can there be between solid orbs? Surely solid bodies must be there. Now behold, reader, here is discovered the matter of all this little work.' There are only five regular solids (Euclid). 'To help the memory I shall describe my ideas in words. The Earth is the circle, the measure of all (by "circle" he must here mean the circle's solid, i.e. the sphere). Circumscribe the earth with the dodecaedron: its circle will embrace Mars. Circumscribe Mars with the tetraedron: its circle will embrace Jupiter. Circumscribe Jupiter with the cube: this circle will embrace Saturn. Now inscribe in the Earth the icosaedron: its inscribed circle will be Venus. Inscribe Venus with the octaedron: its inscribed circle will be Mercury.' And that is why there are that number of planets! Later, of course, this scheme was modified; but the fundamentally closed universe, of harmony etc., remains. Into all this he fits his aspects and house division and so on. At one point in his consideration of aspects he is led to the idea of two sets of five aspects of 36° as more rational than the two sets of 30°. Much of the aspect-material is set out in his book on the *nova* of 1604 (Frisch, vol. II, 1859). He rejects, however, all 'superstitious' astrology of the professionals: divisions in the zodiac and the heavens are man-made, not natural, and the stars are always signs, not causes, and all that can be said of influences in houses and in different aspects must be derived from experience, it must *work*. All these man-made divisions are arbitrary, but they are of course, with their names, necessary to any astrological practice; provided one remembers that they do not actually *exist* 'out there', as it were. *Caput* and *cauda draconis* 'do not represent a natural division, but only geometric or arithmetical points'. The names of the signs are arbitrary, however necessary, and since they have no *natural* qualities ('Why are Taurus and Capricorn feminine signs?') the 'elemental' values of the triplicities are equally unreal. But there is one significant triplicity, of Aries, Leo and Sagittarius, in which the 'great conjunctions' of Saturn and Jupiter recur. This leads Kepler to a consideration of 800-year periods of history – he is not at all sure that the world will last into the period 2400 A.D. on! Behind all this is a wider and firm belief in perfectly right means of divination – divine signs, dreams and so on, all admitted and described in Scripture – which should not be rejected, provided they are divine signs and do not arise in the course of nature, in which case they are to be examined in the usual way. After all, the nova of 1604 did appear with a conjunction of Saturn, Jupiter and Mars, which did not look accidental! On the other hand nothing very special seemed to happen on the historical stage, so . . .?

Kepler and Jean-Baptiste Morin are almost complementary to one another as thinkers. Kepler in a sense wants to look back to a Neo-Platonist, or rather Neo-Pythagorean world of number-forms and

solid mathematical figures, all fitting into a harmony that made sense
of the whole: a view of the world as has been said that Ficino and Pico
would have wholly sympathised with. Morin wants to look forward –
in very much his own way – into the next age, to produce a logical,
coherent whole into which astrology fits with (corrected) modern
scientific ideas and practice as part of the whole pattern, which
includes a proper form of divination. But Kepler belongs to the future,
and his training and experience and even ways of looking at problems
are modern. Whereas Morin's whole background – his geocentrism,
his anti-Cartesian, anti-Gassendi 'science', his alchemy and astrology
– keeps him firmly facing backwards. He could not avoid belonging to
the past any more than Kepler could avoid, even had he tried,
belonging to the future.

Morin was born in Frankfurt in 1583 and died in 1659. His vast
Astrologia Gallica was published two years after his death.[35] He says he
was a doctor, an alchemist and an astrologer. His chief authority in
astrology is Ptolemy, always described in superlatives – *ipse astrologorum princeps*, among other things: 'the prince of astrologers'. His chief
opponents, whom he attacks consistently, are Descartes, Gassendi –
his confrère in religion: Morin was an abbé – Ficino and of course
Pico; he includes among these a few contemporaries, but also Plotinus
and Epicurus, whose physics was revived by Gassendi, and by
implication Copernicus, since he remained firmly geocentric. On page
191 of *Astrologia Gallica* he says categorically: 'Besides, we have
demonstrated that the earth does not move in a great orbit, but is fixed
in the centre of the World'; and it is by no means the only place he is
so clear. The work is set out, with much preamble, in twenty-six Books
of varying length – none very short! The first sixteen are intended as a
theological-philosophical framework on which can depend the rest,
the actual astrology. It is interesting in passing to notice that when he
comes in Book XXII to 'Directions', he describes it as: 'This book is the
most important and the most divine of all Astrology.' It has, in the
past, given much trouble to astrologers, but he has it all sorted out and
settled. He makes precisely the same claim to have got it all right at
last in a fair number of places! The last book of all, Book XXVI, is
concerned with attacking the Arabic 'authorities' and their accretions
to astrology, described as 'false, fraudulent and Diabolical'.

From Book I to Book IX he attempts a deductive scheme on what
were Boethian principles beginning with the existence of God, when
he is Anselmian, and anti-Descartes, and bringing us to an understanding of the metaphysics of the universe, and of physics, including

---

[35] Hagae-Comitis, 1661. Not, so far as I know, lately reprinted.

causation, and matter, notion and time. Book VI, ostensibly on Motion and Time, is actually all concerned with motion with a useless short section on time tacked on at the end. With Book IX we move into *astrologia*, with *Sectio II* on the physical natures of the planets, and a long passage on comets. After a brief excursion into the historical background, he deals in Books XI–XV with the effects of the heavens on the sub-lunary world, with the proper natures of the planets and some of the major fixed stars (since for Morin all heavenly bodies are composite, physically, he has no problems with change in the heavens, as traditional Aristotelians had done), with 'first physical causes' and with the 'essential dignities of the planets'. And then we are into astrology. But before we leave these early books it is worth looking at his general defence of the art against the arguments of Alexander de'Angeli, who was Prefect of the Jesuits in Rome, as he sets it out in the *Praefatio apologetica*.

The Jesuit makes five objections. One, that there are no clear and genuine *principia fundamenta*, 'basic principles'. It is hard to say whether de'Angeli is looking for Cartesian clarity or, more likely, principles for a Boethian deductive science. In either case it is a modern demand. Two, astrologers never completely answer criticism, but are always shifting their arguments: it is all 'Yes, but ...' with more complications. This is really another very modern view: what is objected to, underneath, is the apparent non-refutability of the astrologer. Three, they, the astrologers, are very often simply wrong; with the implication that if their principles were sound and their rules good empirical ones, they ought not to be. Four, many astrologers do not know their business, have not studied it properly, and are ignorant deceivers whose objects are ambition and money, not true divination and guidance. And last, that the authority and the learning of astrology's opponents, past and present, may be contrasted with the ignorance of the astrologers.

Morin's replies are fairly foreseeable, but they are, as much of the book is, very personal. One gets the feeling that Morin feels himself isolated, as a real, educated astrologer, both from the new world unfolding round him and from the vast majority of contemporary practising astrologers, and that he is therefore defending himself as much as his art, throughout the work, so personally involved does he become. To de'Angeli's first objection the work as a whole is an answer: and Morin does not hesitate to say that the Prefect's objection would have been a good one and valid had it not been for himself and his book: now it is no longer true. Ptolemy is his great authority – *Astrologorum Archidux* – and of course a good one from the 'scientific' point of view, as we have seen. Girolamo Cardano is an authoritative Commentator for Morin – again a reasonable choice, of a good mathematician. Both Ptolemy and Cardano err, as must be expected. The same might be said of the developers of all the sciences. To the second objection Morin replies personally. He says he took up astrology late, at the age of forty, having previously been doctor to a bishop. Presumably he was led by a pretty normal path from medicine to astrology. He had then studied the art for ten years, and was convinced of its validity and truth, and now he, Morin, knows the answers to problems that previous generations of astrologers in their ignorance have shilly-shallied round.

To three, that astrologers are often wrong, Morin really produces Ptolemy's answers. He points out that there is bad theology as well as bad astrology, and errors through ignorance are as common in medicine (the old comparison), politics, navigation and so on: all are *artes conjecturales*, arts dependent on instructed and experienced conjecture. Which seems fair, except that, as we shall have to point out more forcibly later, these other arts had, even by the time of Jean-Baptiste Morin, made considerably more evident progress in the value of their conjectures than had astrology. In the course of this section, Morin quotes, from Aquinas, *sapiens dominabitur astris*, still happily attributing it to Ptolemy's *Centiloquium*. Four produces the example of one Nebulo in Paris as an example of just such an ignorant quack as de'Angeli refers to; but as Morin reasonably replies, is that the fault of the genuine astrologer like himself? There are quacks in all professions. For the last objection, on authority and learning, Morin really repeats his reply to the first. Reason, he says somewhat portentously, though he obviously believes it, outweighs all authority: and he, Morin, has now produced astrological reason, as it were. Now it can easily be seen that this is all really merely a statement of objections, some stronger than others, and a contra-statement, largely personal, from Morin. No-one who disagreed with Morin, or whose world-view was antipathetic, was likely to be influenced one way or the other. It was all in fact largely irrelevant, but it does demonstrate that astrology was still worthy of the time and effort of high Roman clergy.

Book XVII of *Astrologia Gallica* is concerned with the division of the mundane houses. Morin insists that they are not entirely man-made, arbitrary divisions of the sky: since the *cardines* – the ASC, the MC, the setting Point and the IMC – are all actual, natural and determinable points in the heavens, then at least so are the four quadrants natural, whatever may be said of the other divisions. Having said that the horizon and the meridian divide the whole into four equal quadrants, he points out that there are various ways of going on from there, and therefore astrologers are divided into *sectae*, 'parties' almost, on this. He asserts – by now a little predictably – that now all will be well since he will settle the problem. He rejects Firmicus and Cardano, and says he learned the true method in Paris in 1622, a method handed down through the cabala from no less an authority than Adam. The rest of *Astrologia Gallica*, except for the last book, which is purely polemical, is simply an outline of Morin's astrology, cleared on Ptolemaic lines of many of the accretions from the medieval revival – almost all, as we have seen, themselves derived from ancient authors – and much more. The important thing about the astrological books is that they are wholly traditional, and indeed might have been written at any time in the four centuries before Morin, had an astrologer set out to 'return to Ptolemy' (plus the Commentator) and tried to follow it through. All Morin's industry and prolixity produced in the end only yet another, differently wrapped, *de astrologia*.

So let us return to house division. The mathematical and mechanical details will not concern us. The point of taking this topic at some length is that it is still not settled, it is a crucial part of the whole of 'personal' astrology, and may be taken as the type problem – one which really, one would have thought, ought by now to have been resolved, at least empirically, after two and a half thousand years of practice, even if it was incapable of resolution on theoretical grounds. That it is not, may be made quite clear by our modern reference work, Margaret E. Hone's *Modern Textbook of Astrology* (revised edition 1968), p. 124: 'Up to the present time, there is no unanimity, even among the most thoughtful and careful astrologers, as to which of the many systems is best'; and one can get no guidance in the matter, 'as there is no book on it'. This was written in 1968: despite the hundreds of books written by astrologers even in the present century there was, she says, no book on so essential a problem! She was in fact, wrong: there is and was one,[36] but it is not a helpful, rather a muddling book. She was also wrong, but by no means alone among the writers on astrology who are or were professional practitioners, in saying that the 'equal house system' – simply dividing off the mundane houses in 30° steps from the ASC – is the oldest form, common for its simplicity, later rejected for more complicated but mathematically 'justifiable' systems. But she could be right about the number of possible variations of systems: 'A mathematician has arrived at the total of fifty-four different methods' (p. 141). It is possible that all of these could be found by a full analysis of all those charts and systems and astrolabe-methods described by past astrological writers and in many anonymous MSS. After all of which it is not surprising that she concludes by saying (p. 281): 'It would be dogmatic to insist on the

---

[36] W. Koch and W. Knappich, *Horoskop und Himmelshäuser*, Teil I, *Grundlagen und Altertum* (Göppingen, 1959).

rightness of any one system of house division to the exclusion of all others, when there is no topic on which astrologers disagree more heartily.' The list of methods and of astrologers having 'a method' gathered from Morin and elsewhere is a long one: the 'Hermetic', equal house system; Porphyry, Rhetorius, Vettius Valens, Firmicus Maternus, Eutokios of Askalon (fl. early sixth century A.D.), Alcabitius and Massa'allah, Guido Bonatti, Campanus, Regiomontanus, Cardano and Placidus de Titis (died 1688); plus the many medieval texts from the twelfth century on, which simply give rules for finding the cusps of the houses (the dividing lines) on the astrolabe – very varying rules, with usually no explanations – as is done by Michael Scot. Ptolemy gives no rules though he does of course refer to and use the mundane houses. He, probably, and Rhetorius, and al Biruni, and a few others, allow for five 'dead' degrees preceding the 25° of each house. Critodemus may have used a curious variant also found in Vettius Valens II.41, with traces in other writers, in which the houses are divided from the Lot of Fortune rather than the ASC. Add to all this the fact that, as we have seen a number of times, in ancient authors especially, there is great confusion in the *terminology* between 'houses' in various senses and 'places' and 'signs' and even 'twelfths', which indicates also some confusion of ideas.

And all of this in one of the most crucial areas of astrological theory and practice. Crucial, because it is the system of mundane houses based on a real point, the ASC, which anchors the chart, as it were, in time and place, fixes it on a subject, and allows all that interpretation which is the point of the whole exercise.[37] More or less by the way, although in earlier centuries there are considerable variations in the 'contents', as it were, the meanings, of the mundane houses, at any rate, from the sixteenth century to the present there is general agreement, so that in practice the agreement among astrologers appears greater than it is. The main lines of the problem are easily described. If the ecliptic were not 'tilted' at 23½° to the equator, there would be no problem. All the signs of the zodiac would rise and set at equal intervals, and an 'equal house' system would be normal and correct. But alas, the 'obliquity of the ecliptic' (which gives us most of what is interesting in our world, from the seasons on) means that different signs rise and set at different times, so that since the mundane house system evolved from a primitive and natural four quadrants through the *octatopos* to the twelve-house system in the

---

[37] I cannot resist the temptation to mention, for those who may at present be thinking that while horoscopes for humans may be all right, horoscopes for your pet dogs are slightly ridiculous, that Morin in Book XXV, c.1 writes of the state of the heavens *circa nascentem hunc hominem vel equum*, 'around this man at his birth, or this horse'.

early centuries of mathematical astrology in Greece, dividing the quadrants has been a problem. The houses are the framework, fixed on the subject by the ASC, within which the zodiac and all in it turns. Therefore the problem is to divide some 'natural' circle by great circles through its poles so that these lines also divide the ecliptic, the zodiac; but which circle, how divided? Since the late sixteenth century there have really only been three or four serious contenders: but they *are* different. Since your conjuncton of Saturn and Mars at your birth means something very different if it is in the eighth house from what it would in the seventh – in the former case it will concern religious beliefs, and so on, or journeys; in the latter, your death! – it could matter a good deal where the cusp between the two actually is. Astrologers attempt to get over such practical difficulties by the use of overlaps and double influences, but it is then difficult to know where the lines are in the 'grey' areas: in one system only about the middle ten degrees of a house was quite clearly one house rather than the next. Yet in modern times, with all the practice and experience, we still have 'no topic on which astrologers disagree more heartily'.

So astrology died, like an animal or plant left stranded by evolution. It was not killed. It had argued with the anti-astrological thinkers ever since its beginnings, and survived. It had survived because in an odd way even those who were most vehement in their attacks actually accepted it: it fitted in with their world-picture. With some, like Ficino, it fitted well, and with others, like Pico, it didn't. But throughout the period to the seventeenth century it remained a genuine possibility, to be accepted or rejected in this or that form, or all of them, but always part of *astrologia, astronomia,* as a whole. Then the world changed, under and round it and over it, and left it behind. There was no need for any 'authority' to condemn it, no real need for anyone to attack it any more. They did, of course, and the debate, if one can so dignify it, went on throughout the seventeenth century. That it was, in educated circles, dead in the eighteenth century is clear not only in its absence from the interests of Newton and his society, and those of the lively circles in London round, for example Samuel Johnson, but also from the fact that the attacks now came not from the natural philosophers but from the satirists, like Pierre Bayle and Swift. It is also demonstrable in a slightly indirect way. In a list of nearly forty astrological writers given by Robert A. Peddie in *Notes and Queries*[38] which covers the seventeenth, eighteenth and nineteenth centuries, only three are named for the eighteenth century: one early, Samuel Penseyre, 1726; and two late, G. Mensforth, 1785, and J. Worsdale,

---

[38] 'A Bibliography of Astrology': *Notes and Queries*, 7th series, November 1891.

1798. In the newly emergent United States, although it all happened a little later, the picture was the same.[39] Serious astrological works were introduced about the middle of the eighteenth century, and even then, although 'natural' astrology – concerned with medicine, agriculture, meteorology and some sorts of 'elections' to do with sailing times – was received with some sympathy, judicial astrology was more sceptically assessed and was of very much less interest and importance. As Leventhal sums it up (p. 64): 'Astrology in eighteenth century America was clearly a subject in a state of decline. It did not have the prestige or importance it had had in Renaissance Europe. Its primary vehicle was the lowly almanac, the literature of the semi-literate. No learned tracts were written about it in the colonies, and those which mentioned it in passing are found only early in the century.'

Almanacs, which varied from the 'lowly' to the base, were indeed almost the only instrument of survival for astrology through the eighteenth and early nineteenth centuries: a situation not unlike that of Late Antiquity, with a less and less understood art in the hands of amateur 'professionals' and charlatans. There is a parallel, too, between the two periods in that in the eighteenth century, as in the early Middle Ages, astrology was deprived of its educated underpinning. The world of learning did not provide that constant contact with and supply of ideas from developments in astronomy which were necessary to the maintenance of a 'properly' based astrology. No art can survive if the understanding of its basic principles is lost: it cannot continue to live on unthinking imitation. Of course, the reasons for this loss of provision were very different in the two cases. The fundamental reason in the earlier period was, in the words of Samuel Johnson, 'Ignorance, Madam; pure ignorance.' The reason in the eighteenth century was that the world of learning had changed. Astronomy was at last separate from astrology. The subject *astrologia* was gone. It is hard, and may indeed be impossible, properly to define the difference between astronomy and astrology. It sometimes seems to be simply assumed that whatever is 'scientific' is astronomy, and whatever is 'unscientific' is astrology. But this raises more difficulties than it solves. No matter. Many ultimately undefinable distinctions are daily drawn and profitably used, and some are of very great importance. There is still, now as in the eighteenth century, a distinction between astronomy and astrology recognised by most people and clear except for the narrow 'grey' area between. When one discourses on the

[39] See Herbert Leventhal, *In the Shadow of the Enlightenment. Occultism and Renaissance Science in Eighteenth-Century America* (New York, 1976). Chapter 2 is concerned with Astrology.

possible interpretations of a natal chart, that is astrology. And it has been so since the late seventeenth century.

The change in the background of educated ideas of the world was the result of the developments in the North Italian schools, particularly Padua, as has been described (in the early part of this chapter, particularly pp. 218–9). That 'Paduan revolution' could not have happened without the new logic and the new texts of the thirteenth and fourteenth centuries. These texts, or the great majority, came from and through the Arabs, on the second 'wave' of what began as the Twelfth-century Renaissance, the same movement that introduced the new, revived, Greek *astrologia*. That same movement of recovery and rediscovery led in one direction to the full development of Renaissance Astrology, and in the other, over a much longer period, since the first was really only a matter of transmission and acceptance, as part of a larger and harmonious world-picture, whereas the second involved a great deal of thinking and the gradual rejection of what had been for many centuries the assumed and authoritative background of ideas, it led to that separation of science and metaphysics, and of astronomy from astrology, that we have seen left astrology dying.

Throughout the period of its life described in this book, one of the chief defences of astrology has lain in its comparison with medicine; the comparison must go back to their beginnings, in the same places and milieux. It is, or rather was, a very natural one to make. Ptolemy says (*Tetr.*, I.2; Robbins, p. 15): 'Every science that deals with the quality of its subject-matter is conjectural and not to be absolutely affirmed, particularly one which is composed of many unlike elements.' Whenever astrology was attacked on the ground that astrologers so often got things wrong – and it was over and over again used in the attack – the reply included a reference to the sister-art of conjecture, medicine. In the early centuries, this was a very plausible appeal. Both arts were new; both largely empirical, with a factual basis – a sick man; a 'subject' in place and time – and having theoretical bases. There were 'schools' of medicine, disagreeing with one another as heartily as any astrological sects. Neither art was very successful in practice, in neither was diagnosis clear and simple. And both could claim, as Hippocrates' maxim said, *vita brevis, ars longa*, 'Life is short, the art is long'. Experience would show the way. It did, of course, eventually. Medicine is still a 'conjectural art'. Diagnosis is informed conjecture; practice is informed trial and error. But even by the seventeenth century it was clear that medicine was improved and improving, with greatly increased and constantly increasing under-standing of the working of the human body and of the material causes which act on it. There is no need now to dwell on the improvement in medicine since the seventeenth century. It would be foolish now for an astrologer to seek justification of his art by appeal to the 'parallel' of medicine: it would merely lay bare for all to see the causes of its own demise. It was only with the beginnings of a rejection in the later nineteenth century of all Western rational thinking in favour of the utterly foreign unreason (*not* irrationalism) of the East, that astrology – of a sort – was revived. Both processes, of rejection and of revival, have continued at an increasing pace, for all kinds of reasons, but that does not concern this book. We have brought the story of Western Astrology down to its second death, at the end of the seventeenth century. Only the servant-girl's laughter rings through the eighteenth.

Index

Writers known by forename and place are normally entered under the forename, e.g. Isidore of Seville

INDEX

This is the story of Western astrology –
that 'ancient art' which covers everything
from a vague acceptance of stellar
influences on the lives of men to precise
and fatalistic predictions of the future.
Astrology, science or art, came into
existence with the discovery of a
mathematical system which enabled men
to plot the relative positions of earth and
planets against the background of the
fixed stars. The story begins in Greece,
in the fifth century BC, with the
absorption into Greece of proto-
astrological ideas from the east. The
Greeks took stargazing and its magic and
added philosophy, geometry and rational
thought; the philosophy of Plato and later
of the Stoics made astrology respectable,
and by the time Ptolemy wrote his
textbook the *Tetrabiblos,* in the second
century AD, the main lines of astrological
practice as it is known today had already
been laid down.

Jim Tester shows how little astrology
changed during its journey from the
Greek world through Islam and back into
the West in the 12th century; even in the
Renaissance and in the 17th century it
preserved its conservative character, until
it was seemingly killed by the shift of
ideas in the late 17th and the 18th century.
The revival of astrology in the 19th and
20th century is outside the scope of this
study, but parallels between the ages of
its greatest influence in the past – late
antiquity and the Renaissance – and our
own times are irresistible.

This is an important book, the first
serious study of its subject. Not only
does it trace the history of astrology over
two thousand years, but it also gives full
weight to man's attitudes to it and its
place in the history of Western society
and ideas throughout that time.